About the author

Nicholas Guyatt is currently a visiting fellow in the department of history at Princeton University. A Cambridge graduate, researching aspects of US foreign policy, he has been a frequent visitor to Israel and Palestine and has worked in Jerusalem at the Society of St Ives (Catholic Human Rights Centre for Legal Resources and Development).

'Only the desperate make good conquerors.'
Theodor Herzl, *The Jewish State*

The Absence of Peace

Understanding the Israeli–Palestinian Conflict

Nicholas Guyatt

The Absence of Peace: Understanding the Israeli–Palestinian Conflict was first published by Zed Books Ltd, 7 Cynthia Street, London N1 9JF, UK and Room 400, 175 Fifth Avenue, New York, NY 10010, USA in 1998.

Distributed in the USA exclusively by St Martin's Press, Inc., 175 Fifth Avenue, New York, NY 10010, USA.

Cover designed by Andrew Corbett
Set in Monotype Dante by Ewan Smith
Printed and bound in the United Kingdom
by Biddles Ltd, Guildford and King's Lynn

Library of Congress Catalog-in-Publication Data

Guyatt, Nicholas, 1973–
The absence of peace : understanding the Israeli–Palestinian conflict / Nicholas Guyatt.
p. cm.
Includes bibliographical references and index.
ISBN 1 85649 579 5 (hc.). — ISBN 1 85649 580 9 (pbk.)
1. Arab–Israeli conflict—1993– —Peace. 2. Palestinian Arabs—Government policy—Israel. I. Title
DS119.76.G89 1998
956'.04—dc21 98–19783
CIP

Transferred to digital printing 2006

A catalogue record for this book is available from the British Library

ISBN 1 85649 579 5 cased
ISBN 1 85649 580 9 limp

Contents

Acknowledgements

This book was principally written in Jerusalem, Cambridge and Princeton in the autumn and winter of 1997. It would not have been possible without the help and generosity of the following people and organisations. In Jerusalem: Lynda Brayer and the Society of St Yves; Uys and Jeanne Viljoen and their family; Jennifer Moorehead and LAW, the Palestinian Society for Human Rights and the Environment; Leonardo Hosh and Jad Isaac at the Applied Research Institute Jerusalem (ARIJ); Denise Burford; and Maysoun Odeh (along with a number of unnamed Palestinian policemen), who managed to retrieve the earliest draft of the chapters from the Ramallah stadium where I'd managed to lose them. In England: my parents and my brother; Catherine, Nancy and Edward Shaw; Richard Serjeantson; and Becca Reeves of Amnesty International. In the United States: Aslı Bâli, Noam Chomsky and Norman Finkelstein.

The book has also benefited, inadvertently, from my association with the University of Cambridge and Princeton University, where I have been researching my Ph.D. thesis when not working on Israel/Palestine. I'd like to acknowledge the kindness and understanding of my doctoral advisor, Professor Peter J. Parish, who has viewed the temporary redirection of my efforts away from American history with enormous patience. I should state for the record that my academic work at Cambridge and Princeton has no relation to the material discussed in this book, and that those institutions should therefore not be seen as responsible for anything that follows.

At Zed Books, I'd like to thank Robert Molteno for having faith in the unlikely manuscript which I brought back from the Middle East; and Anne Rodford for her attentive and skilful editing of the later drafts of the book.

I'd also like to thank the following for their help with specific queries or for their advice, support and encouragement: Rifaat Abou-El-Haj, Tony Allan, Jeff Aronson, Samira Barakat, Ezra Block, Rex Brynen, Wendy Cadge, Meri Clark, Simon Cox, Alec Dun, Marwa and Omnia El-Shakry, William Flemming, Risa Goluboff, Andrew Graybill, Tamara

Griggs, Cathy Grosso, Clare Hariri, Conor Houghton, Jan de Jong, Sarah Kaminker, David Kasunic, Steve Lister, Catharine Macpherson, Jack Martin, Robert Palmer, Daniel Reisel, Ben Schonveld of L'Organisation Mondiale contre la Torture (OMCT), Israel Shahak, Zvi Shulman and B'Tselem, Lisa Siraganian, Anne Strausberg, Matt Thorne, Jane Tienne, Simon Tyler and Lisa Wynn.

Perhaps the best tribute I can pay to many of those who helped me is that they did so even though their own view of the Oslo process diverged from mine. I should conclude, therefore, by stating clearly that the opinions expressed in this book are solely my responsibility, as are any errors of fact or interpretation.

Foreword

1998 marks the 50th anniversary of the founding of the state of Israel. A programme of events, in Israel and around the world, will commemorate the half-century and highlight those areas in which Israel has achieved particular success: its democratic politics, with a multi-party system and universal suffrage; its economic prowess, with an especially strong and promising expertise in computer technology; and its population, estimated to exceed 6 million for the first time during 1998. These aspects of Israel's development will be at the forefront of the celebrations throughout the year.

The focus of this book, however, is on what Israel has conspicuously failed to achieve during its 50-year existence: lasting peace with its neighbours, especially the Palestinians. In this sphere at least, there is very little to celebrate, and much to regret. Even though Israel began negotiations with the Palestinians in 1991, and both sides signed the first Oslo agreement in 1993, violence, hardship and discontent have continued, especially for the Palestinians. News reports from the Middle East over the past few years have very rarely suggested that the 'peace process' is bringing real peace: from the killing of at least 29 Palestinians at a mosque in Hebron by a Jewish settler in 1994, to the bus bombs of February and March 1996 which killed scores of Israelis in Jerusalem and Tel Aviv, through the open conflict between Israeli and Palestinian police in September 1996, and the diplomatic stalemate which prevailed throughout 1997, it is clear that fundamental differences remain between the two parties, and that a just, stable resolution of their dispute has not been achieved.

From the start, the Oslo process has involved more than simply Palestinians and Israelis. The international community, especially the United States, has been instrumental in the negotiations. When Yasser Arafat, the Palestinian leader, shook hands with the former prime minister of Israel, Yitzhak Rabin, in September 1993, the two men were framed by Bill Clinton's welcoming figure, gesturing towards his guests on the White House lawn and the huge television audience. The image underscored the Clinton administration's vital role in shaping

Oslo, and its unstinting support for the process, even amidst violence and recrimination. Since the signing of the first Oslo Accord in 1993, Israelis and Palestinians have been firmly instructed to stay on the Oslo path to an agreement. One of the difficulties of the Oslo Accords, therefore, has been the reluctance of the Israeli and Palestinian leaderships, and especially of the international brokers of the peace deal, to consider other models of peacemaking in the light of Oslo's failure. Scepticism, let alone opposition to Oslo, has been condemned as a threat to peace. Peace and Oslo have become synonymous; to question the latter has implied the abandonment of the former. This argument has been detrimental to the cause of peace, and has led many commentators to ponder over the fine details of Oslo while ignoring the obvious inadequacy of its overall structure. This book will place the Oslo process in its proper historical context; analyse in detail the course of the negotiations and their impact on the ground; and project the likely course of this 'peace' into the immediate future. It will become clear from this evidence that Oslo offers no just or durable solution to the Palestinian conflict, a failure of design rather than of execution. We must then turn our attention to alternative solutions and use the experience of Oslo to fashion a better peace for the future.

In trying to make sense of the absence of peace, observers have tended to seize upon particular factors which have impeded the progress of Oslo. Some have concluded from the unrelenting discord and violence that an ancient hatred animates the sides, and that they will never make peace. Supporters of Israel have, instead, identified Palestinian 'terror' as the immovable threat to an agreement, arguing that Israel's security can never be made compatible with Palestinian hopes of statehood unless these militants are suppressed. Finally, there is a popular view that Binyamin Netanyahu, Israel's right-wing prime minister since May 1996, is the cause of all the trouble. Ever since the murder of Yitzhak Rabin by a right-wing Jew in November 1995, the Israeli Left has depicted itself as the only hope for peace, in opposition to the extremism and rejectionism of its rivals on the Right. When Netanyahu narrowly defeated Shimon Peres, Rabin's successor, in the elections of April 1996, the Left began to mourn, not only the loss of power, but Israel's lost opportunity for peace. Since then, Netanyahu has been the target of particular abuse within and outside Israel. Bill Clinton, desperate to explain to American voters and supporters why Middle East peace seems so flimsy, has done little to discourage the view that the removal of Netanyahu would put the peace process back on track.[1]

These three factors – mutual hatred, Palestinian terrorism and the rise of Netanyahu – have been used by many commentators to describe the failures of Oslo, and to absolve the process itself from any blame for the breakdown of negotiations. However, the facts suggest that none of these can persuasively account for the deterioration of the talks. Although some Israeli Jews[2] claim a right to Palestinian territory based on theology, specifically the promises that God is supposed to have made to the 'Jewish people' three millenia ago, it would be misleading to concede from this that the dispute between Israelis and Palestinians is an ancient and irreconcilable one. Aside from the fact that most Israelis and Palestinians do not approach their dispute from the theological perspective, the present peace process is structured around the norms of diplomacy and negotiation rather than mysticism and biblical claims.[3] The conflict between the sides is barely a century old, and is waged around practical competition for the same land. Meanwhile, the argument that Palestinian terror has destroyed peace ignores the fact that the vast majority of Palestinians have voted for parties that support nonviolent negotiation. Violence is a symptom of the breakdown of peace, not its cause. Finally, as we will see, the scapegoating of Binyamin Netanyahu is both unfair and distracting: unfair, because there is little concrete difference in policy between Netanyahu and his left-wing challengers, at least when it comes to negotiations with the Palestinians; distracting, because it prevents us from seeing what is really wrong with the peace process. If Netanyahu should fall from office at the next scheduled election in 2000, or even if his coalition government should collapse well before then, the fundamental obstacles to a just and lasting peace will remain in place.[4]

The intention of this book is to refute these irrelevant and distracting arguments and to look critically at the Oslo process and the prospects for peace. From this new perspective, Oslo seems less like the solution than the cause of many problems for those genuinely interested in peace. Although Oslo was established on the principle that land conquered by Israel in the Six-Day War of 1967 would be returned to Palestinian control, the crucial question of how much land was to be handed back was never properly answered. Since Palestinian hopes for a stable future rest on the liberation of all the land taken in 1967, the West Bank and the Gaza Strip, this omission carries grave consequences. Palestinians have argued that a sovereign state of Palestine simply cannot exist – economically, socially or politically – unless it occupies virtually all of the territory taken by Israel in 1967. However, Israel, for more than thirty years, has been building on Palestinian land with roads, settlements and military bases, making such a withdrawal highly problematic. Responding to this reality, the major political parties in Israel –

right and left – have envisaged a 'solution' in which Israel retains between 50% and 70% of the West Bank, returning only the leftovers to a possible Palestinian state.[5] The Palestinian leadership, meanwhile, represents a population which insists on a complete Israeli withdrawal as the minimum requirement for a stable, independent state. This is the ambiguity at the heart of Oslo, and the primary reason for the impasse between the sides.

The Clinton administration and the Israeli Left have devised a solution at the end of the Oslo process whereby the Palestinians are given most of the Gaza Strip, while Israel and the Palestinians share the West Bank roughly equally. This sounds like a fair compromise, but there are historical and practical reasons for seeing such a territorial division as both unfair and unworkable in practice. If we are trying to decide upon a reasonable solution to the conflict, it should be remembered that the West Bank and Gaza Strip constitute only 23% of the area known as Palestine before 1948: the other 77% was taken by Jewish settlers and became Israel. The Palestinians would therefore be offered not a 50/50 split, but 50% of less than one quarter of what had once been their land. With the Palestinian population roughly equivalent to the Israeli Jewish population in all of a future Israel and Palestine, Palestinians would thus be crammed into just over 10% of the territory, while Israelis enjoyed the other 90%. When viewed from the historical perspective of Israel's 50-year existence, the compromise is hardly equitable, and heavily favours Israel.[6]

In practical terms, a Palestine comprising approximately half of the West Bank would hardly be a viable entity. As the Oslo process has shown, Israel intends to withdraw from those areas of the West Bank where the Palestinian population is most dense, but to keep the remaining land for itself. A future 'Palestine' would resemble a series of islands in a sea of Israeli control. Freedom of movement for Palestinians would not be guaranteed, and Palestinian economic activity would face debilitating restrictions which would deter investment and stifle growth. Given the certainty of continuing Palestinian protest after any 50/50 split, and the chance of ongoing militant attacks on Israel's cities even after the 'permanent solution' is imposed, it seems probable that the borders of a fragmented Palestinian archipelago would frequently be closed by Israel. This closure would withhold from the Palestinian people the economic and social benefits upon which any permanent peace depends.

Oslo has not brought the two sides any closer on the most crucial issues concerning peace – instead, it has allowed them both to continue to believe in their own conflicting visions of an eventual solution. The

Palestinians expected that Oslo would return all of the occupied territories, including the eastern half of Jerusalem, and lead to a Palestinian state; the Israelis, meanwhile, planned to withdraw from only half of the West Bank at most, and to ensure that the most valuable areas, along with all of the settlements, were absorbed permanently into Israel. Unfortunately for the Palestinians, it has become clear over time that only Israel's view of Oslo will be put into practice. At the beginning of Israel's 50th anniversary celebrations in January 1998, the evidence was clear: the Palestinian Authority still controlled a mere 2.7% of the West Bank, with the prospect of acquiring far less than the remaining 97% over the next few years. If the Oslo process is eventually concluded along these lines, and the peace negotiations are wound up, we can only expect that Palestinians will resort to other means of obtaining redress for their grievances against the Israeli occupation. Even if the Palestinian leadership can be persuaded to sign an agreement ceding a large portion of the West Bank to Israel in perpetuam (an unlikely but not impossible scenario), the Palestinian people will continue to resist their oppression and impoverishment at the hands of Israel. Given that more militant opposition to Israeli annexation of Palestinian land will almost certainly be violent, such a solution at the end of the Oslo process will not resolve the conflict but will simply prolong it.

In 1987, Israeli academic Uri Davis declared Israel to be an 'apartheid state'.[7] In Davis's view, Israel's treatment of those Palestinians who became citizens of the new Jewish state in 1948 has made them second-class members of Israeli society. As in South Africa, where the restrictive laws of 'petty apartheid' preserved separate social systems for blacks and whites, Israel failed to ensure that Jews and Palestinians living in the same state were treated equally and without racial or religious privilege. The consequence has been institutionalised discrimination against the 20% of Israel's citizenship which is Palestinian: more than a million people by 1998.

Writing before Oslo, Davis made no reference to those Palestinians who lived under occupation in the West Bank and Gaza Strip, since their status as an occupied people under international law, bolstered by numerous United Nations resolutions, made clear Israel's responsibilities: a full withdrawal from the territories conquered in 1967. The Oslo process, however, has provided another analogy with South Africa: if the Palestinian citizens of Israel have been the victims of 'petty apartheid' restrictions, the Palestinians of the occupied territories are now suffering under an Israeli plan for 'grand apartheid'. The white

South African government, in an effort to absorb massive areas of land from the indigenous population after the late 1950s, began to offer blacks a form of 'citizenship' in one of several, specially created 'homelands', or 'bantustans', in return for the black renunciation of any claim to South African citizenship or territory. Herding the blacks into these tiny and impoverished bantustans, the white minority simply took the remaining land for itself. The resulting economic and social disaster for blacks is well-documented, and constitutes one of the most terrible chapters in the history of the apartheid era.[8]

Israel has been laying the groundwork for a similar policy against the Palestinians of the West Bank and Gaza Strip since the late 1960s. After occupying these territories in 1967, and taking over the administration of a Palestinian population which today numbers at least 2.5 million, Israel began a comprehensive effort to settle its own Jewish population in these occupied areas. In the West Bank and Gaza Strip there are now more than 300,000 Jewish settlers whose homes surround and divide Palestinian towns and cities. Although many books, articles and speeches have characterised Israel as an occupying power which might soon withdraw, Israel has actually sought to make permanent its presence in the West Bank and Gaza Strip through the building of homes and roads, the creation of what Israel has called 'facts on the ground'. These 'facts' fundamentally alter the nature of the Israeli-Palestinian dispute. Palestinians have long sought a state of their own on the West Bank and Gaza Strip, and full separation from Israel; however, the extent of Israeli settlement and the military superiority of Israel makes full withdrawal extraordinarily difficult. In effect, the state of Israel already stretches from the Jordan river to the Mediterranean: a single economy, infrastructure and political system exists throughout this territory.

Israel is thus faced with a simple question: how can it maintain an exclusivist Jewish state in the face of 1 million Israeli-Palestinian citizens and another 2.5 million Palestinians in the occupied West Bank and Gaza Strip? The Oslo process suggests that Israel has chosen a policy of 'grand apartheid' to answer this dilemma. Seeking to retain control of the land and water while keeping the Palestinians at a safe distance, successive Israeli governments have developed their own bantustan plan for limited self-rule in areas of the West Bank and much of the Gaza Strip. Under the banner of the 'peace process', Palestinians have been offered autonomy over a fraction of their lands in return for recognition of Israeli absorption of and control over the majority of the territory. Oslo has not been an agreement of equals for mutual advantage, but rather a plan stacked heavily in Israel's favour which will cleanse much of the West Bank of Palestinians and allow Israel to extend the domain of its discriminatory system.

The Palestinian leadership has been an unwitting partner in this Israeli plan, keeping alive its hopes of nationhood even as Israel has colonised its heartlands. Hence, Palestinian leaders have made the mistake which the ANC in South Africa avoided: they have legitimised and expedited the Israeli scheme for 'grand apartheid'.[9] As in South Africa, the fragmented and besieged areas of Palestinian sovereignty have made these new bantustans entirely dependent upon Israel. Israel controls all movement between these 'autonomous areas', and Palestinian development is constrained by the cramped conditions of the bantustans and the overriding strength of the Israeli economy. A marked fall in Palestinian living standards since Oslo began suggests that the 'autonomous areas' will become as depressed as the bantustans of South Africa, described by one historian as the 'human dumping grounds of apartheid'.[10] In return for the trappings of a state – a flag, an anthem, a 'national' authority – the Palestinian leadership has allowed Israel to circumscribe entirely the fate of its people.

The South African example proves not only that one population can take the lands of another on a massive scale, but that this process of expropriation can actually be furthered by such superficially liberal concessions as self-rule, or even statehood, for the natives.[11] In the Palestinian case, therefore, we must look beyond the rhetoric of the Oslo agreements and consider who actually benefits from their provisions. The Palestinians are given a measure of autonomy, but only at the expense of even more precious land and further resources, which are ceded to Israel. A genuine commitment to peace compels us, then, to reject a 'solution' which actually exacerbates the problem it claims to be solving. The task of this book is to demonstrate, in the first instance, that Oslo is not a viable prospect for an enduring peace; and then to propose alternatives which offer more hope for a resolution to the Israeli-Palestinian conflict. If Oslo is heading towards disaster, this should also be a concern for every Israeli or supporter of Israel, even amidst the celebrations of 1998.[12]

The chapters that follow offer a general introduction to the Oslo peace process, with an historical overview of its causes and course and a study of its effects on the Palestinians of the occupied territories.

Chapter One deals with the Israeli-Palestinian conflict up to 1991, with particular emphasis on the period after Israel's victory in the Six-Day War of 1967 and the changing ambitions of Israel with regard to the occupied territories. Paying particular attention to the settlement project, this chapter notes the extent of Israel's colonisation and its implications for a complete Israeli withdrawal. Chapter Two continues the story from the Gulf War to the present day, concentrating upon the elements of 'grand apartheid' built into the Oslo peace process and the reasons for and consequences of its imposition.

Chapter Three outlines the political background to Oslo. The first section offers an analysis of the Israeli political scene, and questions the widely held assumption that Israel is divided between 'hawks' and 'doves'. The second section discusses the motivation and interests behind Palestinian participation in Oslo. Finally, the crucial role of the international community – the Arab states surrounding Israel, the European Union and, most importantly, the United States – is explained. In this political context, we begin to see Oslo as very much less than an equitable agreement between equal parties, and we understand more clearly its recent collapse.

Chapter Four returns to the occupied territories, and examines the numerous ways in which Palestinians in the West Bank and Gaza Strip are still governed entirely by discriminatory Israeli laws. Chapter Five focuses on Jerusalem as a model of Israeli control over a large Palestinian population, and suggests that the degree of freedom compatible with 'grand apartheid' is minimal.

Chapter Six charts the likely direction of Oslo into the near future, and suggests that, even if a plan for 'grand apartheid' is successfully implemented, the 'peace' between Israelis and Palestinians will remain fatally unstable. Given the potential for further bloodshed and suffering, and with the benefit of the South African experience of apartheid, the final chapter speculates on the alternative political solutions which will be desperately needed when Oslo has run its course.

Notes

1. As we will see, Clinton's support for Shimon Peres in the 1996 elections in Israel made the American relationship with his winning opponent, Binyamin Netanyahu, substantially more difficult. Since his victory, Netanyahu has been welcomed in Washington a little less extravagantly than his predecessors, even suffering the indignity in January 1998 of being offered equal treatment with Palestinian leader Yasser Arafat. See 'Arafat trims his hopes and pins them on Clinton', *New York Times*, 18 January 1998. A selection of articles criticising Clinton's tougher stance towards Israel was helpfully reprinted in a full-page advertisement in the *New York Times* on 18 January 1998, paid for by the Committee for a Secure Peace under the byline 'Why do so many respected voices say Bill Clinton has turned his back on Israel? Because it's true.' The ad. included quotes from such veteran supporters of Israel as *Times* columnist A.M. Rosenthal and *Washington Post* pundit Charles Krauthammer.

2. Although Israel remains a 'Jewish state', at least 20% of its population is non-Jewish, comprising Palestinians who were not expelled in 1948 and were granted citizenship of the new Israeli state. Throughout this book, therefore, I will attempt to distinguish between 'Israeli Jews' and 'Israelis', since the latter term includes a substantial minority of Palestinians who can be expected to disagree fundamentally with Jewish Israelis on many vital issues relating to the peace process and the fate of the occupied territories.

3. A significant minority of Israelis, especially those who support religious or right-wing parties, argue strongly that the West Bank and Gaza Strip remain God's gift to the Jewish people. This religious argument is then used to oppose any territorial concession to the Palestinian inhabitants of these areas. Although such beliefs enjoy some following outside Israel, especially in the Jewish diaspora and in some fundamentalist Christian circles in the United States and elsewhere, they do not form any part of any diplomatic initiatives (including the Oslo process) or the many resolutions of the United Nations pertaining to Israel. This book will therefore dismiss them entirely as irrelevant to a diplomatic solution within the bounds of international law. For a recent account of Binyamin Netanyahu's efforts to bring the theological argument to bear on his efforts to dispossess the Palestinians of their land on a permanent basis, see 'Falwell to mobilize support for Israel', *New York Times*, 21 January 1998. On his January 1998 trip to Washington, Netanyahu met with many conservative Christian and Jewish leaders who argue that Israel should not give up 'an inch' of land promised by God to the Jewish people around three thousand years ago.

4. Given the resignation of his Foreign Minister David Levy in January 1998, the chances of Netanyahu seeing out his term of office until 2000 seem increasingly remote. See 'Levy quits Netanyahu coalition', *Boston Globe*, 5 January 1998.

5. For an up-to-date summary of the various Israeli plans for withdrawal from parts of the West Bank, see 'Reading the Map', *Report on Israeli Settlement in the Occupied Territories*, Vol. 8, No. 1 (January-February 1998). The three maps under consideration, none of which represents a definite commitment on the part of Israel to make any kind of withdrawal, envisage Israel's retention of at least half of the West Bank, rising to 70% in the case of Infrastructure Minister Ariel Sharon's proposal.

6. It should be recalled here that even this 50/50 plan is considered too generous by many in the Netanyahu cabinet, including the prime minister himself.

7. Uri Davis, *Israel: An Apartheid State* (London: Zed Books, 1987).

8. See A.J. Christopher, *The Atlas of Apartheid* (London: Routledge, 1994), pp. 66ff.; William Beinart, *Twentieth-Century South Africa* (Oxford: Oxford University Press, 1994), pp. 149ff.; William Beinart and Saul Dubow, 'Introduction', *Segregation and Apartheid in Twentieth-Century South Africa* (London: Routledge, 1995), pp. 15–18; and Nelson Mandela, *Long Walk to Freedom* (London: Little, Brown, 1994), pp. 222–4.

9. Nelson Mandela writes in his autobiography that the bantustan proposals

were 'a spurious solution to a problem that whites had no idea how to control', and that they would create 'a cruel jigsaw puzzle out of people's lives'. Although some black leaders agreed to the bantustan plans, the ANC held out against them. Mandela, pp. 223–4.

10. Beinart and Dubow, p. 17.

11. For a detailed comparison of the South African National Party's bantustan plan, and the 'encirclement' agenda of successive Israeli governments since the invasion of the West Bank and Gaza Strip, see Norman Finkelstein's 'Whither the "Peace Process"?', *New Left Review* 218 (July/August 1996), pp. 138–50.

12. Early evidence suggests that the breakdown of the Oslo process, along with such factors as a continuing recession in Israel, may act to dampen the fervour of the celebrations, at least within Israel. See 'Israel is planning a Jubilee party but the people are too nervous to celebrate', *Observer* (London), 18 January 1998. The Israeli ministry of foreign affairs, however, boasted on its website in December 1997 of a programme of hundreds of commemorative events, running from January to December.

1 *Greater Israel*

Zionism and the creation of Israel

The story of Israel has many beginnings, most of them misleading. A history of the modern-day state, for example, would court controversy were it simply to chronicle the foundation of Israel in 1948, and the fate of the nation in the twentieth century. As Israeli politicians have been eager to point out during the 50 years of modern Israel's existence, the heritage of the Jewish nation stretches back to King David across three thousand years of history.[1] Modern Israel, its supporters have claimed, is a triumphant restoration of a national enterprise which was once without parallel; after the unjust expulsion of the Jews from Israel by the Roman Empire in 70 AD, Jewish life had been defined by a yearning to return to those ancient lands, and the success of the Zionist effort in the 1940s was the summation of two millenia in the wilderness. Modern Israel, seen through this prism, is less a polity or a nation-state than the fulfilment of a promise made by God himself.[2]

This overwhelming picture of Israel crowds out many important facts. First, the Jewish nation broken up in the first century AD left behind a land which was far from empty; just as they had lived in the area before the Jewish people established their nation – Israel – so non-Jews continued to live peacefully in Palestine after the Jews had been scattered.[3] In fact, those Palestinians living in what was again to become Israel in 1948 could trace their ownership of the land back at least a thousand years, a significantly longer tenure than the Jews of the first century could claim. Secondly, the Jewish 'people' after 70 AD neither saw themselves as a national unit nor sought a return to the Middle East. Many, in fact, opposed such a move on political and even religious grounds. Only in the twentieth century, under the influence of the new Zionist movement and, eventually, the anti-semitic policies of Hitler, did a mass migration to Palestine seem desirable or feasible.[4] When this migration began in earnest, those Jews 'returning' to a land with which they may have had some connection two thousand years previously faced a large, entrenched Palestinian population which could trace its own ties back through the centuries across an unbroken span.

For the Palestinians, those Jews arriving from Europe in the 1930s and 1940s were no more indigenous than the British who had administered their territory, after the Ottomans, in the twentieth century.

The small number of Jewish settlers living in Palestine before the mass migration paid relatively little attention to the native Arab population.[5] However, relations between the two communities broke down as a direct result of the extent of Jewish population increase around the turn of the century. In the early 1880s, just before the Zionist project in Europe picked up speed, there were less than 25,000 Jews living amongst 550,000 Palestinians (i.e. Jews comprised 4.5% of the population of Palestine), an increase in the Jewish population of at least 15,000 from 1800, but not so alarming an advance as to disadvantage and disturb the Palestinians. However, by 1947, this Jewish community had grown in size to more than 600,000, an enormous increase that placed an impossible strain on the relations between the peoples.[6] An influx of Jews on this scale necessarily meant Palestinian losses, exacerbated by the greater financial resources of the new settlers and their colonial high-handedness towards the native population. Just as other forms of Western settlement had pitted technologically and economically advanced societies against more traditional peoples, so the process of Jewish 'return' led to a strong sense of deception and injustice in the minds of many Palestinians.[7] Their country was being taken from them before their eyes by a group of people who seemed palpably extraneous to the land: no matter how historically grounded the settlers' claims of their distant ancestry might have been, the practical differences between the visitors and the indigenous Palestinian population were numerous and overpowering.[8]

The modern Zionist project also diverged from the Jewish settlement of the nineteenth century in its emphasis on an exclusively Jewish state. Theodor Herzl, the founder of the modern 'resettlement' movement, insisted in *The Jewish State* on the need for Jews to live apart from non-Jews.[9] Although this arrangement had certainly obtained at various moments in European history, and often due more to anti-semitism than to Jewish exclusivism, the concept was alien to many European Jews and even to those settlers living amongst the Palestinians.[10] However, Herzl's Zionist organisations soon began formally to effect this separation, not only by encouraging Jews in Europe to uproot from non-Jewish communities and to settle in Palestine, but also through the actions of agencies like the new Jewish National Fund. The JNF sought donations from wealthy Westerners to buy land in Palestine and to turn it over to the exclusive and perpetual use of Jews. This land could be held publicly and, when it had swollen to the necessary proportions, it might stand as the territorial basis for a new Jewish state.[11]

The twin project of Jewish immigration and land acquisition in Palestine thus led to a growing friction with the Arab community, especially from the late 1920s when the European influx increased once again. Many Palestinians who were tenants on their land experienced the bitter loss of their livelihood as the JNF bought plots from absentee landlords and employed various extra-legal means to secure further territory.[12] Moreover, as the Zionists gathered support for their project from many of the colonial powers, Palestinians awoke to the real possibility that they might lose all of their land in the near future. From Herzl onwards, Zionist leaders made no attempt to disguise their national ambitions, or to conceal the fact that Palestinians could play no part in the desired Jewish state. Although Israel would later claim that the surrounding Arab nations were a persistent threat to its existence, it is more accurate to see Zionism's challenge to Palestinian life, at the individual and societal level, as the primary cause of hostility.[13]

Of course, the re-emergence of anti-semitism in parts of Europe was a strong incentive for Jews to migrate, especially after Hitler's consolidation of power in 1933. However, the terrible developments in Europe should not be allowed to obscure the Palestinian perspective on Jewish immigration. The Palestinian people were clearly not to blame for the rise of Hitler, or for his racist agenda. Although some Israelis have tried to implicate Palestinians in the Nazi genocide, it is undeniable that the indigenous population of Palestine played no part whatsoever in the cleansing of Jewish areas in Europe.[14] Instead, the Palestinians were faced in the 1930s and 1940s with the loss of their own lands at the hands of Jewish victims fleeing to Palestine to escape Hitler. In Palestine, there was no just compromise between the Palestinians and the Jewish settlers; instead, the sins visited on European Jews were subsequently visited on Palestinians entirely innocent of the initial crimes.[15]

Moreover, the Palestinians cannot be held responsible for the exclusivist impulse of Zionism, and the various mechanisms by which newly arriving Jews were prepared, not for co-existence with their neighbours, but for confrontation and separation. A degree of hostility between the communities was circumstantial, stemming from the size of the Zionist effort and the practical consequences of such an enormous colonisation project. However, Palestinians were undoubtedly angered and frightened by the insistence of Zionism on an integral, separate Jewish state, their fears taking practical shape as the JNF acquired more land for solely Jewish use as each year passed.[16] The settlers themselves had been told to expect an empty land for their cultivation: the Zionist mantra held that Palestine was 'a land without a people for a people without a land'. When they arrived to find that this was not the case, many Jews found it hard to adjust to the reality of cohabitation, and were more willing to endorse exclusivist and separatist policies than perhaps they might have been, had they known about Palestine's indigenous population before their arrival.[17]

Hitler's appalling acceleration of anti-semitism in the 1940s led directly, and tragically, to the bloody foundation of Israel in 1948. More and more Jews fled Europe for Palestine, causing even greater tensions between the openly hostile Palestinian and Jewish communities, and strengthening Jewish demands that the immigrant population, now numbering more than half a million, should be given a state of its own. Meanwhile, the horror of the death camps eroded the previous insistence of the international community that the Jewish immigrants had no *a priori* right to build a state on Palestinian land. After 1945, when various European nations had to confront either their direct complicity in the Nazi genocide or their failure to act decisively to prevent it, the moral argument against an exclusivist Israel had virtually disappeared.[18]

In addition, the Jewish community in Palestine had been acquiring sufficient military means to effect its declaration of independence without external assistance. If an Israeli state might be created by Jewish settlers alone, it was even easier for Western nations to recognise its legitimacy and vouchsafe their support. Utilising their connections with wealthy Jewish donors in Europe and America, the settlers in Palestine acquired arms from Czechoslovakia and married them to the new immigrants. Since many Jews had recently fought against the Nazis in various national armies, the settlers could rely on a well-trained core of soldiers to lead the anticipated 'liberation' struggle against the unwitting Arabs.[19]

The British, who had been responsible for Palestine since the First World War, responded to the growing communal violence by passing the issue of a Jewish state to the new United Nations. The UN, composed at the time almost entirely of Western powers, many of them still active in their colonial projects, voted to create three separate areas in Palestine: a Jewish state, a Palestinian state, and an international zone in which the two communities would live side by side under UN supervision. This last zone included the whole of Jerusalem, the site of fiercest confrontation between the sides. The UN plan gave the Jewish settlers, who by then numbered around one third of the population of

Palestine and owned less than 7% of the land, more than half of the available territory for a new state. Palestinians, amazed at the inequitable nature of this proposal, rejected it, whilst the Jewish settlers gladly accepted and began to defend their new gains.[20]

From November 1947 until January 1949, various battles were fought between Jews and Arabs. In the middle of this period, on 14 May 1948, the Jewish settlers proclaimed their independence. The official Israeli view of the ensuing events, expressed for decades following 1948, was that the Palestinians and their supporters in neighbouring Arab nations rejected the UN partition plan because of their greed, then tried to destroy the new Israeli state. In consequence, the Jewish defenders repelled the attack, and many Arabs fled their homes on the assumption that an eventual Arab victory would effect their return. For generations, this received story of Israel's founding has stressed Arab ingratitude, weakness and cowardice, alongside Israel's efforts to accommodate its neighbours and the honest resolve of the Jewish settlers.[21]

In the last decade or so, however, this historical myth has been challenged within Israel by a new generation of historians, the so-called 'revisionists'. Facing up to some aspects of Israel's founding, they have admitted that Israel came into being through well-planned military action and atrocities committed against the Palestinian population. They have conceded the unfairness of the UN plan; admitted that the Jewish settlers tried to expand their area under the partition proposal well before they met with resistance from Palestinian or Arab armies; and they have confirmed that the massive number of Palestinian refugees did not leave their homes of their own volition, but were instead forced out by Israeli massacres and threats.[22] We can see from these new histories that Israeli soldiers fought outside the boundaries of the Jewish state under the partition plan, attempting to create a much greater Israel than the UN had originally intended. As a result, when the outnumbered and overpowered Arab forces finally conceded defeat early in 1949, Israel had swollen to encompass the vast majority of what had been Palestine. The indigenous population, meanwhile, had been scattered comprehensively, with only around 150,000 Palestinians remaining in the new Israel.[23]

This book is largely concerned with Israel's actions in the West Bank and Gaza Strip after 1967. We should pause here in 1949, however, to consider the statistics of Israel's founding. From a population of only 25,000 in 1880, Jewish settlers had grown to almost 600,000 by 1947. These settlers still owned only 7% of the land in 1947, but were offered 56% of Palestine under the UN plan. Moreover, at the end of the fighting in 1949, Israel controlled 77% of what had formerly been Palestine: in only seventy years, the Palestinians had gone from being virtually the sole residents of Palestine to being in control of less than a quarter of it. Anti-semitism in Europe, with Zionism as its consequence, had pushed the Palestinian population into a tiny proportion of its former territory and had created a new, exclusivist state which could hardly enjoy normal relations with its Arab neighbours.

Given the spectacular rate of Jewish migration to Palestine after 1880, and the terrible events of 1947–1949, many Palestinians, and Arabs generally, found it very difficult to make peace with the idea of Israel. The moral argument for Israel's founding was, from a Palestinian perspective, hardly overwhelming; and the conversion of such a large proportion of Palestine into Israel made the Jewish state an even less attractive prospect, especially for the victims of its efforts to 'cleanse' areas of their native populations. For 750,000 Palestinians now exiled from their land, Israel's Declaration of Independence meant the loss of their entire experience: their livelihood, their heritage and their prospects disappeared overnight.[24] And so these people, marooned in refugee camps in the West Bank, Gaza, Jordan and elsewhere, were hardly willing to acknowledge Israel, to make a compromise between their own claims and those of the settlers. The Palestinians had not forced the Jews out of Europe, but were themselves forced from their homeland by Jewish military operations and the exclusivist imperatives of the new Israel. As Israel formalised and fortified its new 1949 borders, Arab resentment also became entrenched, the Palestinians far from satisfied with a territorial conquest that had given the minority Jewish population more than 75% of their land.

Between 1949 and 1967, the indigenous population of the remaining 23% of Palestine continued as best it could, prevented from achieving full autonomy by the administration of Jordan in the West Bank and Egypt in the Gaza Strip. Neighbouring countries had identified Israel as a threat to their own territory, just as Israel claimed that its neighbours sought its own destruction; and so Palestine was once again occupied. Aside from Israel's invasion of Egypt in 1956, and the ensuing Suez crisis, a number of minor skirmishes took place between Israel and the Arab states during this period, contributing to an ongoing atmosphere of tension between the sides. The pattern of defence and attack between Israel and its neighbours continued along these lines until the late 1960s, when Israel decided to take matters into its own hands. Having used the two decades since independence both to increase its population and to invest in expensive military equipment, Israel was well placed to put the threats of surrounding Arab nations to the sword, even if its own strength made these threats more rhetorical than actual. In June 1967, Israel launched a huge pre-emptive strike on its neighbours, obliterating their offensive capability and paving the way for sweeping territorial gains. In the course of 'defending' its 1949 success, Israel occupied the West Bank and Gaza Strip as well as vast areas of the Sinai desert in Egypt. The Palestinian population which had found itself coralled into the West Bank and Gaza twenty years earlier now watched helplessly as the last 23% of what had been Palestine fell under Israeli control.[25]

1967 and its aftermath

By the end of June 1967, the Israeli army controlled the West Bank, East Jerusalem, the Gaza Strip, the Golan Heights and the Sinai peninsula. Supposedly in anticipation of a massive attack on the Jewish state itself, Israel had acquired sweeping territories from all its Arab neighbours. Now it faced the challenge of what to do with these lands taken by war, and how to treat the massive Palestinian population now living under its occupation.[26]

The official Israeli position was that the Six-Day War was a wholly defensive measure, undertaken with the sole intention of preserving Israel. Although the speed of the Arab defeat, and the extent of Israel's land gains, cast doubt on this picture of Israel on the brink of destruction, government officials repeated the message that occupation was solely for security reasons. The captured territories would presumably form buffer zones to help insulate 1949-Israel from further attack.[27]

It was, however, difficult to overlook other motives for the war, or at least to admit that the Israeli conception of the usefulness of the territories was in flux. Before the end of June 1967, the Knesset passed a law to allow for the effective absorption of East Jerusalem, part of the West Bank and under Jordanian administration before the war. On 28 June, the legal process was completed, and an institutional framework was established for the widespread expulsion of Palestinians from some areas and the transfer of Israeli Jews into others.[28]

The 'reunification' of Israel was a distinctly different phenomenon from the 'defence of Israel'. Whereas the latter tapped into negative fears of Israelis that the Zionist project might still be destroyed, Jerusalem's annexation provided positive images of Israel's national achievement, and reopened historical vistas back towards the putative golden age of biblical Israel, a land stretching from the Mediterranean to the Euphrates. If mainstream Israeli politicians had before 1967 concentrated on the practical goal of consolidating the state of 1949, the magnitude of the 1967 victory and the symbolic return of Jerusalem licensed more romantic and ambitious visions of the future Israeli state in the following years.[29]

At first glance, the Palestinian territories acquired by Israel may not have promised much. No Jews lived in these areas, and the indigenous inhabitants had fought bitterly with Israel for control of the land. If the native population was to remain on the land, Israel's opportunities for finding a permanent use for the conquered territory seemed limited. The immediate annexation of East Jerusalem, however, offered some idea of Israel's future strategy. Having first declared Israeli sovereignty over exclusively Palestinian areas, the government and town municipality 'cleansed' the Old City of hundreds of Palestinians and implemented building proposals for the new Jewish areas in the territory recently captured. Despite the protests of the United Nations, Israel quickly secured Jerusalem not against external threats but for the purpose of its own aggrandisement.[30]

The international community responded to Israel's annexation policy in the strongest terms: the UN Security Council resolved in November 1967 that Israel should withdraw 'from territories of recent conflict', emphasising the 'inadmissibility of the acquisition of territory by war'. In accordance with the dictates of international law, the Security Council recognised the illegality of permanent occupation or the annexation of conquered territory, and explicitly ordered Israel to return that which it had taken in the June war. In return, Israel would receive a 'guarantee' of the 'territorial inviolability and political independence of every state in the area', a recognition of its existence from countries that had opposed Israel's formation in 1948.[31]

Since 1967, Palestinians have placed their hope in Resolution 242 and the other UN efforts to force Israel to reverse its gains. Having lost the majority of British Mandate Palestine in 1949, the Palestinians might, if 242 were fully implemented, be able to form a small but viable state on the lands remaining to them. This state would lie alongside Israel but would be free from its army and the forces of its former occupier, Jordan. Those Palestinians who have sought a two-state solution have cast their thoughts back to 1967, when an Israeli withdrawal would have left the basis for an independent state.

The settlement programme

Unfortunately, East Jerusalem did not mark the limit of Israel's territorial ambitions. In the decade following the Six-Day War, the security rationale for retaining the occupied territories was largely replaced by ideological arguments advocating the expansion of the Jewish state. The practical result of this shift in opinion was the settlement programme, which was fundamentally to alter the status of the occupied territories and the prospects for Israeli–Palestinian peace.[32]

By August 1967, a group called the 'Movement for the Whole Land of Israel' had sprung up, advocating the acquisition and absorption of those areas supposedly promised by God to the Jewish people of the Bible. With a membership composed of religious intellectuals and former members of Zionist terror groups, the movement put pressure on successive Israeli governments to colonise the West Bank and Gaza Strip. By the mid-1970s, thousands of settlers had crossed over into occupied territory to establish Israeli settlements amongst the Palestinians. With the tacit and occasionally direct help of the Israeli army, the first Jewish settlements were instated.[33]

Inside Israel, the movement was joined in 1974 by Gush Emunim (the 'Bloc of the Faithful'), a still more influential group with an expanding membership which sought to bridge the gap between ancient religious mysticism and contemporary political practice. The ruling left-wing Labour party, which had confidently annexed East Jerusalem in 1967 but had since vacillated over the colonisation of the other occupied areas, was swept away in 1977 by the Likud government of Menachem Begin. Amongst the new prime minister's first official engagements was a meeting with Rabbi Tzvi Yehuda Kook, spiritual leader of Gush Emunim, at which Begin kneeled with respect and paid tribute to the contributions of the ideological settler movement to his victory.[34]

The effect of groups like Gush Emunim in the 1970s was to push Israel away from an understanding of its occupation as a security measure and towards the recognition of the occupied territories as an integral part of a greater Israel. Those elements within the Labour party that had already opted for annexation of the majority of the occupied territories to Israel found their arguments bolstered from the right; and although there was some debate in Labour circles about the desirability of formal absorption of so much territory and so many Palestinians, the growing Likud party soared in popularity as it offered Israelis the dream of a bigger, better Jewish state. The religious and nationalist elements in society in turn provided the ideological justification for actions which left Israel condemned by virtually every other nation. The international community had interpreted Israel's actions from 1967 as the coercion and, eventually, eviction of a native people by foreign invaders. By reviving historical and mythical memories of the original Jewish settlement two thousand years earlier, groups like Gush Emunim dismissed such charges, and encouraged Israelis to feel proud of their territorial achievements. The new understanding of the territories' importance was based on biblical injunction and a romantic vision of ancient Jewish history: the West Bank was not being occupied by Israel, but rather 'reclaimed' or even 'redeemed'. The Palestinians, if one cast an eye far enough back, were the occupiers of properly Jewish land. With this conception of the gains of 1967 in place, and the security rationale overshadowed, the Likud government was able in 1977 to institute a massive state-sponsored settlement drive.[35]

The settler movement has frequently been regarded, especially outside Israel, as a fringe group, comprising religious or political extremists and not accurately reflecting public opinion. This view is obviously countered by the fact that the Likud party was consistently returned to power in the years after 1977, standing on exactly this platform of expansionist nationalism and irredentism. However, we can also detect more practical or prosaic motives for settlement activity, especially on the left wing of Israel's political divide.

Moshe Dayan, whose father had helped to found the left-wing Labour (Mapai) party in the 1930s, was defence minister during the Six-Day War and had strong links to the left-wing establishment on account of his family and his closeness to David Ben-Gurion.[36] However, in a speech given in August 1967 within the newly captured walls of Jerusalem's Old City, Dayan made clear his support for Jewish settlement throughout the entire occupied territories. Although he spoke from an ideological perspective informed by messianic nationalism, he made the crucial realisation that the settlement programme should be guided by pragmatism, not ideology: 'I favour facts that will bind hands, not only ours, but also those of the other side, and the hands of reality.'[37]

Dayan's genius was to acknowledge that gradual settlement would affect the Israeli public's idea of the potential for Israeli expansion even more than would biblical exegeses and jingoistic propaganda. Moreover, the 'creation of facts' would bind Israelis and Palestinians together by creating a new reality on the ground. Palestinian claims based on international law or the past arrangement in the occupied territories would be irrelevant in the face of this new reality.

Dayan confirmed his influence on the settlement programme by defecting from Labour to Likud during the right-wing landslide of 1977; and he became foreign minister in Begin's cabinet, contributing to the new government's systematic colonisation of the West Bank and Gaza.[38] The state's policy was simple. First, large areas of Palestinian land would be targeted by surveyors or prospectors for settlement. Next, the land would be formally claimed by the state of Israel via many dubious or openly fallacious legal fiats.[39] Finally, the government would massively subsidise the cost of living in the settlement, reducing either the price of a building plot or the rent on a ready-built apartment, and ensuring that the tax status of the area was suitably low. With so many financial incentives to become a settler, and so few of the hardships associated with 'frontier' life in other countries, it is little wonder that the Israeli government was able to persuade thousands of ordinary Jewish citizens to move onto occupied land. Whilst there were those who moved into the territories because of ideology, the majority of settlers moved for financial reasons: their government made them an offer they couldn't refuse.[40]

By the early 1980s, Israel had succeeded in settling tens of thousands of its Jewish citizens on occupied Palestinian land, in violation of international law and the stated opinion of the international community.[41] More importantly, it had begun to change the reality of its territorial relationship with the Palestinians. Finally, it had persuaded the Israeli public to adopt a very different vision of the West Bank and Gaza Strip than had been widely held in 1967. Although Israel's Labour leaders had quickly sensed the opportunities for annexation after the invasions of 1967, the process of selling such a plan to the Israeli people was a more drawn-out affair. Over the following years, the Palestinians came to be seen no longer as the residents of Jordan or Palestine, but as the illegal occupants of 'Eretz Yisrael', Greater Israel; the West Bank became Judea and Samaria on Israeli maps and in the language of the political debate; and the territories themselves, seized amidst rejoicing and triumphalism in June 1967, were no longer 'occupied' but 'disputed'.[42]

Settlements and Israeli public opinion

The consequence of Israel's 1967 gains was an Arab world more than ever convinced of the injustice of the Israeli presence in the Middle East. However, in the wake of the Yom Kippur War of 1973 with Egypt and Syria, and the gravitation of the Egyptian government towards the United States, some Israelis began to see the advantages of peace overtures to consolidate Israel's regional position. Under American supervision, Israel entered into successful negotiations with Egypt, culminating in a peace treaty which promised to address the Palestine question, but which resulted only in an Israeli withdrawal from the Sinai peninsula. Egypt's president, Anwar Sadat, attempted throughout the negotiations to insist on the primacy of the Palestinian issue and Israel's occupation, but Menachem Begin's reluctance to concede any part of the West Bank and Gaza ensured that the peace treaty's provisions for implementing 242 were later ignored.[43]

Sadat's failure to persuade Begin, and particularly the United States, that Israel should pledge to withdraw fully from the occupied territories set an unfortunate seal on his own nation's new peace with Israel. However inadvertently, it appeared over time that Egypt had gone into a peace deal without its fellow Arabs, and the unity of their former approach to Israel was now broken. Although it would be easy to exaggerate the degree to which Arab states had cooperated on their foreign policy aims during this earlier period, it was certainly the case that Sadat's predecessor, Gamal Abdul Nasser, had frightened both the United States and Israel with his talk of 'Pan-Arabism' and a single, vast Arab state. At the Camp David peace negotiations concluded in 1978, Egypt resolved to accept Israel's existence and a weak commitment to advance Palestinian autonomy in return for the Sinai and a huge aid package from the US. Israel, on the other hand, was gifted a more stable environment in which the Begin government could permanently settle the occupied territories.[44]

The peace concluded with Egypt may also have persuaded many Israelis of the compatibility of continued occupation with an Arab peace. If Egypt was prepared to sign an agreement with the 1967 gains intact, Israel's actions in the Six-Day War took on a new legitimacy, even a permanence. Flushed with success, the Likud government launched its biggest settlement drives to date, committed to restraining its ambition only in the Sinai, which was to be returned to Egypt under the peace agreement. However, by the time the Israeli army came to dismantle the Sinai settlements in 1982, even this minor concession seemed too great. The Sinai settlers clashed openly with the troops sent to evict them, and enjoyed widespread support throughout Israel for their principled stand against negotiated withdrawal.[45]

While the Sinai settlements were being dismantled, settlement activity in the West Bank was reaching record levels.[46] There was some evidence in the early 1980s, however, that public opinion in Israel was split over the desirability of annexing the entire occupied territories.[47] For his part, Menachem Begin resolved to answer this uncertainty with a display of Israeli military might and Palestinian/Arab weakness. Less than two months after the Sinai settler protest, Israel launched its spectacular assault on Lebanon, aiming both to destroy the Palestinian leadership-in-exile and to crush the spirit of the Palestinians in the occupied territories as a precursor to further Israeli settlement.[48]

Begin's objectives were not entirely realised. Although he did succeed in killing a large number of Lebanese and Palestinian civilians, and in driving the PLO from the region, the sheer brutality of the offensive forced many in Israel to take stock of Likud's policies.[49] Aside from official investigations into some of the bloodier actions of the military, the liberal community inside Israel threw its weight behind organisations like Peace Now, which rejected the Likud's advocacy of brute force and sought negotiations with the Palestinians over the future of the occupied territories. The Likud and Gush Emunim supporters fought openly with Peace Now and some members of Labour, a dispute which itself descended into violence with a grenade attack on a Peace Now march in 1983. As settlement building in the occupied territories continued unabated (the number of settlers almost tripled between 1982 and 1985), the real possibility of civil disorder, even civil war, gripped Israel's leaders.[50]

Although it would be simple to extrapolate from these tensions two distinct blocs in Israeli society, one opposed to and one promoting settlement activity, this would present a distorted picture of the actions of Israel's various elected leaders during this crucial period. The Labour party, for example, resolved its difficulties with Likud, not by challenging and isolating the agenda of the Right, but by forming in 1985 a 'national unity government' which remained committed to all of Begin's plans for the ongoing Jewish settlement of the occupied territories.[51] More generally, Dayan's pragmatic advocacy of 'fact creation' offered all Israelis an opportunity to reconcile the annexation of the occupied territories with their own beliefs. Whether one believed in a biblical idea of Greater Israel, or a nationalist conception of more living space for Israelis, or the view that Israeli society could only survive with the land and water resources of the West Bank (and South Lebanon), Dayan's policy of creeping annexation offered the means by which one could effect these ends. Crucially, the 'facts' in the occupied territories also bound those Israelis who might oppose annexation in the abstract to a historical acceptance of Israel's action: to oppose settlement was to hold an anachronistic argument, to rule oneself out of the practical discussions necessary to the future of the settlement programme.

As the settlements expanded, and the sheer number of 'facts' made effective opposition within Israel more difficult, so the material conditions within and around the settlements disarmed the attacks of those who had linked the West Bank and Gaza projects to Israel's adventures in Lebanon. The early settlements had been heavily dependent on ideology and obvious military might, religious or nationalist occupants guarded by soldiers from the encroachment of the nearby Palestinians.

As the settlement programme advanced, some of the more obvious differences between life in 1949-Israel and life in the occupied territories were dissolved. The Israeli government confiscated more land and the areas immediately around the settlements were cleansed of Palestinian inhabitants or labourers. The ramshackle early settlements were replaced with permanent structures, made more secure by design and by the greater numbers of settlers. A separate infrastructure for the settlements was laid down and linked to Israel, providing a physical and psychological continuity between Israel 'proper' and its new outposts.[52] Given that the vast majority of settlers were flocking to the occupied territories for economic rather than ideological reasons, it was much more important to emphasise this continuity rather than to stress various pioneer or redemptive ideas which had fired the early settlers. Although some ideological settlements remained (such as the tiny enclave in the centre of Hebron), the Israeli government made deliberate and extensive efforts to model the majority of settlements closly on the pattern of existing Israeli towns.[53]

It was easy, therefore, for those opponents of the Lebanon war to castigate the Hebron settlers or the zealots of Gush Emunim for their extremism and refusal to compromise; but it became more difficult to deal with the tens of thousands of more moderate Israelis who migrated to occupied East Jerusalem or the settlements of the central West Bank. In these crucial areas, upon which a viable Palestinian state would depend, the Israeli government did all in its power to make the process of annexation as smooth and unremarkable as possible.[54]

The intifada and the road to Oslo

The consequences of the settlement programme for Palestinians were grave and extensive. Those who had already lost their land and their homes in the 1940s during Israeli expulsions had now to come to terms not only with another occupation, but with another systematic process of eviction and dispossession. Already-crowded cities and refugee camps were filled still further beyond capacity with those Palestinians cleared away by Israel to make room for Jewish settlement. From being majority residents in the whole of Mandate Palestine, the occupants of the West Bank and Gaza had to accept the possibility that they might again lose their livelihood and identity, this time with nowhere to retreat to in defeat. As it became clear that Israel intended not to occupy but to colonise the last remaining Palestinian areas, so the settlements became the chief target of Palestinian protest and the chief obstacle to peace.[55]

The ongoing building projects of the Labour/Likud administration

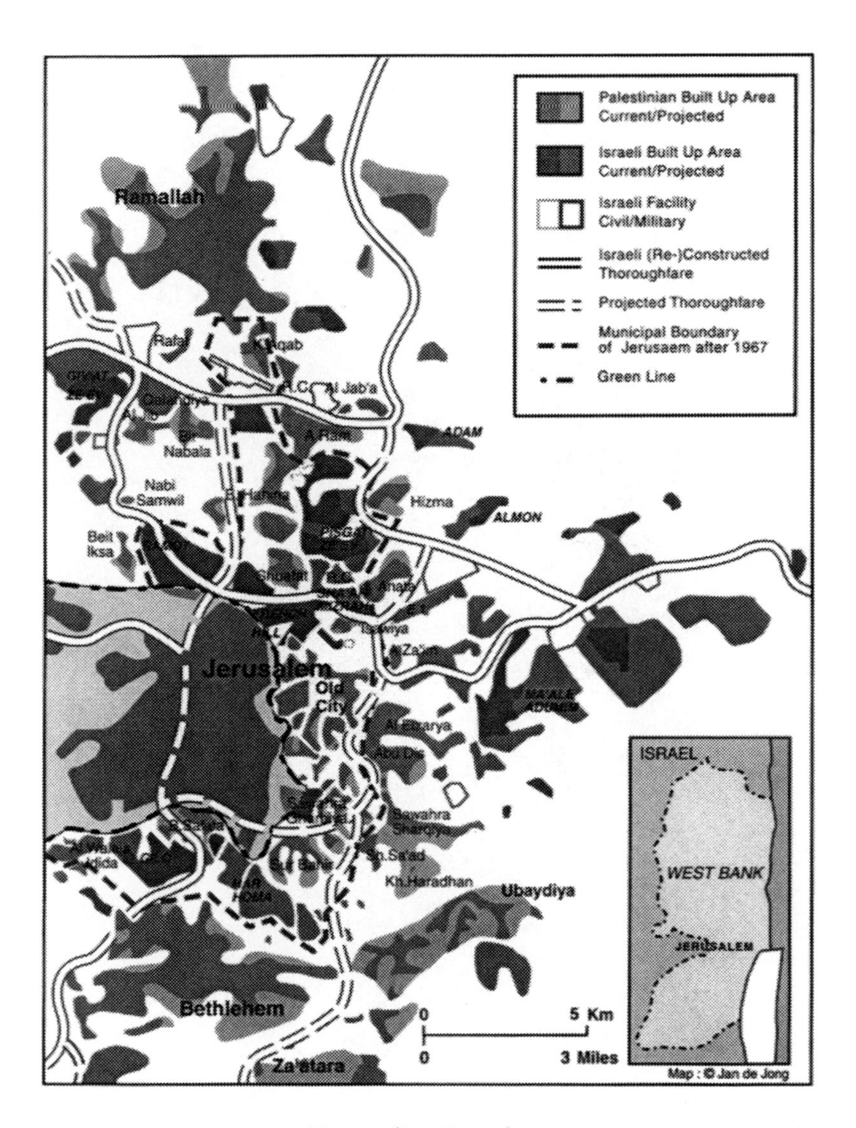

Metropolitan Jerusalem

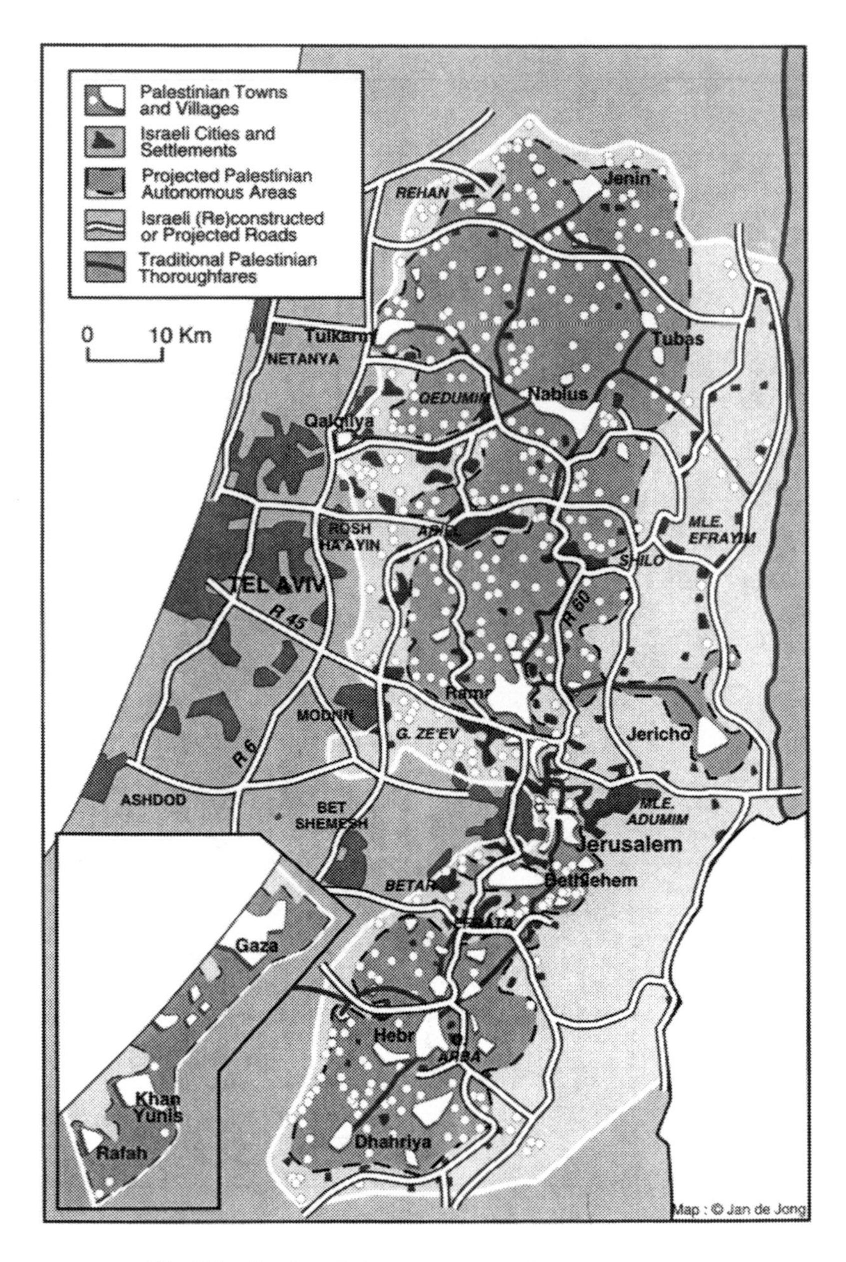

The West Bank and Gaza: Projection for the year 2010

in the mid-1980s eventually provoked organised resistance from Palestinians. Although Israel had pushed the PLO as far as possible from its home, and killed many of its leading lights in an effort to stymie effective Palestinian responses to its policies, the weight of dispossession and eviction ultimately produced a grassroots reaction to the occupation. From small beginnings in December 1987, the Palestinian uprising, the intifada, spread throughout the territories and offered the occupying forces the stiffest opposition they had encountered in twenty years.[56] As the Israeli army followed Yitzhak Rabin's infamous dictate to 'break the bones' of the stone-throwing protesters, international opinion was again focused on the brutality of the occupation and the continued refusal of Israel to facilitate Palestinian national aspirations.[57]

Having occupied the West Bank and Gaza Strip for twenty years, Israel cannot have been prepared for the intensity and extent of Palestinian resistance evident in the intifada. If successive governments had believed that they could treat the occupied territories as de facto extensions of Israel, the intifada taught them that they had an angry native population to deal with as well. The strength of Palestinian resistance, coupled with domestic and international protest at the repressive tactics of the Israeli army, forced Israel to consider a more permanent, de jure solution to the occupation.

In the main, Israeli settlements had avoided the centres of Palestinian population and were instead situated on good agricultural land, near the best water supplies. Although the Jewish residents of Hebron were a powerful symbol of one constituency inside the settler movement, most of the existing and expected West Bank settlers would be put off by the prospect of daily, face-to-face confrontation with the people they had expelled. The everyday migrants envisaged by the enormous colonisation programme sought just the opposite: they wanted reassurance that the Palestinians were as far away as possible. The targets for most new developments, therefore, were those lands from which it was relatively easy to expel the Palestinian population, especially the rural areas away from the major Palestinian cities.[58] The experience of the intifada confirmed the wisdom of this strategy. Whilst the Jewish enclave in Hebron and the various Israeli buildings inside Nablus and Bethlehem were vulnerable to Palestinian crowds, the bulk of the settlements were easy to reach (via the new road links with Israel) and simple to defend. Although it was difficult to police a Palestinian population in the cities, it was not hard to seal off those same cities to prevent the population from mobilising against the vast majority of settlements situated in the Palestinian countryside.

As more and more Israeli soldiers were injured in urban street battles with Palestinians, and Israel's international reputation was increasingly defined by its army's brutality in the occupied territories, a solution began to crystallise: why not take the Israeli army out of the Palestinian cities altogether? To redeploy from the urban areas, comprising only around 3% of the West Bank, would protect Israeli soldiers from the full force of the intifada without compromising the further progress of the settlement programme. In addition, this apparently generous gesture would offset much of the criticism levelled at Israel abroad, and would enable the Israeli government to claim that the occupied territories were occupied no longer.

Palestinians believed that they had won something through the intifada: they had humbled the mighty Israeli military and earned a new respect after the disastrous Arab defeat of 1967. However, Israel was not about to elevate their urban intransigence into a threat to its entire occupation. It had become difficult for Israel to maintain order in the cities, but this experience helped to focus Israeli minds on the real objective of the occupation: the settlements. The intifada taught Israel's leaders that a degree of Palestinian self-rule in the cities might actually consolidate Israeli control over the land elsewhere, forcing the Palestinians to police themselves and enabling the army to control the Palestinian population from a distance. In retrospect, the intifada contained a terrible irony for Palestinians: it proved the compatibility of Palestinian self-rule with the furthering of the Israeli settlement programme. In many respects, this irony lies at the heart of the Oslo process and best explains its failure.

Notes

1. For an example of this, see Shimon Peres's memoirs, *Battling for Peace* (London: Weidenfield and Nicolson, 1995), in which the former prime minister speaks of 'Israel's collective consciousness' as 'built out of millions of pent-up memories'.

2. This is made explicit in Israel's Declaration of Independence: 'Exiled from the Land of Israel, the Jewish people remained faithful to it in all the countries of their dispersion, never ceasing to pray and hope for their return and the restoration of their national freedom.' Walter Laqueur and Barry Rubin (eds), *The Israel–Arab Reader* (London: Penguin Books, 1995, 5th edition), pp. 107–9.

3. For accounts of this period, see Charles D. Smith, *Palestine and the Arab–Israeli Conflict* (New York: St Martin's Press, 1992, 2nd edition), pp. 4–15; Benjamin Beit-Hallahmi, *Original Sins: Reflections on the History of Zionism and*

Israel (London: Pluto Press, 1992), pp. 4–16; and Keith W. Whitelam, *The Invention of Ancient Israel* (London: Routledge, 1996).

4. Israeli historian Israel Shahak has chronicled Jewish thought in this period and has overturned the assumptions of many Israeli scholars; see 'The weight of history', in *Jewish History, Jewish Religion* (London: Pluto Press, 1994), pp. 50–74; and Beit-Hallahmi, pp. 32–45. See also Lenni Brenner, *Zionism in the Age of the Dictators* (Westport, Connecticut: Lawrence Hill, 1983).

5. Beit-Hallahmi, p. 65. See also Walter Lehn with Uri Davis, *The Jewish National Fund* (London: Kegan Paul, 1988), pp. 18–19.

6. These figures are from the 'Survey prepared for the Anglo-American Committee of Inquiry into the question of Palestine' (Jerusalem, 1946), cited in Lehn, p. 6; and the United Nations Survey of 1947, cited in Smith, p. 135; and Donald Neff, *Fallen Pillars: United States Policy towards Palestine and Israel Since 1945* (Washington: Institute for Palestine Studies, 1995), p. 37.

7. Beit-Hallahmi, p. 62, refers to a Zionist rally in London's Royal Albert Hall in 1919, where leading Zionist Max Nordau told a British audience including Prime Minister David Lloyd George that the Jewish settlers 'know what you expect of us. We shall have to be the guards of the Suez Canal. We shall have to be the sentinels of your way to India.' Incredibly, this is almost exactly what happened 35 years later, as Egyptian nationalist leader Nasser was attacked by Israel, with British support, after trying to assert Egyptian sovereignty over the canal.

8. For settlers' dismissive treatment of Arabs, see the Hebrew sources cited by Lehn, pp. 12–13; and Nur Masalha, *Expulsion of the Palestinians* (Washington: Institute for Palestine Studies, 1992), pp. 6–7.

9. Herzl rejected those who sought to integrate Jews with non-Jews as 'amiable visionaries'; the compulsion of anti-semitism would eventually prove his argument, he predicted. 'Universal brotherhood is not even a beautiful dream. Antagonism is essential to Man's greatest efforts.' *The Jewish State*, p. 153.

10. See, for example, Beit-Hallahmi's account of the Dreyfus affair in France, and the success of the Jewish community there after Dreyfus' eventual pardoning; *Original Sins*, pp. 34–5. Israel Shahak has argued that Zionist leaders not only grew in popularity because of anti-semitism, but were actually complicit in its aims. Referring to the 'conservative alliance' between Zionism and anti-semitism, Shahak cites leading Zionist figures (including Joachim Prinz, vice-chairman of the World Jewish Congress and president of the American Jewish Congress) who were quietly contented with Hitler's rise in the early 1930s because it threatened the 'liberalism' on which Jewish integration depended. Prinz declared triumphantly in 1934, after Hitler's victory: 'The only form of political life which has helped Jewish assimilation is sunk.' Shahak, p. 79.

11. This process of systematic land purchase and exclusive use is the subject of Lehn's *The Jewish National Fund*. The Fund's intention, according to Lehn, was 'to acquire and retain in Jewish hands ownership of land in Palestine for the purpose of settling Jews on it'; p. 14.

12. Lehn, pp. 54–7, outlines the JNF's policy changes and its various efforts to establish a de facto Jewish state.

13. Nur Masalha has revealed a wide consensus on the part of even nineteenth-century Zionists that the Jewish state could not emerge in Palestine without a major transfer of the Palestinian population away from their homeland. The idea of transfer was thus an integral part of Zionist political thought from the earliest days of the twentieth century. Israel Zangwill, perpetrator of the myth that Palestine was 'a land without a people', recommended an 'Arab exodus' in his 1920 book *The Voice of Jerusalem*, insisting that 'we cannot allow the Arabs to block so valuable a piece of historic reconstruction.' See also, *Expulsion of the Palestinians*, pp. 13 –14. Beit Hallahmi, pp. 68–74, views the Arab 'problem' through a colonialist rather than a moral lens: the difficulty for Zionists was not how to transfer large numbers of natives, but how to persuade the colonial powers to let them execute the scheme.

14. The British journalist Robert Fisk has criticised Yad Vashem, Israel's holocaust museum in Jerusalem, for its efforts to present the Mufti of Jerusalem, spiritual leader of many Palestinians, as an important figure in Hitler's project of Jewish extermination. Whilst the Mufti met with Hitler in Germany during the war and tried to persuade him to stop the immigration of Jews to Palestine, Yad Vashem presents the Mufti (and the Palestinians he is supposed to represent) as complicit in the holocaust. For Fisk, this turns the museum into 'an instrument of propaganda': 'the inference is clear: the Muslim religious leader of the Palestinian Arabs is also a war criminal. So why should not his political successors be war criminals?' See Robert Fisk, *Pity the Nation* (Oxford: Oxford University Press, 1992, 2nd edition), p. 16. In fact, Hitler was also receiving embassies from militant Zionist groups fighting the British in Palestine. The National Military Organisation, composed from these militant groups, told the Nazis in a communiqué of January 1941 that Zionist fighters in Palestine were 'well acquainted with the goodwill of the German Reich government and its authorities towards Zionist activity inside Germany and towards Zionist immigration plans'; the NMO also claimed to be 'of the opinion that [c]ommon interests could exist between the establishment of a New Order in Europe in conformity with the German concept, and the true aspirations of the Jewish people'. This document is translated into English by Lenni Brenner in *Zionism in the Age of the Dictators*, (Zed Books Ltd, 1984), pp. 267–8.

15. The meeting of Arab heads of state in October 1944 produced a document which offers a proper balance to Israel's efforts to insinuate Arab complicity in the holocaust. The Alexandria Protocol declared that Arab states were 'second to none in regretting the woes that have been inflicted upon the Jews of Europe by European dictatorial states', but that 'there can be no greater injustice and aggression than solving the problems of the Jews of Europe by another injustice.' Quoted in Smith, p. 124.

16. Smith confirms that JNF land, once purchased by Zionists, became 'inalienably Jewish, never to be sold to or worked by non-Jews, as part of a program to establish a dominant Jewish presence in the area'. Ibid., p. 31.

17. Israel Zangwill coined the slogan 'a land without a people for a people without a land', and he and other Zionist leaders perpetuated the myth long after they knew that the reality was very different. See Beit-Hallahmi, pp. 60 ff.; Lehn, pp. 10–13; and Masalha, *Expulsion of the Palestinians*, pp. 5–8.

18. Although Benjamin Beit-Hallahmi argues that Zionism's triumph was assured long before the holocaust (p. 172), he concedes that the genocide reinforced Zionism's contention that anti-semitism was inevitable, especially amongst the colonial powers whose consent was crucial to Israel's foundation; p. 170. Donald Neff makes the same point from a different perspective, showing how Harry Truman's support for Israel strengthened in the light of the holocaust, and how American public opinion rallied to the idea of a Jewish state after confronting the images of the death camps and the masses of displaced people. *Fallen Pillars*, pp. 44–5.

19. Michael Palumbo attacks the 'David' myth which suggests that the Jews in Palestine were a tiny, outnumbered force in the 'War of Independence', detailing the Zionists' material and logistical superiority over the Arabs; *The Palestinian Catastrophe* (London: Faber and Faber, 1987), p. 39. Charles Smith even suggests that the Zionists 'had an advantage [over the combined Arab forces] of roughly 1.5 to 1 among males in the twenty to forty-five age group'; p. 140.

20. Israeli historian Tom Segev notes that the first UN partition plan gave 62% of the territory to the Jews, and only 38% to Palestinians; this ratio was so flagrantly inequitable that it was supplanted by a new division of 55% Jewish to 45% Palestinian. Moshe Sharett, a leading figure in the Jewish Labour party which was to dominate Israeli politics in the following years, told his colleagues in 1947 to suppress these ratios, 'or they might serve as a dangerous weapon against us, like oil on the fire.' Segev, *The First Israelis* (New York: Macmillan, 1986), p. 21.

21. Paul Findley collects a number of these historical fallacies, expressed by Israeli leaders from David Ben-Gurion to Golda Meir, in *Deliberate Deceptions*, (New York: Lawrence Hill Books, 1993), pp. 9–18.

22. The 'revisionists' include Simha Flapan, Tom Segev, Benny Morris, Avi Shlaim, Ilan Pappé and Gershon Shafir. Morris has overturned the myth of a spontaneous Arab exodus in 1948/1949, asserting instead that the Israeli army played a major role in the process: *The Birth of the Palestinian Refugee Problem 1947–1949* (Cambridge: Cambridge University Press, 1987). Shlaim has argued that the Zionist leaders in Palestine drew up a secret agreement with King Abdullah of Jordan to partition Palestine according to their mutual interest: *Collusion Across the Jordan: King Abdullah, the Zionist Movement and the Partition of Palestine* (Oxford: Oxford University Press, 1988). Gershon Shafir, meanwhile, has defined Zionism not as a liberation movement but as a form of settler colonialism, its goal 'to successfully colonize Palestine while at the same time justifying the creation of a homogeneous Jewish settlement through an intensifying denial of Palestinian national aspiration': *Land, Labor and the Origins*

of the Israeli–Palestinian Conflict 1882–1914 (Berkeley: University of California Press, 1996, 2nd edition), p. xiii. For all the advances of the 'revisionists', it has been argued that many of their reassessments do not go far enough towards redressing the historical balance between Israeli and Palestinian claims. For example, Norman Finkelstein has criticised Benny Morris for the latter's attempts to attribute equal blame to the Israeli and Arab armies for the Palestinian refugee crisis of 1948/1949; *Image and Reality of the Israeli–Palestinian Conflict* (London: Verso, 1995), pp. 51–87. I am grateful to Noam Chomsky for pointing out that the revisionist scholarship merely confirms many of the earlier conclusions of Arab and non-Israeli scholars, such as Walid Khalidi and Michael Palumbo, who make use of Arab sources which Israeli 'revisionists' often disregard.

23. Nur Masalha offers the figure of 150,000 in *A Land Without a People: Israel, Transfer and the Palestinians 1949–1996* (London: Faber and Faber, 1997), p. xi.

24. The figure of 750,000 has been contested by both sides, although Benny Morris presents evidence in *The Birth of the Palestinian Refugee Problem* that the Israeli government knew that the lower figures it had published were erroneous. The estimate of the UN Relief and Works Agency (UNRWA) of 726,000 refugees was thought too low even by Walter Eytan, the Director General of Israel's Foreign Ministry. See Morris, appendix I, 'The number of Palestinian refugees', pp. 297-8.

25. For general accounts of the pre-1967 period, see Smith, pp. 151–203; Noam Chomsky, *The Fateful Triangle: The United States, Israel and the Palestinians* (Boston: South End Press, 1983), pp. 98–103; Benny Morris, *Israel's Border Wars 1949–1956* (Oxford: Oxford University Press, 1993), pp. 173–99; and Sara Roy's account of Israel's attack on the Gaza Strip in 1995: *The Gaza Strip: The Political Economy of De-development* (Washington: Institute for Palestine Studies, 1995), pp. 69–71. Israel's conduct in 1967 is described by Smith, pp. 195–203; and Donald Neff, *Warriors for Jerusalem: The Six Days That Changed the Middle East* (New York: Simon and Schuster, 1984). Norman Finkelstein brilliantly refutes the contention of Israel's former Ambassador to the United Nations, Abba Eban, that Israel's attack on Syria and Egypt in June 1967 was both 'preemptive' and 'retaliatory': *Image and Reality of the Israeli–Palestine Conflict*, pp. 125–49. Finkelstein contends that Israel 'faced no significant threat, let alone mortal danger, in June 1967', and that the Six-Day War was waged to avoid a diplomatic solution to the Arab-Israeli dispute, to crush Arab nationalism, and to enable Israel to appropriate even more Palestinian territory. This claim should be borne in mind as we examine the fate of Israel's West Bank and Gaza settlement project in the rest of this chapter.

26. William Wilson Harris estimates that a total of 1.4 million Arabs lived in Gaza, the West Bank, the Golan Heights and the Sinai in May 1967; approximately 430,000 fled these areas between June and December of that year (31% of the total), leaving around one million people under Israeli occupation. *Taking*

Root: Israeli Settlement in the West Bank, the Golan and Gaza–Sinai, 1967–1980 (Chichester, England: John Wiley and Sons, 1980), p. 16.

27. Most Israeli historians have stressed the threat posed by the Egyptian president, Gamal Abdul-Nasser, and emphasised Israel's need to strike first in 'self-defence'. Bernard Avishai's *The Tragedy of Zionism* (New York: Farrar Straus Giroux, 1985), although critical of some aspects of Israel's conduct after 1967, holds that the Six-Day War was 'forced upon' Israel, p. 248. Michael Walzer, philosopher and political scientist, argued in his *Just and Unjust Wars* (New York: Basic Books, 1977) that the Six-Day War was the only war in human history to have been started by the 'just' side, since Israel's actions amounted to 'a clear case of legitimate anticipation'; p. 85. Paul Findley, in his *Deliberate Deceptions*, pp. 35 ff., takes a different view, holding up the official pronouncements of Abba Eban and others to the later reminiscences of Yitzhak Rabin, Menachem Begin and David Ben-Gurion, all of whom doubted the likelihood or danger of an Egyptian attack. See also supra note 25.

28. For details of the legal measures enacted by the Israeli government on 27 and 28 June 1967, see Michael Dumper, *The Politics of Jerusalem Since 1967* (New York: Columbia University Press, 1997), p. 38 ff. Dumper details successive waves of forced Palestinian migration and eviction in 1967, encompassing a displaced Palestinian population of between 10,000 and 20,000 in Jerusalem alone, pp. 74–5.

29. Shmuel Dayan, the father of Defence Minister Moshe Dayan, called the 1967 offensive 'a war to regain the land of Israel's forefathers'; meanwhile Naomi Shemer's song 'Jerusalem of Gold', which was played repeatedly in celebration of Israel's gains, referred to the ancient Jewish Jerusalem and the new possibilities for its modern revival: Avishai, p. 244. Moshe Leshem, in *Israel Alone* (New York: Simon and Schuster, 1989) captures this romantic mood in Israel, telling of the 'delights' of the occupied territories which Israelis 'quickly discovered', oblivious to the fact that 'not a single country in the world' would be prepared to see Israel's occupation as 'anything more than temporary'; pp. 173–4.

30. The legal moves by which Israel annexed East Jerusalem are recounted by John Quigley, 'Jerusalem in international law', in *Jerusalem Today*, ed. Ghada Karmi (Reading: Ithaca Press, 1996). See Dumper, p. 39, for the confiscation of an enormous area in the West Bank for inclusion within a new, 'united' Jewish Jerusalem; p. 74 for the expulsion of Palestinians in the Old City for the creation of a new plaza in front of the Western Wall; and pp. 109–11 for the first steps towards massive Jewish settlement in East Jerusalem.

31. The text of Resolution 242 is contained in Laqueur and Rubin (eds), pp. 217–18. Israel and its supporters have frequently claimed that the resolution encourages only a partial withdrawal from the occupied territories: see, for instance, the essay of Eugene V. Rostow in Michael Widlanski (ed.), *Can Israel Survive a Palestinian State?* (Jerusalem: Institute for Advanced Strategic and Political Studies, 1990). Paul Findley rejects Rostow's 'Historical Perspective'

and demonstrates from US State Department policy and the authors of the UN resolution that the withdrawal stipulation applies on all three fronts to all the land conquered. Problems with this interpretation only began, according to Findley, after 1977 and Israel's initiation of a plan to colonise the occupied territories (*Deliberate Deceptions*, pp. 42 ff.). See also Donald Neff's 'The differing interpretations of Resolution 242', *Middle East International*, 13 September 1991. Norman Finkelstein points out that the American-led Rogers Plan of 1969 and the Israeli–American rejection of Anwar Sadat's 1971 initiative proved at an early stage that different visions of 242 were incompatible with each other (*Image and Reality of the Israel–Palestine Conflict*, Chapter 6).

32. The account of the settlement programme which follows draws largely on the extended and more detailed accounts in Ian Lustick, *Unsettled States, Disputed Lands* (Ithaca: Cornell University Press, 1993); David Newman (ed.), *The Impact of Gush Emunim* (London: Croom Helm, 1985); Geoffrey Aronson, *Israel, Palestinians and the Intifada: Creating Facts on the West Bank* (London: Kegan Paul International, 1990); Robert I. Friedman, *Zealots for Zion: Inside Israel's West Bank Settlement Movement* (New York: Random House, 1992); and David J. Schnall, *Beyond the Green Line* (New York: Praeger Publishing, 1984).

33. Lustick, p. 354 and Lilly Weissbrod, 'Core values and revolutionary change', in *The Impact of Gush Emunim*, p. 96, introduce the movement (also known as the 'Land of Israel Movement') and define its early support base. See also Friedman, p. 14, and Aronson, pp. 33 ff.

34. The essays in Newman's book each draw on some aspects of Gush Emunim's rise and its effects on Israeli society. Ehud Sprinzak's essay 'The iceberg model of political extremism', the second chapter of the book, provides a concise introduction to Gush Emunim and draws upon interviews conducted in the mid-1970s with some of its key members. Lustick, pp. 355–7, charts the influence of Gush Emunim on the Likud party, and relates the story of Begin's homage to Tzvi Yehuda Kook. For a partisan introduction to Kook's 'pioneering spirit', and an apologia for Gush Emunim, see Schnall, pp. 19–21.

35. Lustick, p. 367, sees the Likud government of 1977 rejecting the idea of territorial compromise under the influence of its 'extragovernmental allies, especially Gush Emunim'. The various essayists in *The Impact of Gush Emunim* disagree on the extent of the movement's influence over government policy, but agree that it practised what Yosseph Shilav calls 'territorial indoctrination' on its own members and on the Israeli public: 'Interpretation and misinterpretation of Jewish territorialism' in Newman (ed.), p. 113. Bernard Avishai notes Gush Emunim's ability to mobilise large crowds inside Israel in opposition to territorial compromise during the early 1970s: *The Tragedy of Zionism*, pp. 278–9. See also the careful narrative of Aronson, pp. 59–76.

36. Lustick, p. 357. Schnall claims, as he relates the rise of Gush Emunim, that support for settlements came from ordinary people as well as elements of the Labour party disaffected by the government's apparent vacillation. Schnall is at pains to present the settlement movement as other than a coalition of extremists: p. 7.

37. Lustick presents this quotation, from Dayan's Hebrew *A New Map: Different Relations*, p. 357.

38. Ibid., p. 358.

39. These Israeli techniques of confiscation will be discussed in detail in Chapters 4 and 5.

40. Gershon Shafir offers an analysis of the Likud's major settlement blueprint, the 'One-Hundred-Thousand' plan of 1981, which concludes that financial incentives were much more essential to settlement expansion than 'territorial indoctrination'; these incentives are summarised in 'Institutional and spontaneous settlement drives: did Gush Emunim make a difference?', in *The Impact of Gush Emunim*, pp. 166–7. Meron Benvenisti, former Deputy Mayor of Jerusalem, points out in his *Conflicts and Contradictions* (New York: Villard Books, 1986), pp. 141–2, that observers of the settlements tend to ignore their economic dimension and to concentrate on military or ideological motives for an ongoing presence in the occupied territories. Benvenisti's *West Bank Handbook* (Jerusalem: Jerusalem Post, 1986) outlines the various tax breaks and financial concessions available to Israeli settlers in the occupied territories; see the entries for 'Taxation of Israelis', pp. 203–4, and 'Incentives for settlement', pp. 111–12. The latter entry suggests that in the 'high demand' areas of the West Bank, the Israeli government has subsidised apartment-building up to around 75% of the total cost of a unit; and that 'in more distant areas the assistance in its various forms covers the entire cost of the apartment and its development.' See also Schnall's analysis of the Likud's public presentation of the 'One-Hundred-Thousand' plan: the 'Build Your Own Home' scheme. Schnall summarises the 'two-page spreads in major Israeli newspapers', paid for by the government: 'if the people won't come to the territories out of ideological commitment, let's appeal to their desires for creature comforts'; pp. 136–7.

41. Lustick, p. 12, claims that from around 12,000 settlers in 1980, the Israeli population in the occupied territories increased to almost 30,000 in 1983 and 45,000 in 1984. Gershon Shafir's essay confirms these figures: *The Impact of Gush Emunim*, p. 169.

42. Bernard Avishai refers to this 'new Zionist vocabulary of double-think names for occupied territory' in *The Tragedy of Zionism*, p. 250. 'Eretz Yisrael' literally means 'the land of Israel', but it has always been used to denote a much grander territorial arrangement than the state created in 1949; hence, 'Greater Israel' is the usual translation of the phrase. David Schnall, at once the victim and the perpetrator of this linguistic fiat, makes a bid in his 1984 book to be 'semantically neutral' by promising that 'the West Bank and Judea/Samaria will be used interchangeably', and 'both "occupied" and "liberated" will be avoided'. Schnall, p. x.

43. There is a wealth of literature on this topic, and a wide variety of theses as to why Israel and Egypt chose to make peace with one another, especially after the election victory of the right-wing Begin in 1977. William B. Quandt's *Camp David: Peacemaking and Politics* (Washington DC: The Brookings Institute,

1986) offers the most comprehensive view of the peace negotiations, and demonstrates the commensurately great desires of Sadat to resolve the Palestinian issue and Begin to retain the occupied territories. Paul Findley, in *Deliberate Deceptions*, p. 200, records Jimmy Carter's frustration in his diary entries for 1978 with Begin's unwillingness 'to withdraw politically or militarily from any part of the West Bank.'

44. Quandt also suggests that Camp David enabled Israel to pursue such appalling adventures as its 1982 invasion of Lebanon without fear of Egyptian response: p. 321.

45. Myron J. Aronoff suggests that the Likud government and Gush Emunim had an interest in making the Sinai withdrawal 'as traumatic as possible', on the understanding that this trauma would then make a withdrawal from Gaza and the West Bank unthinkable. Aronoff notes that Sinai occupied a less central position in the romantic and theological visions of Gush Emunim, but that it was effectively used to protect the more desirable colonisation in the rest of the occupied territories; 'The institutionalisation and cooptation of a charismatic, messianic, religious-political revitalisation movement', in *The Impact of Gush Emunim*, p. 46. Schnall's account of the Sinai withdrawal is a good example of the usefulness of the event to proponents of further settlement (like Schnall himself): 'Though the territory was returned, the experience toughened the resolve of those who were there and those who only watched from the sides'; for Schnall, Sinai was the moment when Gush Emunim moved 'from the edges of Israeli society to its core'; p. 11.

46. See Aronson, p. 268: 'For the Begin government, the Sinai was being sacrificed for the West Bank.'

47. Lustick, p. 367, lists a series of public outcries from 1980 onwards against Begin's government and its behaviour in the occupied territories. Michael Palumbo details the interest of 'Peace Now' in the Egyptian peace process and, by 1979, in Israel's settlement programme. Peace Now organised a rally against West Bank settlement on 16 June 1979 which was attended by forty thousand Israelis; *Imperial Israel* (London: Bloomsbury, 1990), p. 205.

48. Lustick, pp. 367–8, links the Sinai evacuation to the Lebanon War, and confirms Begin's aim to destroy the Palestinian spirit and leadership to facilitate settlement expansion. Israel's motives for invading and occupying Lebanon have also encompassed its desire to take water from the Litani river in the south of the country: see, for example, Rosemary Sayigh, *Too Many Enemies: The Palestinian Experience in Lebanon* (London: Zed Books, 1994), p. 18.

49. Begin's offensive confirmed many in their thinking that Israel was heading in the wrong direction: Avishai, p. 323, describes the resentment of traditional Labour Zionists at the hijacking of their state-building agenda by religious and romantic nationalists; Aronoff suggests that even former supporters of the Likud from Israel's religious community were brought to question its actions by the barbarity of Israel's Lebanon invasion: *The Impact of Gush Emunim*, pp. 57–8. The Lebanon War marks the high-water mark of

internal Israeli criticism, the obvious misdemeanours of the government and army almost impossible to ignore. Some prominent Israelis did choose to ignore them, of course: aside from the unapologetic conduct of Ariel Sharon and Rafael Eitan, generals in the Israeli Defence Forces in 1982 and newly rehabilitated ministers in the Netanyahu cabinet of 1996, Moshe Leshem gives some idea of the reluctance of many Israelis to confront their country's misdeeds: he refers to the Lebanon War merely to accuse some American newspapers of anti-semitism in their criticism of Israel's bloody actions; *Israel Alone*, pp. 229–30.

50. Lustick describes the activity of the Jewish terror groups on the West Bank and inside Israel (against their liberal opponents) at 368ff; he also reprints Shimon Peres' remark in 1985 that the struggle inside Israeli society over the fate of the occupied territories might lead 'even to the point of, heaven forbid, civil war', p. 371.

51. Lustick again quotes Peres: 'I say that the solution is to guard the nation's unity, to also guard unified frameworks and, from this aspect, I think the national unity government, with all its problems, is contributing to the nation's unity.' Ibid., p. 371. The unity government did nothing to halt settlement building in the territories: see the report of the Israeli think-tank The International Center for Peace in the Middle East, *Jewish Settlement in the West Bank and Gaza Strip* (Tel Aviv, 1993): 'The years of the National Unity Government were the years of the greatest migration to the territories, from then up until the present day [...] the National Unity Government under Shimon Peres did not either politically or ideologically stand in its [the settlement movement's] way'; p. 16. See also Aronson, p. 307, for the vital distinction between building entirely new settlements and the extension of existing ones.

52. *The West Bank Handbook* contains entries for 'Electricity', 'Roads' and 'Water' which confirm that the West Bank's various infrastructural systems were definitively absorbed by Israel in the early 1980s. The purpose of this absorption was to expropriate Palestinian resources for use inside Israel (in the case of water) but also to ensure that the settlements were part of a single Israeli network. A shift in road planning from a north–south to an east–west axis in the late 1970s and early 1980s was one of the most obvious manifestations of this policy. Two systems remain in place on the West Bank, but these are now a unified Israeli/Jewish settler system and a separate Palestinian infrastructure: the new road network 'is not intended to serve Arab settlements and, indeed, is characterised by its avoidance of them.' See pp. 75–7, 193–5 and 223–5.

53. Lustick describes Israel's extension of its essential services and infrastructure to the occupied territories at p. 360: 'A wide variety of measures was taken to foster perceptions by the settlers and other Israelis that life in the territories was governed by the same norms and expectations as prevailed within the Green Line.' Michael Palumbo outlines the efforts of West Bank settlements like Ariel and Efrat to present themselves as 'normal' Israeli towns in the hope of attracting new citizens from 1949-Israel: *Imperial Israel*, pp. 188–

91. 'We are a cross-section of average Israel,' offers Ariel's Ron Nachman, 'a real melting pot.'

54. Palumbo, p. 188, suggests that the rationale of the settlement programme has always been to make the Israeli government's annexation plan unavoidable in practice: 'the original goal of those who favoured large-scale West Bank settlements – that it would create a sizeable group of people with a vested interest in annexation – began to be achieved in the 1980s.' Thus, for Palumbo, even those who came to the West Bank as Labour voters or 'doves' were hardened in their political views by the proximity of Palestinian anger at land expropriation and settlers' own fears that their new homes be taken from them by a government offering 'land for peace': 'Although most of the people in the West Bank suburban communities were drawn by economics rather than ideology, polls indicate that they often changed from doves into hawks after living there for only a short time.' The expansion of East Jerusalem for Jewish settlement offered a particularly strong incentive for many Israelis to suppress their doubts about Israel's right to the 1967 acquisitions.

55. Virtually every account of the intifada makes reference to the increasing Palestinian population of the occupied territories and the decreasing quality of their living standards. Even Aryeh Shalev, a former commander of Israel's forces in the West Bank, concedes in his *The Intifada: Causes and Effects* (Jerusalem: Jaffee Center for Strategic Studies, 1991) that the 'squalid living conditions in the refugee camps' were an 'underlying cause' of the uprising, the refugees' lives 'made increasingly unbearable due to rapid population growth'; pp. 14–15.

56. David McDowall's *Palestine and Israel: The Uprising and Beyond* (London: I.B. Tauris, 1990) offers a general account of Israeli and Palestinian history in the context of the intifada; more specific discussions of different aspects of the uprising are contained within *Intifada: The Palestinian Uprising against Israeli Occupation*, Zachary Lockman and Joel Beinin (eds) (Boston: South End Press, 1989); and *Intifada: Palestine at the Crossroads*, Jamal R. Nassar and Roger Heacock (eds) (New York: Bir Zeit University and Praeger Publishers, 1991). The emphasis of all these accounts is on the intifada, not as a response to Israeli occupation planned well in advance by a Palestinian leadership, but a spontaneous reaction on the part of the Palestinian grassroots to terrible and enduring conditions. See McDowall, pp. 2, 11 for the feelings of the local organisers of the intifada that the exiled PLO was too far from their struggle to take an active part or claim credit. Palumbo makes a similar point at p. 240 of *Imperial Israel*, and also contends that the intifada saw a remarkably high level of participation and organisation from ordinary Palestinian children, who consequently bore the full force of Israel's armed response to the stone-throwing. Helga Baumgarten argues in '"Discontented people" and "Outside agitators": the PLO in the Palestinian uprising' that the PLO did make efforts to capitalise on the intifada as soon as the extent of support for the uprising became evident; and that the PLO's efforts to play some role intensified as resistance continued over months and years; Nassar and Heacock (eds), pp. 207–6

57. In January 1988, as it became clear that the national unity government would not be able to contain the uprising without a major increase in its forces in the occupied territories, Defence Minister Rabin declared that Israel would use 'force, might and beatings' against the Palestinians in an effort to produce 'broken bones': Aronson, *Israel, Palestinians and the Intifada*, pp. 327–8, and Findley, pp. 78–9. In September of 1988, Israel introduced plastic bullets into its armed response to the uprising, Rabin stating explicitly that 'it is our intention to wound as many of them as possible ... inflicting injuries is precisely the aim of using plastic bullets' (McDowall, p. 15). Throughout the intifada, Israel's intention was to terrify the Palestinians into submission, and to make them understand the practical consequences of Israel's superior firepower. Rafael Eitan, former Likud member and Lebanon War chief-of-staff, founded his new political party Tzomet on a simple response to the intifada: 'a bullet in the head of every stone-thrower'; Azmi Bishara, 'The uprising's impact on Israel', Lockman and Beinin (eds), p. 221. International outrage at Israel's brutality and continuing occupation is summarised in McDowall, p. 13 and in Fouad Moughrabi, 'The intifada in American public opinion', in Nassar and Heacock (eds), pp. 241–56. Findley, pp. 81–5 and 191–4, lists the resolutions passed or proposed against Israel by the international community and international non-governmental organisations during the period of the intifada. McDowall stresses that, even for those governments that routinely supported Israel and had tacitly accepted its conduct in the occupied territories before 1987, 'routine scenes of troop brutality demanded a response'; p. 13.

58. The settlement plans of the 1980s and later have not envisaged a concentration of far-flung outposts, but instead the appropriation of Palestinian agricultural land outside the big Palestinian cities and close to the Green Line with Jerusalem and 1949-Israel. The central West Bank and Green Line borders have therefore been most popular with settlers; see *Jewish Settlement in the West Bank and Gaza Strip*, pp. 21–31.

2 *Oslo*

The Declaration of Principles

In addition to the intifada, the Gulf War of 1991 played a major part in the instigation and fashioning of the Israeli–Palestinian peace process. Aside from confirming the supremacy of American power in the Middle East, the victory of the coalition forces over Saddam Hussein once again split those Arab nations which had formerly been united. With Egypt, Syria and Saudi Arabia backing the winners, and Lebanon, Jordan and the Palestine Liberation Organisation supporting Saddam, further evidence had been offered that there was no natural Arab consensus on regional issues. With an eye to this division, the US and Israel were quick to seize the opportunity to launch a new diplomatic process. As before, Israel would negotiate with each side separately, making a series of single deals rather than an agreement amenable to all the parties. Since Israel's closest enemies – Jordan and the Palestinians – had backed the wrong horse, Israel might hope for a more favourable resolution (given American supervision) in the light of these parties' embarrassing mistake.[1]

The road to an agreement was a long and hard one for the Palestinians. The most public element of their leadership, the PLO, had been on the run from Israel for more than twenty years, condemned generally in Israel and the US as terrorists or worse. Only after elaborate arrangements for indirect talks had been made did Israelis and Palestinians begin to negotiate in earnest. One of the legacies of Israel's occupation had been the expulsion of the Palestine Liberation Organisation: first to Jordan, then to Lebanon and finally North Africa. The absence of the PLO had inevitably distanced the movement from the people living under occupation, and a new cadre of political leaders, people like Hannan Ashrawi, Faisal Husseini and Haidar Abdul-Shafi, had come to prominence at the head of NGOs, educational or charitable institutions. It was these people who went to Madrid to conduct the negotiations, well versed in the actual situation in the occupied territories by virtue of their own experiences there during the decades of Israeli rule.

By all accounts, the Madrid negotiators concentrated on the realities of Israel's presence in the West Bank and Gaza Strip, and showed a reluctance to become involved in any peace process which did not promise an immediate and substantive withdrawal by the Israeli army.[2] Israel's response to this principled stand, however, was to find other Palestinians that it could do business with. The need to find someone who would do things differently, and would make less of an issue of standing on principle, best explains the re-emergence and rehabilitation of Yasser Arafat. The exiled PLO leader was a much better prospect as a negotiating partner than the 'internal' leaders who had taken charge at Madrid, since Arafat was considerably more naïve and out of touch than those who had stayed in the territories; not to mention his substantial personal interest in returning from exile to reestablish his own political career in the West Bank and Gaza Strip. Thus Israel sent another team of negotiators to begin talking to the PLO in Oslo, unbeknownst to the Palestinian team in Madrid and, later, in Washington.[3] Arafat's representatives were more open to Israel's suggestions for a protracted withdrawal, alongside various 'trust-building' measures which would act as a precondition for the continuation of the process. Whereas the Palestinians in Madrid and Washington were unlikely to accept anything other than clear guarantees of Israel's intentions to leave the occupied territories, the Oslo negotiators accepted Israel's jargon of flexibility and mutuality, leaving an enormous number of vital Palestinian claims at the mercy of interpretation and, most dangerously of all, Israeli good intentions. An ominous note of what was to follow was struck as the Madrid team distanced themselves from Oslo and Arafat's new approach, thinking aloud that the Palestinians had perhaps signed up to the wrong kind of peace.[4]

Of course, these events seem clearer in retrospect than they did at the time. When the first phase of the Oslo process, the Declaration of Principles, was presented in September 1993, many Palestinians imagined that the long Israeli occupation would soon end. The Declaration of Principles (DoP) contained many statements of good will and intent, but explicitly committed the parties to a solution based on UN Resolutions 242 and 338.[5] Issued by the Security Council after the 1967 and 1973 wars respectively, 242 and 338 had long called on Israel to leave the occupied territories, in return for recognition from and peace with its neighbours. However, a crucial shift in the interpretation of 242 had taken place after 1971, when Anwar Sadat's apparent willingness to make peace with Israel on the basis of a full withdrawal from the occupied territories threatened to call Israel's bluff, and to force an abandonment of land which was already being expropriated and settled. From this time onwards, both Israeli and US officials stressed that 242 urged Israel to leave not 'the occupied territories' but simply 'occupied territories', a semantic evasion which might allow Israel to give back all of the West Bank and Gaza or a mere fraction of it. Although this reading hardly represented the original intent of those diplomats who had framed 242 at the United Nations, or even the US position before 1971, the provisions of 242 would always be conditioned not by an 'authentic' interpretation but by the will of the strongest powers.[6]

As we have already seen, Israel's hopes for peace at the outset of Oslo were rather different from those of the Palestinians. By 1993, almost 300,000 settlers were living on land conquered in 1967. The success of the settlement programme had made compliance with 242 virtually impossible. More than one half of these settlers lived in Palestinian East Jerusalem, illegally annexed by Israel just after the Six-Day War. How could an Israeli government uproot so many potential voters? Conversely, if these settlers were allowed to stay, how could others be removed? On what principle could a single settlement be destroyed if a single settlement was left standing? 242 had been drafted at a time when there were no settlements in place, and envisaged a solution to the conflict as it was then. Unfortunately, the Israeli action addressed by 242 had mutated into something immeasurably worse by 1993, making a solution based on a simple Israeli withdrawal both anachronistic and impracticable.[7]

The solution to this difficulty was thus to reinterpret 242 as allowing for only a limited return of parts of the West Bank and Gaza, a strategy which would isolate Israel within the international community, but which might still succeed, given the support of the United States. In the drafting of the Declaration of Principles, therefore, the US and Israel cleverly installed 242 at the centre of the peace process (knowing full well that the resolution's wording was sufficiently ambiguous to allow for a minimalist interpretation) and simultaneously excluded from Oslo the many other UN resolutions on the Israeli–Palestinian conflict. Those resolutions – demanding Israel's withdrawal from East Jerusalem, for example, or the return of refugees – were ignored, and 242 was left as the sole guarantor of Palestinian rights. Given the extent of the Israeli settlement programme, and the proven ability of the US and Israel to advance an interpretation of 242 that was entirely at odds with a full Israeli withdrawal, the foundations of the peace process were far from secure.

Rabin: Oslo falters

Although the current peace process began under Yitzhak Shamir's tenure, it came to be identified most closely with Yitzhak Rabin, who became prime minister in 1992. The return of the Labour party to power inspired hope in some quarters that Israel was on course to make a lasting peace. George Bush had been withholding some $10 billion of American loan guarantees (the financial pledges necessary for Israel to borrow huge sums from banks) from Shamir on condition that the Israeli government suspend its settlement building programme; since the bulk of this borrowed money had been ploughed into the settlements since the early 1980s, the request was a logical one. With Rabin's election, promises were made by Israel that America's concerns had been noted; and so the money was made available as soon as the Labour leader took office.[8] For his part, Rabin acknowledged the important role played by settlements in the search for peace and declared to the world that his government would halt its settlement plans. News of the 'settlement freeze' inspired further hope for the future, suggesting that Israel had at last conceded the incompatibility between peace and its efforts to colonise the West Bank and Gaza.[9]

It soon became apparent, however, that Rabin's 'freeze' was far from a prohibition on Israeli construction in the occupied territories.[10] Firstly, Rabin excluded Arab East Jerusalem from the restrictions, arguing that, even though this territory had been invaded in 1967 and held by military force ever since, Jerusalem was the unified and integral capital of Israel and therefore exempt from consideration as occupied territory.[11] The only 'frozen' developments were entirely new settlements, where there had been no settlers at all previously. Those settlements which already existed, even if they consisted of simply a few houses, were excluded from the putative freeze. Rabin therefore set himself at liberty to turn settlement villages into cities, and to expand further those towns which already contained tens of thousands of settlers. Since there were already so many settlements in 1992, there was hardly any need to break turf on any new ones. Even so, Rabin gave the go-ahead for more than 10,000 apartments that had been planned by the previous government, some of them forming entirely new settlements in contravention even of this limited freeze. By expanding the existing developments without restraint, Rabin could happily extend the settlement programme indefinitely.[12]

Most calamitously for the Palestinians, Rabin imposed no restriction on the continued confiscation of land in the West Bank and Gaza. In fact, the Labour administration seized at least as much territory as any of its predecessors, pursuing a major housing programme and Rabin's pet project: a system of by-pass roads intended for Jewish settlers only, circumventing Palestinian towns and linking the various settlements with each other and with Israel.[13] The by-pass road project had long appealed to Israeli leaders seeking to shift the axis of West Bank travel from north–south to east–west. However, the roads have been identified by human rights and environmental groups, as well as organisations supporting a land-for-peace solution to the conflict, as a disastrous compounding of the existing settlement problem: new highways have cut across Palestinian land and agriculture, carrying only settler traffic and reinforcing the permanence of the Israeli presence in the occupied territories. Despite the freeze on entirely new developments, Rabin's administration contributed enormously to the consolidation of the settlements and the effective annexation of still more Palestinian land.

After reaching agreement on limited autonomy for 65% of the Gaza Strip and the West Bank town of Jericho in 1994, the Israelis and Palestinians produced the most comprehensive measure thus far in 1995: the Interim Agreement, more commonly known as Oslo II. For the first time, Oslo II provided a view of the entire West Bank and the planned progress of an Israeli withdrawal. Although much was made of the establishment of a Palestinian parliament under the agreement, with elections to take place in the occupied territories for the first time, the more significant provision of Oslo II was the territorial arrangement outlined alongside proposals for Palestinian autonomy.[14]

Although the parties still agreed in the Preamble to Oslo II upon a commitment to Resolution 242, the Interim Agreement offered ample evidence that Israel intended to withdraw from only a part of the West Bank. Officially, the land was divided into three zones: A, consisting of Palestinian towns and urban areas and comprising a little less than 2.8% of the total West Bank land which was occupied by Israel in 1967; B, Palestinian villages and less densely populated areas, comprising around 22.9% of the West Bank; and C, consisting of Palestinian agricultural lands and areas confiscated by Israel for roads and settlements. The third zone comprised the overwhelming majority of the West Bank, some 74.3%, and contained many key agricultural regions and water supplies.[15]

All three areas would be essential to Palestinian autonomy, and Oslo II contained provisions for Israeli withdrawal from A, B and C. Moreover, 1995 and 1996 saw Israel keep its promise to withdraw entirely from Area A (except for Hebron), and to give a measure of control to the new Palestinian Authority over Palestinians living in Area B.[16] However, buried in the stipulations about Area C was a simple but devastating provision: Israel would withdraw from Area C over time, but not from the parts which related to 'issues that will be negotiated in the permanent status negotiations'. 'Permanent status' talks were envisaged as the final stage in the Oslo process, with negotiations lasting no more than two years and commencing no later than 4 May 1996.[17] Elsewhere in the agreement, these issues were listed: 'Jerusalem, refugees, settlements, security arrangements, borders, relations and cooperation with other neighbors, and other issues of common interest.'[18] Amongst this list, settlements and 'security arrangements' were of particular relevance to the occupied territories. With hundreds of settlements and military outposts in Area C, Israel had negotiated the right to remain in a large portion of the West Bank and Gaza even after the interim period; and since the declaration of a military area or settlement depended wholly on Israeli legal or military fiat, this modest clause changed fundamentally the nature of the agreements. It subsequently emerged that these 'Israeli' parts of Area C would be decided not by negotiations but by unilateral Israeli deliberation.[19] In contrast to the stated aim of the Oslo process to return the conquered territories under 242, the documents signed in September 1995 gave Israel the right to hold on to at least 75% of the West Bank and still claim that it was abiding by the agreements.[20]

If Area C was to be returned to the Palestinians only when Israel had annexed its own share, it made little sense to talk about the West Bank as an integral entity any more.[21] Amazingly, the official map of the Oslo II bears this out: whilst areas A and B are shaded, Area C is left unshaded, exactly the same colour as Israel. If further confirmation were needed, the map offers no demarcation of the Green Line marking the pre-1967 border with Israel. Just as Rabin's by-pass roads enabled settlers to drive from Tel Aviv or Jerusalem into occupied territory without noting the difference, so his 'peace' map extended Israeli sovereignty deep into Palestinian territory, without pausing to observe the line crossed in 1967 and its enduring significance to the Palestinian people. Even the tourist maps offered to new visitors in Israel show Area C as part of 1949 Israel, with Palestinian sovereignty limited to the scattered, separate islands of areas A and B.

Although Oslo's principal aim was to negotiate an Israeli withdrawal from the occupied territories, the various stages of the process consistently failed to address the biggest obstacle to this outcome: Israeli settlements. In fact, the agreements allowed this problem to worsen considerably. Oslo's intention, according to its framers (and American sponsors), was to encourage the sides to agree on smaller issues in the first instance: if Israelis and Palestinians could learn to trust each other from the outset, the most difficult negotiations could come later, benefiting from an improved working relationship. In this spirit, Oslo II envisaged final negotiations after the interim period, the 'permanent status' talks referred to in the provisions for Israel's continuing occupation of Area C. The permanent status issues – borders, the return of Palestinian refugees, statehood for Palestine, Jerusalem, water and Jewish settlements – were deliberately deferred until the end of the negotiating process, supposedly to allow for the sides to build trust before discussing the most contentious problems in an atmosphere of mutual respect. However, Rabin's government did all in its power to consolidate Israel's mastery in many of these important areas, then rejected the Palestinians' complaints by saying that these permanent status issues were not affected by existing agreements. Even though the entire peace process would stand or fall on the extent of Israeli withdrawal from the occupied territories, Rabin was happy to expropriate thousands more acres of land in the West Bank and to build many more roads and settlements during the interim period, constraining still further the possibility of a meaningful Israeli pull-out and a viable Palestinian state.[22]

Given the violent nature of his death, Yitzhak Rabin has acquired near-mythical status as a peacemaker and visionary.[23] The record of his three years in office, however, paints a different story. He gave the Palestinians limited autonomy in around 65% of the Gaza Strip, but he preserved the remaining 35% for the Jewish settlers there. On average, each Gaza settler enjoys 36 times as much land as each Palestinian, and an inequitable share of Gaza's precious water supply.[24] Rabin also succeeded in carving up the West Bank, and giving Israel the negotiated right to retain 75% of the land and virtually all of the water. The settlements, recognised as illegal by the entire international community, with the crucial exception of the US, were expanded further, and their importance and permanence were confirmed by the new settler road network. Jerusalem, comprising some of the most important Palestinian areas (economically and socially) and essential to mutual trust and cooperation, was ignored entirely, deferred to permanent status talks along with the mushrooming settlements. Finally, Rabin had begun to bring those vulnerable Israeli army units out of the Palestinian cities, where they had been easy targets for Palestinian unrest, and to regroup them outside the major population centres, where they could more effectively contain and coerce as Palestinian discontent increased. From an Israeli perspective, Rabin achieved enormous gains at relatively little cost. However, the effect of his policies was to throw Palestinians deeper into despair, and to make an equitable peace far less likely.

Netanyahu: Oslo adrift

An important legacy of the 1967 Israeli victory was a triumphalism towards the occupied territories which could not countenance their return to the Palestinians, or any form of Israeli withdrawal. As we have seen, religious and nationalist groups spearheaded the settlement movement in the 1970s on the understanding not that the land was to be colonised, but that it was to be 'reclaimed'. A significant minority in Israeli society saw the settlements not as practical extensions of 1949-Israel but as the completion of a biblical promise. Up until the early 1990s, while both the more pragmatic and the ideological proponents of settlements were at least agreed on a general policy of Israel's complete occupation of the West Bank and Gaza, tensions between the two could be contained. As the Israeli government began to broker a long-term solution to the present situation, however, these tensions were once again to surface.

Rabin's policies between 1992 and 1995 were disastrous for the Palestinians and very favourable to Israel. He had somehow succeeded in turning around Israel's international isolation while still holding on to virtually all of the West Bank and a wholly disproportionate slice of Gaza. Rabin's genius was in appearing to compromise whilst in fact securing all of Israel's objectives: the Oslo II agreement would save Israeli lives in Palestinian cities, whilst preserving every settlement and consolidating Israel's grip on the land and water of the West Bank. However, Rabin's pragmatic conquests put him at the mercy of those elements in Israel which could not countenance the return of a single acre of Palestinian territory, for the simple reason that they did not concede that the land of Greater Israel could be owned by any other people than the Jews. As long as Israel occupied the whole of Gaza and the West Bank, these ideological supporters of settlement could imagine that the Palestinians would soon be expelled from the land entirely, and Jewish settlers could 'return' in huge numbers to Nablus, Bethlehem and Hebron. By allowing the Palestinians to administer their own cities, Rabin had dashed this hope, and betrayed this ideology.[25]

Consequently, in November 1995, Yitzhak Rabin was murdered by Yigal Amir, a student in a religious college (or *yeshiva*) with links to the ideological settlement movement. Amir claimed that, by making even the smallest territorial concession to the Palestinians, Rabin had failed the Jewish people and earned his demise.[26] Israel was gripped by grieving and soul-searching in the aftermath of the murder, but its circumstances offered a false perspective on Rabin's achievements as leader. Although Amir stood for the most militant sectors of Israeli society, implacably committed to the retention of all the occupied territories and the furthering of the settlement programme, he was far from the antithesis of Rabin. The prime minister was also fully committed to the settlement programme, and had arguably done more to further its aims than the

Israeli Right through his Oslo accords. The killing of the Jewish leader by another Jew licensed the media in Israel, but especially outside the Middle East, to speak of Israeli 'doves' and Israeli 'hawks' in the context of Oslo; this seriously distorted the true picture, which was of Rabin as a staunch supporter of settlement expansion killed by an even more extreme proponent of the same policy.[27] Many of the subsequent problems in the Oslo process, both of negotiation and media analysis, stemmed from this idle quest for Rabin the peacemaker, and the policies he had followed which would guarantee justice and freedom for all sides. Rabin was murdered before the consequences of his annexation policies became fully clear, and in circumstances which indemnified his memory against responsibility for the situation he had created.[28]

Although some Palestinians had opposed Oslo from the start, believing that its postponement of the most vital issues at stake could not be a sure foundation for peace, many others went along with the process in the hope that it might generate its own momentum. Since Israel under Rabin intended to withdraw from at least some of the occupied territories, Palestinians were given opportunities to dream that a massive withdrawal might be imminent. Watching the Palestinian flag, banned until 1993, rise over Jericho and Gaza City was irresistible; and it would be hard not to feel that such an event marked the beginning of better things.[29] Even after Rabin had expanded the settlements and by-pass roads of the West Bank, Palestinians could still look in 1995 and 1996 to their first democratic elections, another sign that their condition was at last improving. The new Palestinian Authority had an electorate, a measure of diplomatic representation and a national flag; all contributed to the sense that Palestinians were inexorably moving towards statehood.

Against these trappings of state, however, was the constant and further expropriation of Palestinian land in the occupied territories, especially the West Bank. Whilst the Palestinian leadership focused on the gradual autonomy won from Israel in the cities, ordinary people could not ignore the overwhelming evidence of dispossession in the rural areas. The idea of a Palestinian state, which enjoyed such currency in the cities, was constantly undermined by the experience of those who witnessed the building of new settlements and roads elsewhere. If Rabin was serious about peace and a Palestinian state, why was he erecting infrastructure which would link and strengthen the settlements? If urban autonomy was to be the first, rather than the last stage of Palestinian self-rule, how could one make sense of the ongoing, even accelerated Judaisation of the West Bank? Against the efforts of the Palestinian leadership to keep its people focused on the gains and possibilities of Oslo, a grassroots disillusionment developed during 1995 and 1996, a sense that the promise and reality of Oslo were steadily diverging.

This divergence best explains the phenomenon of the Palestinian militant groups, Hamas and Islamic Jihad, which rose on the back of Oslo's inadequacy.[30] Those Palestinians who had counselled against dealing with Israel, excepting a full withdrawal from the occupied territories, were vindicated as the settlement programme continued, and the victims of dispossession proved easy recruits for the militants. For Hamas and Islamic Jihad, Israel was taking everything it wanted from the occupied territories and leaving Palestinians with the scraps: and so Israel would be made to suffer as the Palestinians were suffering, even if that meant killing crowds of civilians. The bus bombs of 1995, and especially February and March 1996, were a terrible attempt by militant Palestinians to hit back at Israel in the only way available to them. Since the Palestinian leadership did not have the power to force Israel to end its occupation, let alone to uproot the settlers, the Palestinian extremists exercised their own agency in the most visceral and disastrous fashion.

Had Yitzhak Rabin survived, it is hard to believe that he would have been spared the bus bombs of early 1996 which proved fatal to his successor, Shimon Peres. Rabin exited the political arena a little before the consequences of his policies became apparent, and Shimon Peres became their victim. The Israeli public had been led to believe that the Palestinians would be grateful for the limited Israeli withdrawal from the West Bank and Gaza; the notion that an occupied people would be dissatisfied with the return of less than 3% of their land seems not to have disseminated widely through Israeli society. The public response inside Israel to the bus bombs, then, was one of betrayal: first by the Palestinians, who had rewarded Israel for its generous territorial concessions with appalling violence; and second by the Labour government, which had endangered Israelis by giving the Palestinians too great a degree of freedom.[31]

When the Oslo talks began in 1991, Israel did not of course find itself compelled to leave the occupied territories. The strength of the Israeli army would certainly contain the Palestinian people even through a prolonged intifada, and Israel had at its disposal as much firepower as was needed to resolve the Palestinian issue once and for all. Many inside Israel opposed the idea of even limited withdrawal, with various claims of Israeli ownership and the practical argument that Israel's occupation had been militarily unchallenged for 25 years. Since Israel had not been forced from the occupied territories, but had left of its own volition, the temptation within some Israeli circles was to see any withdrawal as a compromise, a major concession. The fact that so much of the West Bank and Gaza Strip had been taken from Palestinians since 1967, or that three-quarters of a million Palestinians had been expelled from Israel after 1948, had dropped from the reckoning. The bombings inside Israel were widely interpreted not as the desperate response of extremists to the ongoing occupation, but as proof of the ingratitude and untrustworthiness of a Palestinian people dependent on Israel's good grace for their continued survival. A Hamas operation suggested, for a fleeting second, that Israel was militarily threatened; and so the Israeli response was often to hit back at the Palestinians, to make them understand the true power relations between Israel and the occupied territories. This psychological bar offers some explanation for Shimon Peres' disastrous invasion of Lebanon in April 1996, vengefully entitled 'Operation Grapes of Wrath'. The Hizbollah guerillas in South Lebanon, who had been fighting another Israeli occupation of almost twenty years' duration, were convenient targets for a large-scale military operation against Arabs in the wake of the bus bombs.[32] Unfortunately, as has often been the case in Israeli military adventures, the victims of Israel's awesome firepower turned out not to be Islamic militants: around 200 Lebanese civilians were killed, half of that number slaughtered by Israeli artillery whilst taking shelter in a United Nations compound.[33] In addition, the targeting of Lebanese infrastructure ensured that Israel's wrath was directed not at Hizbollah but towards the civilian population at large, creating hundreds of thousands of refugees and crippling electricity and water supplies. The international condemnation of Israel's actions ensured that Peres' war offered little catharsis to the Israeli public, which promptly removed him from office a few weeks later in favour of the Likud leader Binyamin Netanyahu.[34]

The Likud party had been largely demonised after Rabin's death, accused of encouraging rejection of the peace process and courting the Greater Israel advocates of the religious Right. The bus bombs, however, led people to question whether the Labour peace policies had not been too lenient. Netanyahu adeptly exploited the moment: Peres could not argue that the bombing proved the folly of Israel's peace moves, or suggest that the best way to stop further attacks was to improve the material conditions in the occupied territories and expand Palestinian autonomy. Instead, Peres tried to toughen his stance towards the Palestinians, alienating Palestinian Israelis and his left-leaning supporters. Peres had never been considered anything other than a dove within Israel, and his failure to capitalise on this reputation forced him to compete with political hawks on their terms, rather than his own.[35] In the absence of the argument for more concessions on Israel's part, Netanyahu drilled home his message that less should be given away. Telling Israelis that peace should not be sought at the expense of security, he broke the intuitive bond between the two and suggested that what Israel needed was less peace and a good deal more security. In an election campaign in which the two seemed frequently to be opposites, Netanyahu persuaded enough Israelis to put security ahead of peace and defeated Peres. By the time Netanyahu and Peres had agreed on the primacy of security, the Israeli voters had a clear sense of who would be the best man for the job.[36]

Netanyahu had been elected on the basis of slogans suggesting that he was 'good for the Jews', and he himself claimed that, although he had only just scraped to victory because of support for Peres, his mandate to govern was a clear one, since he enjoyed 55% of the Jewish votes cast in the election.[37] This prompted many to suspect that the Oslo accords were doomed with his acceptance of the premiership. In fact, the new Likud government surprised its detractors and quickly vowed to continue the peace process which Rabin had shaped. In part, this was a concession to international opinion, especially pressure from the United States, but it was also a tribute to the brilliance of Rabin's plan contained in Oslo II. Netanyahu inherited a policy of limited withdrawal and settlement expansion from Rabin and Peres, and continued it faithfully. Some of the new faces in his cabinet caused alarm, given their reputations as hawks and settlement supporters, but the Likud government pursued essentially the same course as Labour.[38]

Just as Shimon Peres had increasingly to deal with Palestinian despair over the ongoing occupation, so Netanyahu's election ensured that he was responsible for inevitable displays of Palestinian discontent. Likud ministers were less adept than their Labour counterparts at pursuing hawkish ends with dovish words, but it was those ends themselves that provoked Palestinian opposition. In September 1996, in a move partially to appease his backers on the religious Right, Netanyahu allowed the opening of a new entrance to a tunnel alongside the Temple Mount in Jerusalem, the site of the holy Islamic shrines. Although this tunnel had been used by foreign tourists and Israelis for many years, the carving of a new entrance was a politically symbolic act. The right-wing mayor of Jerusalem, Ehud Olmert, lent ceremonial weight to the proceedings, and the public presentation of the event was in part responsible for the Palestinians' subsequent anger. The Temple Mount has been the scene of numerous protests and occasional massacres of Palestinians since the Israeli invasion of 1967, and its religious and political significance make any Israeli activity in the area especially explosive. The tunnel opening seemed to confirm, if not to trumpet, Israel's sovereignty over Jerusalem; a provocative reminder of an ongoing injustice. The consequence was Palestinian protest, followed by an Israeli army response, followed by further Palestinian protest. As some observers had feared, the creation of the tiny Palestinian enclaves provided a focus for the discontent, and the Israeli units stationed outside the big Palestinian cities were in the vanguard of the fighting that followed. With the aid of tanks and even combat helicopters, the Israeli army displayed its military might over unarmed Palestinian civilians, whilst the Palestinian police force vacillated between protecting its people and preventing them from responding to the Israeli attacks. More than 60 Palestinians, virtually all civilians, had been killed before the fighting was over, as well as 12 Israeli soldiers.[39]

Netanyahu received some criticism inside and outside Israel for provoking Palestinians in this way, but to focus on the immediate cause of the disturbances is to ignore their underlying rationale: since the peace process began, Israel had continued to confiscate and build on land in the occupied territories. Every Israeli prime minister since 1967 had overseen and endorsed settlement building in the occupied territories, and the continuation of the settlement programme throughout the Oslo period gradually persuaded more and more Palestinians that Israel was not serious about peace. The autonomy enjoyed in the Palestinian cities was heavily circumscribed by Israel's continuing siege of these areas, and Palestinians could not believe that they might one day see a meaningful state in the occupied territories when they witnessed further annexation and Jewish settlement on a daily basis.

It was fitting that the Oslo process should grind to a complete standstill in March 1997 over the issue of settlements. Netanyahu agreed to a partial redeployment of the Israeli army from Hebron in January, but he left the settler group in the city centre untouched: a garrison of troops would remain at the heart of the Palestinian town, Israeli soldiers guarding 400 Jewish settlers amidst 120,000 Palestinians. This arrangement was far from satisfactory for those 20,000 residents of Hebron who now lived in a new Israeli zone of occupation, or the other Palestinians who went to pray or work in the central area.[40] Netanyahu's refusal to disband the Hebron settlements ensured ongoing tensions in the town, and a continued belief on the Palestinian side that Israel intended to make permanent its occupation. In March, Netanyahu gave the go-ahead for an enormous settlement to be built in East Jerusalem at Jabal Abu Ghneim, the site of a nature reserve and a monastery, overlooking Bethlehem. The new development, to be named Har

Homa, would complete the circle of Israeli settlements which had been built around East Jerusalem, and effectively close off the city to the West Bank. If construction went ahead, the last gateway to a prospective Arab capital would be blocked.[41]

Ground was broken at Har Homa on 18 March, with intense protests from Palestinians bringing an armed Israeli response and a curfew on the population of Bethlehem. A few days later, a suicide attack on a Tel Aviv café reconfirmed the pattern of Israel settlement expansion and armed resistance from militant Palestinian groups. The Oslo talks were broken off from the Palestinian side, and the peace process came to a complete stop. Meanwhile, yet another area of Palestinian East Jerusalem, Ras el-Amud, was threatened with an Israeli settlement. Since Ras el-Amud lay deep in the heart of Palestinian residential housing, the plan to build a settlement was criticised even by Prime Minister Netanyahu. However, the combined pressure of Jerusalem's right-wing mayor, Ehud Olmert, and the American businessman, Irving Moscowitz, who claimed to have purchased land in the area, forced through the development even against Netanyahu's supposed resistance. By the end of 1997, Palestinians were confronted by the destruction of the forest of Jabal Abu Ghneim and the sight of new Jewish settlers in Ras el-Amud. Militant elements chose to renew their attacks on Israeli cities, and so Israeli West Jerusalem was once again, in July 1997, the target of bombers. As the peace process remained frozen, Palestinian land was confiscated and built upon for Jewish residents in the occupied territories, and the peace of Israeli cities was threatened in return.[42]

In more ways than one, the settlements of Har Homa and Ras el-Amud brought the Oslo process full circle. Support for a peace on the Palestinian side could only be guaranteed if an Israeli withdrawal from the occupied territories was completed. Successive governments of Israel, inheriting a massive settlement programme from their predecessors, refused even to freeze all construction of new homes, let alone to dismantle existing houses. The response of the Palestinian people to the continuing confiscation of their lands was frustration and despair, manifested widely in the clashes of September 1996; and, in extremis, in the bomb attacks of Hamas and Islamic Jihad in 1996 and 1997. In turn, the action of the Israeli government was to arrest more Palestinians, suspend peace negotiations and continue the confiscation and annexation of Palestinian land unabated. Since the novelty of Oslo had worn off for the Palestinian people, and the government of Israel was inclined to pursue its settlement policies exactly as it had done before the peace process, this cycle of dispossession, protest, violence, suffering and repression had acquired a momentum of its own.

Conclusion

Four years after the signing of the Declaration of Principles, and two years after the Interim Agreement, the pattern of Oslo had become clear. Israel had succeeded in withdrawing from the most populous Palestinian areas, and had consolidated its grasp on the remaining territory of the West Bank. The Gaza Strip, home to only 5000 Jewish settlers but containing valuable water resources desperately needed by its one million Palestinian citizens, had been partitioned to allow one third of the land and all of the water to be controlled by Israel. If Palestinians had hoped that the momentum of a peace process would force Israel to end its occupation and recognise its Palestinian neighbours, the experience of Oslo proved that such an outcome was fantastical. The Palestinian Authority controlled less than two thirds of Gaza and only 3% of the West Bank; water supplies were still subject to military orders and controlled, inequitably, by Israel. Meanwhile, settlement building throughout the West Bank and in East Jerusalem continued unabated, whilst the newly completed by-pass roads stretched around the West Bank settlements, choking the possibility of Palestinian sovereignty. The Palestinian population languished in the cities, frequently confined there by Israeli border closures and always subject to the scrutiny of troops stationed outside each town; and the Palestinian leadership found that its own survival depended increasingly on the passage of a peace process which was anathema to the Palestinian people. With the continuation of terrorist attacks inside Israel, the ongoing repression of Palestinians by the Israeli army or the Palestinian Authority, and the accelerated construction of the settlements which had caused the conflict in the first instance, the Oslo process has actually worsened the situation in the occupied territories and confounded the possibility of a lasting peace.

Notes

1. Hugh Carnegy in the *Financial Times* (London), 13 August 1990, summarises Saddam's linkage of an Iraqi withdrawal from Kuwait with an Israeli withdrawal from the Occupied Territories, describing the manoeuvre as 'a shrewd and awkward weapon cleverly dispatched'. The risks of Saddam's strategy were much greater for the Palestinians, after they had chosen to back the Iraqi leader's stance. Writing in *The Guardian* (London) as early as 14 September 1990, Ibrahim Abu-Lughod predicted that 'of all actual and potential victims of this conflict, the Palestinians stand to lose the most.' These losses would be registered not only in political weakness but in the drying-up of financial contributions to the Palestinian cause from countries such as Saudi

Arabia, which had lined up against Saddam: see Michael Theodoulou's article in *The Times* (London), 21 August 1990.

2. Haidar Abdul-Shafi's insistence on certain preconditions to an agreement survived even the euphoria over Rabin's 1992 victory: 'We are ready to negotiate the interim self-rule government in the first phase but we have made this contingent on [the Israelis] stopping appropriating land and establishing settlements. Autonomy loses its meaning if this is not conceded.' 'Palestinians await proof from Rabin', *The Guardian*, 15 July 1992.

3. Several accounts of this clandestine process have now been published: Mohammad Heikal's *Secret Channel* (London: Harper Collins, 1996) offers a detailed narrative of the open and secret negotiations; whilst Mahmoud Abbas's *Through Secret Channels* (Reading: Garret Publishing, 1995) outlines the personal experiences of Yasser Arafat's deputy.

4. The three Palestinians mentioned above all distanced themselves from Oslo and from the new Palestinian Authority after the Madrid process was discarded. Although Ashrawi and Husseini have been persuaded to return to the fold and accept portfolios in the PA, Abdul-Shafi remains outside the government, as he said he would after the Oslo news was announced; see the 'Interview with Haidar Abdul-Shafi', *Journal of Palestine Studies*, Vol. XXIII, No. 1 (Autumn 1993), pp. 14–19. Shimon Peres gives a remarkably candid confirmation of Israel's motives for choosing the PLO and Oslo rather than the 'internal' Palestinian leadership and Madrid in Connie Bruck's extended essay 'The Wounds of Peace' (*New Yorker*, 14 October 1996): 'Peres was convinced that if Arafat was allowed to return and rule in Gaza and in Jericho [...] he would yield, for the time being, on virtually everything else. This included the Palestinians' core issues'; p. 70. See also Bruck's treatment on p. 72 of Joel Singer, another Oslo negotiator for Israel, who 'told Rabin that they would get a far better deal with the PLO than with the "inside" Palestinians, in Washington, whose demands were far more extreme'; and Tanya Reinhart's 'The man who swallowed Gaza', in *Yediot Aharonot* (Hebrew), 7 April 1997.

5. *Declaration of Principles*, Article I. The DoP is reprinted in Laqueur and Rubin (eds), pp. 599–612.

6. See supra Chapter 1, note 31, for a summary of Resolution 242 and the limited Israeli interpretation of the same. Resolution 338 is reprinted in Laqueur and Rubin (eds), p 310. Both Norman Finkelstein and Noam Chomsky have written about the changing interpretation of 242, and have stressed the importance of power in determining the meaning of the resolution at any moment, as opposed to 'original intent'. See Chomsky, *World Orders Old and New* (New York: Columbia University Press, 1996, updated edition), pp. 272, 274; and Finkelstein, *Image and Reality of the Israel–Palestine Conflict*, pp. 152ff.

7. The Washington-based Foundation for Middle East Peace, in its *Report on Israeli Settlement*, Vol. 3, No. 5 (September 1993), estimated a total of 284,000 settlers at the time of the signing of the DoP – 4,000 in Gaza, 120,000 in the West Bank and 160,000 in occupied East Jerusalem.

8. See Paul Findley, *Deliberate Deceptions*, pp. 116–23. America's threat, delivered by James Baker, secretary of state, was reported in the *Daily Telegraph* (London), 25 February 1992.

9. Rabin told the British Channel Four News before his election victory that he would 'freeze the settlements in those areas where building there serves only political issues and not the security problems of Israel'; 24 February 1992. In fairness to Rabin, he seems not to have promised a 'complete' settlement freeze in various speeches and interviews, content for that interpretation to be drawn from his remarks but never committing himself fully: see, for example, his interview with Sarah Helm and David Horovitz in *The Independent* (London), 17 April 1992. Of course, Rabin did show enormous bad faith in allowing virtually all settlement projects to come within his definition of 'strategically necessary' Jewish areas, a concept which was hardly challenged by the international media, let alone the Israeli electorate. The insistence of the US on a total settlement freeze wilted when Rabin announced his partial restrictions in July 1992, and Rabin soon got his money; see Sarah Helm, 'Rabin hedges bets on settlements freeze', *The Independent*, 17 July 1992.

10. Rabin's failure to keep his promise is the subject of Peter Demant's 'Settlers and Settlements under Rabin and Peres: Obstacles on the Road to Peace', *Amsterdam Middle East Papers*, No. 5 (May 1996). The Foundation for Middle East Peace estimates that 50,000 new settlers moved into the occupied territories during the first two years of Rabin's administration: 'Settlement pace picks up', *Report on Israeli Settlement*, Vol. 5, No. 6 (November 1995). See also the report of LAW, the Palestinian Society for Human Rights and the Environment, 'Palestinians in Wonderland: a report on the human rights violations of the Labor and Likud governments during the Oslo process', 9 October 1996. LAW notes that between the signing of the first Oslo agreement in September 1993 and the Labour party's defeat in May 1996, more than 73,000 acres of land (some 5% of the total land area of the West Bank) were confiscated by the Israeli military authorities.

11. See Demant, p. 6. Rabin made clear that 'the Jerusalem area' (i.e., the West Bank areas around the illegally annexed eastern side of the city) would be the site of new settlement building, reaffirming this position throughout June 1992; see *The Guardian*, 27 June 1992, for an example. See also LAW's report 'Palestinians in Wonderland', p. 5.

12. Demant, pp. 9–10. See note 26 of Chapter 1 for the convenient distinction between 'new' developments and the massive expansion of existing ones, a tactic which came into its own for Israeli governments from the mid-1980s onwards.

13. See LAW's 'Palestinians in Wonderland', p. 2; 'By-pass road construction in the West Bank: the end of the dream of Palestinian sovereignty', 23 February 1996; and 'West Bank road plans leave nothing to negotiate', *Middle East International*, 25 June 1993.

14. The Preamble to the Agreement makes no mention of the division of

the West Bank into three areas, the largest of which is to remain under Israeli control; instead, the sides are said to be 'desirous of putting into effect the Declaration of Principles on Interim Self-Government Arrangements ... and in particular Article III and Annex I concerning the holding of direct, free and general political elections ... in order that the Palestinian people in the West Bank, Jerusalem and the Gaza Strip may democratically elect accountable representatives'. *Israeli–Palestinian Interim Agreement on the West Bank and the Gaza Strip*, Washington DC, 28 September 1995, p. 7.

15. These percentages are derived from the 'Consolidated Map of the West Bank', supplied with the *Interim Agreement*. The Applied Research Institute, Jerusalem (ARIJ) has calculated that Area A comprises 159 km^2, Area B some 1334 km^2, and Area C totals 4328 km^2. The percentages above are based on the assumption that the West Bank includes all those parts of Jerusalem which were seized by Israel in 1967. Israeli figures exclude the Jerusalem area as a matter of course, and consequently exaggerate the degree of planned withdrawal from the occupied territories.

16. In the first phase of redeployment, Israel was to retain a substantial military presence in Area B but to cede control of some civil affairs to the Palestinian Authority. It was imagined that full Palestinian security control over Area B would follow, necessitating a complete Israeli withdrawal; but this has yet to happen, and the Israeli occupation continues. See Article XI for details of A, B and C, and the respective responsibilities of the sides in each; and Annex III, 'Protocol Concerning Civil Affairs', for a full delineation of Palestinian jurisdiction over Area B, including planning authority: *Interim Agreement*, pp. 14–15 and pp. 128 ff.

17. See ibid., Article XXXI, Paragraph 5, p. 27.

18. The provisionary clause on Area C makes the first of many appearances in the *Interim Agreement* at p. 15, Article XI, Paragraph 2e. The permanent status issues are listed in Article XXXI, Paragraph 5, p. 27.

19. This vital fact was established in writing as part of the January 1997 Hebron accords, which were only signed after Israel obtained reassurance from the US that its redeployments required no negotiation with the Palestinians, and that it was free to withdraw from as much or as little of the occupied territories as it wished. See Warren Christopher's 'Letter of Assurance to Israel', 15 January 1997, and the Israeli cabinet's 'Communiqué' of 16 January 1997, reprinted in the *Journal of Palestine Studies*, Vol. XXVI, No. 3 (Spring 1997), pp. 139–40.

20. To summarise Israel's commitments to withdraw from the occupied territories under Oslo: Israel could retain control of its 30% of the Gaza Strip at least until a permanent status agreement, and was committed to return Areas A, B and C of the West Bank except for 'permanent status' issues within eighteen months of the inauguration of the Palestinian Legislative Council. Since Israel could technically declare all of Area C to be territory affected by permanent status issues, the Israeli army was in effect required to withdraw

from only the 25% of the West Bank included in Areas A and B by August 1997, in three six-monthly phases. When this deadline passed, Israel had in fact withdrawn from less than 3% of the territory. Israel was still occupying over 97% of the West Bank in March 1998, with no further withdrawal in sight. See *Interim Agreement*, Article XVII, Paragraph 2a, for confirmation of the withdrawal plan and timetable; p. 20.

21. The Interim Agreement did, in fact, contain a provision explicitly defending the territorial integrity of the occupied territories: 'The two sides view the West Bank and the Gaza Strip as a single territorial unit, the integrity and status of which will be preserved during the interim period.' Article XI, Paragraph 1, p. 14. This statement has formed the cornerstone of the argument that Israel's partition plan is in violation of the spirit of the Oslo agreement; however, the Israeli government has pointed to the letter of the document elsewhere to justify its policy. See, for example, the Israeli Government Press Office statement 'Jewish Communities in Judea, Samaria and Gaza', 21 January 1997, which argues that Israel's policy of settlement building is 'fully consistent with the terms of the Oslo accords'.

22. In his Knesset speech of 5 October 1995, urging ratification of the Oslo II agreement, Rabin not only declared that the Interim Agreement allowed for 'natural growth' of existing settlements, but also that 'activity for providing security measures for the Israeli communities — fences, peripheral roads, lighting, gates – will continue on a wide scale.' Rabin was explicit about his scheme for massive land expropriation and Jewish construction in the occupied territories: 'By-pass roads will be built, whose purpose will be to enable Israeli residents to move about without having to pass through Palestinian population centers.'

23. Only the latest of many plaudits offered to Rabin is the posthumous 'Rabin–Peres Peace Prize', to be awarded each year to a person who has made outstanding efforts in the search for Middle East peace. Given Rabin's own checkered record in this regard, it is fitting that the first recipient of the prize should be US President Bill Clinton. Clinton has pledged to dedicate the $75,000 prize to a support fund for 'students of Middle East peace', which should ensure that such ironies continue. 'Peace Prize for Clinton', *Yediot Aharonot*, 29 July 1997.

24. Jad Isaac's survey 'The water conflicts in the Middle East from a Palestinian perspective' (Bethlehem: Applied Research Institute Jerusalem, 1997) outlines at least three ways in which Israel has seriously compromised Gaza's water supply: first, the Israeli settlers in the Strip are located on top of the most plentiful supplies, and pump from them inequitably; second, Israel itself takes water not only from Gaza itself but from a coastal area to the north which ensures that the Gaza aquifer yields less; and finally, Israel is responsible for the enormous refugee population and overcrowding in Gaza which exacerbates the water shortage by increasing demand. See also Sara Roy's account of the 'devastating' effect of Israeli water management in Gaza on the indigenous agricultural economy; according to Roy, the settlers consume around eighteen

times more water per capita than the Palestinians, a ratio which does not include the water siphoned off to Israel before it reaches the Gazan population; *The Gaza Strip*, pp. 162–75.

25. Of all Israeli Jews, it was the settlers who objected most violently to Oslo, and even organised their own militia in September 1993 dedicated to defending the settlements from Palestinians and, in the last resort, the Israeli army. Meanwhile, Shlomo Goren and other well-known rabbis called upon soldiers to disobey any order to disband settlements, since such an order would be against Jewish law. Demant, 'Settlers and Settlements Under Rabin and Peres', pp. 11–12. Demant links the 1994 Hebron massacre of at least 29 Palestinian worshippers by a Jewish settler, Baruch Goldstein, to the more general problem of settler violence and Jews 'lording over their Palestinian neighbours'.

26. According to his confession, signed days after the murder, Amir had declared that it was permissible 'to kill anybody who was giving up the land of Israel'; *The Independent*, 6 November 1995.

27. The picture of a peace-loving Rabin murdered by an extremist opponent, made more resonant by Rabin's attendance at a Peace Now rally just before his death, was so easily intelligible to a Western audience that very few newspapers diverged from it in their editorials and editorial pieces. See, for example, the leader articles 'Death of a peacemaker', *The Times*, 6 November 1995, and 'Shalom to the fallen', *The Guardian*, 6 November 1995; Michael Walzer's eulogy to Rabin and his 'visionary politics' in 'Reasons to mourn', *The New Yorker*, 20 November 1995; and Henry Kissinger's otiose tribute, 'My Fallen Friend', in *The Washington Post*, 12 November 1995, in which Rabin is compared to Moses. See also the tributes of world leaders to Rabin at his funeral, collected in 'The bullet that killed you cannot kill what you started', *The Guardian*, 7 November 1995. Robert Fisk's 'Palestinians will not weep for Rabin', *The Independent*, 8 November 1995, is a notable exception to this trend.

28. See Geoffrey Aronson's essay 'Rabin assassination' in *Report on Israeli Settlement*, Vol. 5, No. 6 (November 1995): 'Rabin attempted to build an Israeli policy for the West Bank's future on what he rightly considered to be a broad national consensus – a policy that left the Israeli army in strategic control of the occupied territories and the settlers, despite their apocalyptic visions, with an unprecedented measure of protections aimed at securing their future.'

29. Although the transfer of control of over 60% of Gaza was a chaotic and ill-organised affair, Israeli withdrawal from the West Bank cities produced a more spectacular and euphoric response from Palestinians. See Sarah Helm's optimistic assessment of Israeli withdrawal from Jericho: 'History breaches walls of Jericho', *The Independent*, 14 May 1994. Even though the other cities were not transferred for more than eighteen months, the departure of Israeli troops still produced hope and joy: see 'Israelis leave Nablus in haste', *The Guardian*, 13 December 1995.

30. The link between Israel's oppressive tactics and the growth of Hamas is

widely accepted; see, for example, 'Security chiefs warn Netanyahu', *Foreign Report*, 7 August 1997, in which Israeli army and secret police chiefs are quoted as fearing that Netanyahu's treatment of the Palestinians threatens Arafat's legitimacy among Palestinians, and 'without Arafat it will be virtually impossible to achieve a negotiated settlement.' Moshe Ya'alon, the head of the army's Intelligence branch, confirmed to a Knesset committee that Palestinian support was flowing to Hamas because of oppressive closure measures by the Israeli government; *Middle East News Items*, 10 July 1997. Dilip Hiro's thoughtful article 'Hamas the key factor in the peace equation', *Inter Press Service*, 6 August 1997, outlines the many ways in which Israeli policies, from the expulsion of 400 Palestinians to Lebanon in 1992 to the closures of August 1997, have served only to strengthen Hamas: 'For Netanyahu to pile up pressure on Arafat seems like a recipe for destroying the secular, nationalist mainstream among Palestinians, paving the way for the Islamists to fill the consequent political vacuum.'

31. See Patrick Cockburn's article 'Has peace been blown apart?', *The Independent*, 5 March 1996.

32. See Peres's justificatory speech in the Knesset, 22 April 1996, for his attempts to link the activities of Hizbollah, resisting Israel's occupation of south Lebanon, with Hamas, fighting a different war by different means on the streets of Israeli cities: 'The firing of Katyushas [Hizbollah rockets], like the actions of Hamas, was intended to undermine the peace process in the Middle East. The incidents in Tel Aviv, in Ashkelon and in Jerusalem [the bus bombs], like the firing on our northern settlements, stem from the same source and the same logic.'

33. See Shyam Bhatia's article 'Children killed in Israeli attack', *The Observer* (London), 14 April 1996 for the link between Peres's Lebanon War and his desire to enhance his 'security' credentials ahead of the May 1996 elections; see also 'A war the Israelis can all support', *The Independent*, 18 April 1996 and 'Strong man Peres fights his last battle', *The Guardian*, 24 April 1996.

34. The bombing at Qana focused the minds of international commentators on the repercussions of Peres's policies in the context of his re-election campaign: see, for example, the editorial of the *Independent on Sunday*, 21 April 1996: 'It is hard to imagine a worse perversion of the idea of peacemaking than Operation Grapes of Wrath, or a greater insult to the idea of democracy than killing foreigners to win votes.'

35. Peres's campaign slogan gives some sense of his change in tone and emphasis: 'Israel is strong with Peres'; see *The Independent*, 12 April 1996. The narrowness of Peres's eventual defeat, and the abstentions of many Palestinian Israelis who might otherwise have backed him, suggests that this tactic was doubly mistaken.

36. Peres's achievement in losing the May 1996 election was a colossal one, given the huge Labour lead after Rabin's death, and the well of sympathy for his 'path of peace'. From the evidence, one can only conclude that Peres's repeated attempts to remodel himself as a tough character in the mould of

Rabin were a huge mistake. This new image was first advanced in the extra-judicial murder of Yahya Ayyash, alleged Hamas suicide bomber, who was decapitated by an exploding mobile phone in a baroque Israeli secret service operation of January 1996, for which Peres took the credit. Hamas claimed after the assassination that Ayyash would be avenged, and Peres's operation was cited by the militants as the immediate cause of the appalling bus bombs of February and March 1996. That Peres should choose to respond to this lesson with yet more violence in Lebanon demonstrated how little he had learnt from his first adventure and from the deaths of innocent people in the buses of Tel Aviv and Jerusalem.

37. The slogan was described as 'racist' by some members of the Labour party; 'Peres edges ahead', *The Guardian*, 29 May 1996 and 'Labor and Likud clash over what is "Good for the Jews"', *Jerusalem Post*, 28 May 1996.

38. See the new government's 'Guidelines', issued by the Government Press Office, 17 June 1996, for Likud's commitment to the continuation of peace negotiations within the Oslo framework. Fears were raised when it became apparent that the Netanyahu cabinet included roles for Rafael Eitan and Ariel Sharon, chief of staff and defence minister respectively during Israel's roundly condemned invasion of Lebanon in 1982. Both men were condemned by the official Kahan investigation into the Lebanon War, particularly for their role in the massacre of at least 800 Palestinian refugees, virtually all elderly men, women and children, in the Sabra and Shatila camps of Beirut on 16 September 1982. Most estimates of the death toll in the camps were higher than this official Israeli number. Amnon Kapeliouk, Israeli journalist and former correspondent for *Le Monde*, put the figure at 3,500; see *Sabra et Chatila: Enquête sur un massacre* (Paris: Seuil, 1982) pp. 93–4.

39. LAW's report, 'Palestinians in Wonderland', contains a detailed summary of the events leading up to the September violence, and the human rights violations of the Israeli army during the fighting itself. See Chapter 3, note 51 on the conduct of the Palestinian police during the disturbances. See also Israeli human rights organisation B'Tselem's report 'Playing with fire on the Temple Mount' (Jerusalem, December 1996), which concludes that Israeli police actions in Jerusalem on 27 September 1996, during a demonstration in which three Palestinians were shot to death and more than 100 wounded, 'paint a dismal picture of the excessive and illegal use of force, including lethal force.'

40. For details of the partition plan and population distribution under the new arrangement, see 'A new Berlin on the West Bank', *The Independent*, 18 January 1997.

41. See 'Bulldozers roll in', *The Guardian*, 19 March 1997. Daoud Kuttab offers an overview of the Har Homa issue in 'The bulldozers arrive', *Los Angeles Times*, 19 March 1997.

42. For a succinct analysis of the Ras el-Amud affair, see 'The mayor and the millionaire', *Jerusalem Report*, 16 October 1997.

3 *Peacemaking and Politics*

Before we examine the effects of the Oslo process in more detail, we should look more carefully at the political circumstances in which it was produced. If Oslo has been a failure, can we ascribe its lack of success to particular political factors, or political parties, which might have enjoyed a different emphasis if events had taken a different turn? Specifically, we might be able to think more optimistically about the future if we can locate a source of optimism, or a reversible cause of pessimism, in past events. Those inclined to defend Oslo often suggest that there is an unrealised political potential in the region: a different political party may assume power, a leader may change his or her policy, the course of peace will inevitably triumph over the exigency of political strife.

In fact, a close analysis of the political situation reveals both that Oslo's failure was always likely and that there is little chance that the process can be saved within the existing political framework. Oslo has collapsed not because of the victory of Binyamin Netanyahu, or the murder of Yitzhak Rabin, but because certain ideas and policies, especially within Israel, have remained constant from 1967 and before to the present day. Oslo has seen the onset of a new vocabulary of peacemaking, but has offered remarkably little in the way of genuinely original thinking which might lead to a just and stable resolution of the Israeli–Palestinian dispute. As we will see, this has implications not only for our understanding of recent events but for our hopes of a more successful peace agreement in the future.

Israel: in search of the 'doves'

One of the most common assumptions in the discussion of Israeli politics, both domestically and outside Israel, is that there is a meaningful distinction in Israeli society between those elements in favour of peace with Israel's neighbours, and those who seek only to contain the supposedly hostile Arabs all around. It is hard to date exactly when this division was first drawn. In 1978, when Israel's right-wing government announced its readiness to sacrifice a land-for-peace deal in the name of further settlement building, a number of former soldiers banded together to establish 'Peace Now,' a movement dedicated to a more constructive relationship with surrounding Arabs. By the time of the invasion and bombing of Lebanon in 1982, Peace Now had persuaded many Israelis to recognise the excesses for which their government was responsible. Although Israel's leaders had successfully presented its previous wars as a threat to the nation's continued existence, the sheer one-sidedness of the Lebanon assault induced some Israelis to express their dissent as never before. Peace Now soon targeted the more militant elements of the settlement programme, correctly identifying the religious and nationalist settlers as antithetical to their own vision of an Israel at least at peace with itself. In the international clamour over atrocities in Lebanon, these more liberal Israelis attracted praise and support for their dedication to conscience in the face of a brutal military assault. The prime minister, Menachem Begin, was an archetypal 'hawk', and to oppose his extreme strategy was instantly to become a 'dove'.[1]

More recently, the comparison between more and less liberal Israelis has again come to the fore. When Yitzhak Shamir, prime minister of the Labour–Likud unity government from 1987 to 1990, and the Likud administration of 1990 to 1992, declared a massive expansion of the settler programme in the early 1990s, he raised an international outcry and ensured that observers would define him unequivocally as a 'hawk'. Yitzhak Rabin adroitly exploited the moment to oppose Shamir's policy, and therefore satisfied the need of commentators to balance Shamir's combativeness with an Israeli 'dove'. Since 1992, the pattern has remained the same: opponents of Oslo inside Israel are 'hawks'; Rabin, Shimon Peres, and their successors are 'doves'. Events have been largely amenable to this framework: Rabin defeated Shamir in 1992, a 'victory for peace'; Rabin and Peres drafted Oslo, peace itself; the Royal Swedish Academy bestowed the Nobel peace prize on Oslo's architects, enshrining their status as 'doves'; Rabin was murdered by an opponent at a peace rally in Tel Aviv, now a martyr for peace as well as a dove; and Shimon Peres lost the 1996 election to Netanyahu, a 'defeat for peace' and the supposed cause of Oslo's recent decline. This understanding of Israeli politics is coherent, persuasive and appealing, enabling us to commit ourselves to Oslo and to construct a strategy for its redemption: remove Netanyahu from office and return to the Rabin–Peres 'path of peace'. Unfortunately, it is also false and profoundly dangerous, offering a skewed vision of Israeli politics exactly when we need to examine Israel's priorities and beliefs most clearly.

Yitzhak Rabin

Since Rabin has been most lovingly and powerfully presented as a 'dove', it is proper that we begin a survey of 'moderate' Israelis with him. As he was himself to admit, he came to peacemaking late in life. Israel's most famous soldier, he took an active part in the campaigns of 1948/9 and 1967, and made his contribution to the process which removed more than a million Palestinians from their ancestral lands. To his credit, he made little effort to deny this, at least earlier in his career. In a passage of his *Memoirs* which was actually excised from the first edition by the Israeli military censor, he confessed to having 'cleansed' the Arab areas of Lod and Ramle of around 50,000 Palestinian civilians in 1948. Admitting that the population 'did not leave willingly', and that his soldiers had found 'no way of avoiding the use of force', he confessed that the action had demanded 'prolonged propaganda activities' after the event to 'explain' why this transfer had been 'necessary'. Rabin's earlier career, at least, was not marked by an effort to reach out to the Palestinians, except to force them from their land.[2]

Even in the 1980s, Rabin did little to suggest that he would later emerge as a champion of peace and accommodation with the Palestinians. In the first instance, he served from 1984 in the Likud–Labour unity government which pursued an enormous settlement programme in the occupied territories. The man who would later present himself in Israel and abroad as the proponent of a settlement freeze happily played a leading role in a cabinet which pushed Israel's presence in the West Bank and Gaza closer to permanence. More notoriously, Rabin also led Israel's repressive response to the Palestinian intifada from 1987 onwards. Whilst much of the international criticism of Israel's fierce tactics was directed at Yitzhak Shamir, the Likud prime minister, it was Rabin who bore responsibility for devising Israel's hard-line strategy and implementing it on the ground.[3] As late as 1991, Rabin's chief contribution to Israeli politics was as a soldier prepared to use any means to consolidate Israel's control over both its 1949 gains and the additional territories seized in 1967. Even though Rabin belonged to the left-wing Labour party, one could hardly think of him as a dove.[4]

All this appeared to change in 1991 and 1992, as Israel approached a general election and Shamir began yet another new settlement drive. Rabin had assumed leadership of the Labour party and, with the benefit of his intifada experience and the lessons of the Gulf War, he saw the opportunity to formalise Israel's hold over the occupied territories and to return the less useful areas to Palestinian control. As we have seen, the intifada brought home powerfully to Israelis that their occupation of the large Palestinian urban centres could not be sustained without a cost in addition to the lives and livelihoods of so many Palestinians: Israelis would also have to die, albeit in far smaller numbers, to preserve Israel's hold over such exclusively Palestinian towns as Nablus and Ramallah.[5] Rabin had the intelligence to see that, on the very limited issue of Palestinian autonomy in the cities, the interests of Israelis and Palestinians overlapped. This was the moment of his conversion to the cause of 'peace'.

Before Oslo came into being, Rabin asserted his new credentials as peacemaker by standing squarely against Shamir's new plans for settlements. Given the reluctance of George Bush and Secretary of State James Baker to bankroll an Israeli government bent on settlement expansion, Rabin's call for a settlement freeze quickly endeared him to international opinion. One of Shamir's final acts as prime minister before his defeat by Rabin was to approve 11,000 new homes in the occupied territories, which would house around 50,000 settlers. It seems reasonable to expect Rabin, elected on a platform of peace and opposition to Shamir's settlement policy, to cancel these building orders and to approach the Palestinians as genuine in his desire for territorial compromise and an end to the conflict.

In fact, Rabin approved every new house, and made virtually no effort to cut back Shamir's expansion plan.[6] He also gave the go-ahead to around 10,000 new homes in East Jerusalem, again on land seized in 1967 and occupied in contravention of international law. These extraordinary facts bear some emphasis. As Palestinians sat down with Israelis to negotiate the future of the occupied territories in Washington, the new, liberal, 'dovish' government of Israel accepted without major alteration a plan to expand Jewish colonisation massively. If Palestinians had placed any faith in a meaningful distinction between hawks and doves in Israel, Rabin's actions proved this to be spurious. The new prime minister's embarrassed excuse, when some commentators questioned the compatibility of up to 100,000 new settlers with a settlement freeze, was that these contracts had been signed by the previous government and would be hard to cancel.[7] This explanation amounts to the most spectacular chutzpah: Rabin would put at risk an immediate agreement with the Palestinians and endanger the prospects of a long-term peace, because he feared the wrath of the Israeli construction industry? It is hard to believe that it would have been more expensive to cancel the new apartments than to build them, or that the United States, which had linked its aid to Israel with the success of Israeli efforts to limit settlements, would not have picked up the tab.[8] It is impossible but to conclude that Rabin built these new homes because, like Shamir, he believed passionately in a future for settlers and settlements in the occupied territories.

This was confirmed explicitly in his justification of his actions: his freeze applied only to entirely new settlements – not to new houses, but to apartments built on land which had not previously been settled by Israel or which was not adjacent to land which was settled. The existing settlements, which the unity government of Shamir, Rabin and Peres had expanded assiduously in the 1980s, were to be encouraged in their 'natural growth'. By 1992, there were already so many settlements in the occupied territories that this provision for natural growth could happily house 50,000 or 500,000 new settlers. The pattern for widespread colonisation had, by this time, been established: in fact, it is hard to imagine that large-scale development and construction would have taken place away from existing settlements. As long as one was committed to the expansion of existing neighbourhoods, any freeze on new settlement was worth virtually nothing.[9]

And so Rabin's tenure as prime minister marked one of the largest expansions of Jewish settlement in the occupied territories since their acquisition in 1967.[10] Although Rabin could plausibly argue that his style was different than that of Shamir, his settlement policy was substantially the same. Since, as we have seen, settlements are at the centre of the Israeli–Palestinian conflict, Rabin's claims to be either a dove or a genuine peacemaker seem, in the context of his premiership, to be threadbare. He not only refused to remove the principal obstacles to a just territorial arrangement with the Palestinians, he actually worked enormously hard to erect more obstacles which would complicate this just arrangement in the future. His legacy therefore would be more accurately described as a confounding of prospects for peace, rather than the vision of peaceful co-existence which his eulogists have ascribed to him.

Those still wedded to his memory might point to the spirit of his political approach, or the possibility of his uprooting some of the settlements had he lived longer, and decry this account of Rabin's hawkishness as disingenuous. However, it should be remembered that Yitzhak Rabin not only refused to dismantle a single settlement, but also created over 10,000 new apartments on occupied Palestinian land, even as he was claiming to the Palestinians that he was genuine in his desire for peace. As for the possibility of his becoming more radical at a later stage of negotiations, there is no evidence to suggest that this would be the case, and overwhelming evidence to the contrary. In his speech recommending ratification of Oslo II, delivered in the Israeli Knesset just a month before his death, Rabin declared unequivocally that Israel 'will not return to the June 1967 lines', before outlining in detail the permanent solution which Israel would accept:

> And these are the main changes, not all of them, which we envision and want in the permanent solution:
>
> a) First and foremost, united Jerusalem, which will include both Ma'ale Adumim and Givat Ze'ev – as the capital of Israel, under Israeli sovereignty, while preserving the rights of the members of the other faiths, Christianity and Islam, to freedom of access and freedom of worship in their holy places, according to the customs of their faiths.
>
> b) The security border of the State of Israel will be located in the Jordan Valley, in the broadest meaning of that term.
>
> c) Changes which will include the addition of Gush Etzion, Efrat, Beitar and other communities, most of which are in the area east of what was the 'Green Line', prior to the Six-Day War.
>
> d) The establishment of blocs of settlements in Judea and Samaria, like the one in Gush Katif.[11]

Rabin's explicit demand extended to virtually every existing settlement, and made no compromise whatsoever to Palestinian demands that the settlers should vacate occupied land. Rabin confirmed that, under Oslo, Israel's new border was not with Palestine but with Jordan. His reference to 'united Jerusalem' incorporates territory so far eastward of the existing boundaries that the West Bank is cut in half; the central West Bank areas, colonised as the Gush Etzion settlements, are formally taken into Israel; and even the exposed Gaza settlements of Gush Katif receive the reassurance of Rabin's permanent protection. This is the clearest, most accurate and up-to-date impression we will ever have of Yitzhak Rabin's conception of peace, and it provides no basis whatsoever for believing either that Rabin was a dove or that he could have reached an equitable agreement with the Palestinians. In this respect, the Oslo process was for Rabin not a late conversion to the cause of peace but the culmination of his life's work.

Shimon Peres

Although the circumstances of Rabin's death ensured that he was closely identified with the cause of peace, Israel's most famous 'dove' remains his long-time rival and partner, Shimon Peres. Whilst Rabin retained his reputation as a soldier first, even during the Oslo process, Peres presented himself as a statesman and, occasionally, a philosopher. Their partnership was billed as the best of both worlds: the strong approach of Rabin, trusted general of the Israeli army, and the insight and vision of Peres, the civilian who yearned for peace.[12] After Rabin's assassination in November 1995, Peres reaffirmed the strength of their combined approach and pledged to continue Rabin's work during his own tenure as prime minister. Peres's narrow defeat in June 1996 was therefore viewed in the international media as an enormous blow to peace. Israel was now denied the benefit of Peres's sincerity and forced to rely on his opposite, the hawkish Netanyahu.[13] As Peres himself had warned in his memoirs, *Battling for Peace*, a 'yawning ideological chasm' existed between Labour and Likud, and the defeat of the former could have terrible implications for the prospects of a lasting peace.[14]

This picture of Peres is no more accurate than the one of Rabin. Although it is true that Peres has employed the language of peace more often than any other Israeli leader, and has been more willing to admit some claims of the Palestinians than his predecessors as Israeli prime minister, he offered nothing to the Palestinians that Israel could not happily live without. His vision of Oslo, like Rabin's, was of a process of gradual Israeli disengagement from those areas of the occupied territories which held no interest to Israel's colonisation plans or security needs. The existing settlements, in their entirety, were to be preserved, even though they made impossible the establishment of a genuinely sovereign and viable Palestinian state. Responding to the erroneous question that Oslo forced settlers to 'give up their homes', Peres confirmed in the Knesset that his vision of peace was compatible with ongoing settlement:

> The explicit answer is that nobody has been asked to give up his home. Contrary to Camp David, we conducted negotiations that do not require the evacuation of even one settlement. The edifice we are building is based on a change in relations, not in locations. If the two sides were to develop a different relationship, the whole problem would take on a totally different form. Hatred would give way to wisdom. If relations improve, there will be no problem. If relations continue as they are, there will be no solution.[15]

Peres was the architect not of substantive 'land for peace' negotiations, but of a disingenuous form of diplomacy which sought 'a change in relations, not in locations'. With this simple phrase, Peres indicated his reluctance to make the genuine concessions necessary for a stable peace. How could the Palestinian Authority persuade its people to reverse their hostility towards Israel if Peres was to extend and formalise the massive occupation of Palestinian land? The entire conflict was based on Israel's aggressive acquisition of 'locations', and yet Peres sought to downplay this primary cause and to elevate the words of peacemaking above concrete actions. The result was not a meaningful foundation for reconciliation but an empty shell, devoid of the practical measures essential to a genuine agreement.

Aside from his misleading reputation as a dove, Peres also became identified with a specific economic agenda for recasting the relationship between Israelis and Palestinians. Although Peres sought to maintain settlements, he was not comfortable with an indistinct dividing line between Palestinian and Israeli areas. He sought instead to draw new lines of separation, and to stem the flow of movement from Palestinian areas into Israel, principally caused by the absolute dependence of a Palestinian economy on its Israeli master. Tens of thousands of Palestinians had been flooding into Israel every day to work in Israeli-owned factories, many staying overnight (illegally) to maximise their paltry wages. Since Peres was committed to an effective separation of Israelis and Palestinians he planned instead to relocate the Israeli factories on the border between an expanded Israel and the new Palestinian autonomous areas, thereby hoping that Palestinian discontent with Oslo would affect neither Israel's economic opportunities nor the security of its major cities.[16]

Aside from the fact that this solution would resemble closely the factories of white South Africa, with black labourers forced to work for minimal wages in white-owned factories, the course of Oslo has demonstrated that even this model of so-called co-existence is not possible. As we shall see in later chapters, Israel has chosen to import non-Palestinian labour from Europe and Asia to replace its Palestinian workforce, and Peres's 'industrial estates' have remained a figment of his imagination. Successive Israeli governments during Oslo, including Peres's own, have imposed severe closures on the Palestinians of the occupied territories, cutting them off from labour inside Israel, and so Peres's dream of an 'economically advanced and politically just' Middle East has come to nothing.[17]

More than any other Israeli politician, Shimon Peres invites scrutiny into the quality of his personal character. His speeches are infused with references not only to the political expediency of peace with the Palestinians but to its ethical implications. Addressing the United Nations General Assembly in October 1995, just after the signing of Oslo II, Peres declared that Israel had made the 'moral choice not to dominate another people'.[18] Later that month, in the Knesset, he put the case for Oslo still more strongly: 'Israel has gained moral liberation, the Palestinians have gained democratic freedom.' In the same speech, he cast this message in the practical example of Gaza:

> Israel has managed to seize the political initiative and return to its moral and political self. Practically speaking, Gaza in reality looks better than the Gaza described in the agreement. Our soldiers need not risk their lives, and Katyusha missiles have not been hurtling from Gaza into Ashkelon or Kiryat Gat. Israel without the Gaza Strip is more Israeli and stronger than an Israel burdened with Gaza.[19]

The only problem with this sentiment is that Israel is not 'without the Gaza Strip', but still in possession of around 35% of it. Even though Peres conceded in his memoirs that 'our rule over Gaza was an ongoing, ghastly mistake', and that he 'was frankly sorry that we had created any Jewish settlements there at all', he and Rabin had fought in 1994 to preserve the Israeli army's influence and, of course, to ensure the 'ongoing, ghastly' presence of every Israeli settler.[20] This fact drops conveniently from Peres's memoirs, of course, replaced by his obviously more important regard for the 'endearing qualities' of the Gazan people, noted on one of Peres's 'pleasurable and memorable' boat trips 'with the Gaza fishermen'. (One wonders whether these trips were made before or after the systematic harassment of, and restrictions upon, the same fishermen by Peres's own Labour government.)[21]

If we are forced by Peres's own boasts to extend our analysis of his achievements to the moral sphere, we can hardly avoid noting the hypocrisy of his public statements on the subject of Gaza, and his quiet defence of the other Israeli settlements alongside his stated advocacy of 'land for peace'. His final political testament, however, reached new depths of moral dereliction: Operation Grapes of Wrath, Peres's bombardment of the people and infrastructure of Lebanon in 1996, killed at least 200 civilians and forced around half a million people to leave their homes.[22] The Lebanese economy and infrastructure were, once again, left in tatters, and Israel found itself on the receiving end of criticism from the international community. The Israeli army's shelling of a United Nations base at Qana, on 18 April, caused particular revulsion. The sight of around 100 people, burned alive or blown to pieces, being carried from a building flying the blue flag of the UN prompted many people to reassess the dovish claims of Shimon Peres.[23] The new prime minister, however, was bullish in the Knesset a few days later, boasting tastelessly of the surgical precision of the Israeli army and laying the blame for Qana at the feet of the Lebanese movement resisting Israel's occupation:

> The operation relies on the use of sophisticated and precise weapons. It accords expression to the IDF's [Israel Defense Forces'] advantage in human and technological quality, in mobility, and intelligence, and in precise and

> accurate hits. ... The Qana tragedy and any other harm done to civilians are, first of all, a terrible human tragedy, and we regret them very much. But we know that it was not intentional. It did not serve our objectives, and it is completely contrary to the nature of the operation.[24]

To most observers, the indiscriminate bombing of Qana seemed entirely compatible with the 'nature of the operation', and although for Peres the matter was closed, the investigating committee of the UN Security Council eventually concluded that the Israeli attack was not the result of a mistake. Thanks to the courage of a UN soldier who smuggled a videotape of the bombardment to the press, the presence of an Israeli drone aircraft over the UN base during the attack, guiding the artillery shells into the compound, could clearly be seen.[25] Far from possessing an 'advantage in human and technological quality' over the Lebanese people under assault, the Israeli army, directed by Peres, used its overwhelming military superiority to blow to pieces 100 innocent civilians taking shelter in a UN 'safe haven'. Although this certainly proved Israel's 'advantage in technological quality', it is hard to see anything human in the action.[26]

If, as so many international observers had hoped, Shimon Peres had defeated Binyamin Netanyahu in 1996, Peres's record offers little to suggest that the cause of peace would have been significantly advanced. Peres had refused to move against the settlement project, thereby ensuring that any land ceded to the Palestinians would be fractured and patchy; his model of economic rejuvenation had collapsed completely and the prospects of Palestinian economic recovery had receded still further from view; further, his bombardment of Lebanon had seriously questioned his ability to lead Israel away from its past towards a more 'moral' relationship with its neighbours in the future. Although Peres certainly yearned to be lauded as a man of peace, his actions confirm him to be as hawkish as Netanyahu on the most vital issues of difference with the Palestinians. That Netanyahu did not reject the Oslo framework bequeathed him by Rabin and Peres confirms the degree of consensus in the mainstream of Israeli politics, and refutes the common assumption that a new Peres government would have delivered a lasting peace. After surveying both Rabin and Peres, our search for a genuine dove must continue.

After Rabin/Peres: the future of the Israeli Left

Both Rabin and Peres have now departed the political scene, but their successors as Labour party leaders have been cast in remarkably similar terms.[27] Ehud Barak, the new party leader, is a former army chief-of-staff who presents himself as a soldier-turned-peacemaker in Rabin's mould. His deputy, Yossi Beilin, adopts the Peres role, having played a large part in the development of Oslo and appearing more as statesman than general. Together, their opposition to Binyamin Netanyahu represents no real change from the position of Rabin and Peres: there are no new initiatives, no major concessions, no approaches to the Palestinians of any real substance. As such, a critique of their credentials as doves follows a similar pattern to our treatment of their mentors above.

Ehud Barak, like Rabin, has defended the rights of settlers to remain in the occupied territories. Like Rabin, he envisages a Palestinian entity that will be wholly conditioned by the extent of the existing settlement programme (with allowances, of course, for 'natural growth'):

> We are never going back to the 1967 borders, we expect most of the Israelis in the West Bank to be under our control even after the agreements on permanent status are achieved.[28]

As Barak has correctly surmised, such an attenuated Palestine could hardly consider itself 'sovereign', politically or economically, and so his conception of a permanent status for Palestine depends upon its merger with an external sovereign state: Jordan.

> Personally, I believe the right solution is a certain kind of affiliation between the Palestinians and the Jordanians to emerge before we make the final steps in negotiation or decide what type of relationship we should have. I prefer confederation of Palestinians and Jordanians as an entity with which we're going to deal, but it's up to them.[29]

Jordan has long appealed to Israeli leaders, since the massive expulsion of Palestinians by Israelis in 1948 and 1967 swamped the neighbouring state to such an extent that the existing Arab community, the Hashemites, became a minority. Barak, like many of his predecessors, would like nothing more than the formalisation of Palestinians' ties to Jordan, since then their refugee status might be effaced.[30] Barak seeks to promote Jordan as a Palestinian 'homeland' because Israel has so comprehensively colonised their actual indigenous lands; if Oslo could persuade the Palestinian leadership to enter confederation with Jordan, Israel might be spared the messy and embarrassing task of denying responsibility for the millions of refugees it has created in its short lifespan. As Barak points out, it is important that this decision should appear to be 'up to them', in case cynical observers saw Israel engineering a final and permanent rejection of the refugees' rights under international law.[31]

Barak's Jordanian dream hardly suggests that he will pursue dovish ends should his party return to office. Interestingly, his plan is also shared by his chief rival, Binyamin Netanyahu. Netanyahu has written extensively on the relevance of Jordan to an adjudication of Palestinian claims, and his conception of a just resolution of the conflict sounds uncannily like Barak's:

> The land of Palestine comprises the modern states of Jordan and Israel. It is large enough to accommodate both a small Jewish state, Israel, and a substantially larger state for the Arabs of Palestine, which is today called Jordan. This is a two-state solution to resolve a conflict between two peoples.[32]

With Barak and Netanyahu in such close agreement on the most desirable course for Oslo, it is difficult to look forward to Labour's eventual return to power with any optimism. If there is a more just solution on the Israeli side, it will not emanate from either of the major parties in the near future.

Looking further still to the left, and moving into the peace groups on the fringes of Israeli society, we can see a minor improvement on the Labour position, but no immediate cause for hope. The Meretz party lies on the edge of acceptable political debate in Israel, and its members have to contend with abuse and intimidation from many Israelis who find their degree of sympathy with the Palestinians to be unacceptable.[33] Although they gained a respectable nine seats in the Knesset elections of May 1996, they cannot be considered a mainstream force in Israeli politics. The radicalism of Meretz depends upon their proposal to disband at least some of the settlements and to relocate settlers within 1949-Israel. However, whilst Meretz claims 'to completely oppose' the settlements in the occupied territories, the party's most recent platform commits itself only to 'the dismantling of small and isolated settlements'.[34] The largest West Bank settlements of Efrat, Ariel and Ma'ale Adumim are not covered by this promise.[35] Similarly, Meretz cannot bring itself to answer a central Palestinian demand: some form of sovereignty over Jerusalem. Given the massive expansion of the city under successive governments since 1967, a form of shared political control is absolutely essential to a stable two-state solution. The Israeli expansion of Jerusalem as its 'undivided capital' has divided the West Bank into two, and excluded Palestinians from a vital engine of a future, sovereign economy. Even assuming that Meretz could greatly increase its support base, the absence of this cession to a new Palestine would seriously threaten the prospects of any peace agreement.[36]

The same hesitancy before Jerusalem has gripped Peace Now, which continues to catalogue settlement expansion outside 'Greater Jerusalem' but is wary of disturbing the more than 150,000 settlers in the

Palestinian areas of the city to the East. The zeal with which such 'doves' as Peace Now advocate a two-state solution is not matched by a careful and equitable assessment of the territorial implications of that concept. The rhetoric of the peace movement comes to sound very much like the mainstream platform of Labour, and the settlement programme rolls on.[37] The breakdown of Oslo appears, if anything, to have driven some more famous Israeli liberals to the right. Amos Oz, for example, who has long basked in his image as the 'conscience of modern Israel', responded to the Hebron agreement of 1997, which preserved the settlement enclave in the centre of the Palestinian town, by recommending a substitute settlement to be inhabited by Israeli peace activists:

> Now that the Palestinians have accepted, in accordance with the Oslo agreement, that there can be a Jewish section in Hebron – let us the doves renew it. ... Let the Peace Now oriented Israelis, the pro-peace Orthodox groups, the dovish religious movement volunteer to take shifts in inhabiting the Jewish quarter in Hebron.[38]

Given the fresh memory in Hebron of Baruch Goldstein's mass murder in 1994, and given Oz's long-term commitment to a putative two-state solution, this plan for a settlement of 'doves' seems extraordinary, although not unrevealing of the crises and confusion of Israel's peace movement. Oz's mistake is an example of the wider danger which threatens all efforts to find a way out of the present impasse: to confuse unsavoury individuals with unsavoury actions is to lose sight of the root cause of the problem. It is not simply the ideology of the Hebron settlers that is at fault, but their very presence within a town of 120,000 Palestinians. To substitute them for more liberal Israelis will not affect the central contention, which is that any settlement is illegal and anathema to Hebron's Palestinians. Similarly, it is not Binyamin Netanyahu who prevents a meaningful peace from emerging, but his actions as prime minister. If one proposes simply to remove him from office, but then to accept virtually all of his policies towards the Palestinians, it is unlikely that a dovish peace will look very different from a hawkish one.

Yitzhak Rabin's murder has indeed set back the cause of peace, but not because of the absence of his wisdom in the difficult years ahead. His assassination has been most harmful in its suspension of the debate about Rabin's progress and the worth of his political vision. Many people inside and outside Israel who are sympathetic to the idea of peace have been unable to see past the long shadow cast by Rabin over his successors, and to engage critically with his policies. As we have seen, Rabin's platform was not based upon a just and lasting peace but upon the annexation of large parts of the occupied territories, along with the settlements, to Israel. Rabin, like every other major figure in Israeli politics, was unable to conceive of anything but the most modest 'land for peace' scheme. Consequently, his policies have brought very little peace, as Shimon Peres discovered in the first months of 1996.

Far from being a villain to Rabin's hero, Binyamin Netanyahu's conduct since becoming prime minister has been broadly congruent with the goals of Rabin and Peres. When he has clashed with the Palestinians, such as over the opening of a new entrance to the tunnel beneath Jerusalem's Old City in September 1996, or over the building of settlements in East Jerusalem in 1997, he has been completely within the mainstream of Israeli political beliefs. Since Jerusalem is, in Rabin's words, Israel's 'eternal and undivided capital'; 'under our sovereignty forever', as Ehud Barak recently declared; or even 'the indivisible capital of Israel', as the far-left Meretz platform puts it; why shouldn't Israel open as many tunnels as it sees fit? Or build wherever it likes? Har Homa and Ras el-Amud are both within the precincts of expanded Jerusalem, and the Har Homa settlement was approved by Rabin's government; as Netanyahu wryly pointed out after the barrage of criticism over the new settlement, its construction would hardly have displeased Rabin.[39]

To blame Netanyahu for the breakdown of Oslo is to ignore the evidence of a wide consensus within Israeli politics around the course of action which Netanyahu has taken. It would be idle to attribute Oslo's failure to Netanyahu's May 1996 election victory, just as it would be wrong to suggest that, had Peres defeated his rival, subsequent events might have gone much differently. The problem in Israeli politics lies not with individuals, or even with party platforms, but with a series of deeper assumptions about the legitimacy of the settlement programme and the permanence of Israel's annexation of Palestinian East Jerusalem. Until these assumptions are generally challenged within Israel, there is little hope that a better peace will emerge, regardless of 'dovish' or 'hawkish' politicians.

The Palestinians and Oslo

Although we have so far reviewed the Oslo process in the context of Israel's objectives and policies, we must confront the issue of the Palestinians' relationship to the peace agreements if we are to understand the magnitude of Oslo's failure. In the first instance, before cataloguing the many ways in which Oslo has disastrously undermined the Palestinian people and their rights, we should consider how and why the Palestinian leadership became involved in the peace process in the first place, and to what degree the Palestinian people can be held responsible for what has happened to them.

As we have previously seen, Oslo has effectively disguised a fact essential to a proper understanding of peace between Palestinians and Israelis: the sides did not enter negotiations as equals, or anything resembling equals. Although it could be argued that the intifada had restored pride to the Palestinian people and dignified their resistance, they remained firmly under Israeli occupation. Palestine had no army, navy or air force; Israel boasted one of the best trained and most technologically advanced military forces in the world. In return for the Israelis leaving the occupied territories, the Palestinians could only offer to stop throwing stones. Israel, on the other hand, could offer the Palestinians a range of options up to and including an independent state, and had the military might to impose any option with or without Palestinian consent. The occupying power had not been forced out, but was leaving of its own volition and on its own terms. Perhaps the simplest explanation for why the Palestinians embarked on such a deleterious peace process was that they had no option but to, and no agency to effect the peace talks for their own advantage once negotiations had begun.[40]

Reviewing the early discussions between the sides, even the 1993 Declaration of Principles, one might forgive the Palestinian negotiators for being optimistic, despite evidence that Oslo was falling short of their expectations. Aside from the words of the various accords themselves, both sides (and the American broker of the treaties) referred to the 'spirit' as well as the letter of Oslo, suggesting that the parties would be bound beyond what had been literally spelled out to more wide-ranging responsibilities.[41] Even though the Israeli–American interpretation of Resolution 242 did not guarantee a full withdrawal from the West Bank and Gaza, there were hopes that, over time, Israel would come to accept it. It was only with the evidence of settlement expansion during the Oslo process that the Palestinians could rule out this possibility: Rabin was to prove to them that his understanding of the 'spirit' of Oslo bore no relation to theirs.

Away from honest misinterpretation, Israel introduced several factors into the negotiating situation which were intended to disadvantage the Palestinians. From the first days of peace talks in Madrid and Washington, where Israel rejected a tough Palestinian team and went looking for a more compliant alternative, the Israelis exerted a strong hold over their negotiating partner. Since the sides were meeting because Israel had chosen to do so, to decide the circumstances of a possible Israeli withdrawal, it is not altogether surprising that Israel sought to regulate the Palestinian delegation in its own interests. The most brazen example of this came with the Palestinian elections of January 1996, which Rabin had presented as a major concession by Israel in Oslo II, and the international community had heralded as a great step forward for peace and democracy in the region. Elections took place for a president and a legislative council, and Palestinians eagerly cast their votes for the new apparatus. However, Oslo II had chosen carefully not to balance these offices against each other but to place the legislature entirely at the mercy of the executive. Arafat was to control the Palestinian Authority with his own unelected appointees, and the legislative council was rendered little more than a talking shop.[42] Palestinians had cast votes for both president and council, but the latter had no influence whatsoever on the most crucial issue facing Palestinians, the peace process. As the effects of the Oslo Accords encouraged more debate and argument amongst Palestinians, Oslo II imposed upon them a 'democratic' system which marginalised parliamentary debate and privileged executive power. Internal opposition to Arafat's policies was suppressed as a structural consequence of Oslo; and so the true plurality of Palestinian opinions towards Oslo was stifled just as it became most important.[43]

The presidential election of 1996 confirmed a pattern of Israeli policy which had taken Yasser Arafat from sworn enemy and terrorist to Israel's partner and would-be statesman. After decades as the symbol of resistance to Israel, it is hardly surprising that Arafat should be elected by the Palestinian people as their first president. However, by offering to recognise Arafat as the legitimate leader of the Palestinians, Israel had bound its former opponent in a dependent relationship. After agreeing to the Oslo process, Arafat had won acceptance on the world stage, as well as the personal kudos and warmth that his new position brought. All this was dependent upon his continued acquiescence in a process dictated by Israel. If he stood up to the Israelis, they could suspend their arrangements for Palestinian self-rule and send Arafat back into exile or worse. If he accepted what was offered, he would be vilified by his own people. Arafat thus found it necessary to conduct negotiations in secret and to repress internal dissent to his own handling of the peace process. Having gambled his own legitimacy, at home and abroad, on the Oslo process, Arafat was unwilling or unable to act upon the fundamental flaws of that process as they became obvious in 1995 and 1996; and so he began to resemble merely a puppet leader, ensuring that the Israeli vision of Oslo was imposed, however brutally, on the Palestinian people.[44]

The Palestinian leadership was already tarnished in 1996, as the timetable for limited Israeli withdrawal was postponed by Peres and Netanyahu. In early 1997, however, evidence of widespread corruption within the Palestinian Authority began to emerge. A British newspaper charged Arafat with having done a secret deal with Israel to enrich his own bank account at the expense of the Palestinian Authority.[45] Later in the year, Arafat's own investigative committee suggested that corruption in the various ministries of the PA had reached unacceptable levels, and that some of those responsible should consider their positions.[46] Given the inexperience of the new Palestinian bureaucrats and politicians, a measure of mismanagement, if not corruption, was inevitable; but talk of secret deals with Israel suggests that the very institutionalisation of the Palestinian struggle, through the creation of the PA, had brought its own problems. Many Palestinians who worked for the new PA were now offered the opportunity to put personal gain before the good of their people: with the autonomous cities providing a measure of freedom from immediate Israeli occupation, and PA officials enjoying much greater freedom of movement than the people they represent, the spirit of unity which had sustained the Palestinian people throughout the occupation was seriously eroded. With the news in May 1997 that some Palestinians had acted as agents in land sales to Israeli Jews, it became apparent that self-preservation and advancement had become an easier option for some than a continuing commitment to the collective struggle. A sad corollary of limited self-rule was that the hopelessness engendered by ongoing Israeli occupation could be alleviated by and for a tiny minority; unfortunately, as they enriched themselves with the profits of land sales or embezzlement, they impoverished the Palestinian people still further.[47]

The Oslo process has been a disaster for the Palestinian people. Although the odds were stacked in Israel's favour from the start, the participation of the Palestinian leadership in negotiations and agreements has legitimised not only the status quo of occupation but the further annexation of Palestinian land. The decade following the intifada has seen the Palestinian people's hopes of freedom dashed definitively.

As we have seen, one of Israel's intentions in beginning the negotiations was to mask the absolute degree of its own agency. As the occupier and (overwhelmingly) superior power, only Israel could decide upon the extent of its withdrawal from the occupied territories, and so that withdrawal did not depend upon a negotiation process. With the Palestinians on board, Israel could frame its strategies for redeployment as territorial concessions, bargaining chips for which it sought some recompense. The Palestinians had nothing to give and nothing to threaten Israel with; and yet, as Oslo continued, it became apparent that Israel sought Palestinian approval for its continuing occupation of some areas in return for withdrawal from others. In 1996 and 1997, reports suggested that Arafat had made major territorial concessions to Israel in secret, in return for 'concessions' from Israel which should have belonged to the Palestinians by right: Arafat had allegedly agreed to many of Rabin's by-pass roads in 1995 in 'return' for Israel's allowing the Palestinian elections to take place; some sources even claimed that he was prepared to compromise in the summer of 1997 on the settlement of Har Homa, which he would stop opposing if Israel allowed the long-promised Gaza port and airport to open. Both cases leave us with the picture of Arafat as a desperate man, prepared to compromise the Palestinian cause in secret to breathe fresh life into his moribund presidency.[48]

By claiming that the Palestinians were their 'partners' in the peace process, Israel attempted to efface its own history of belligerent occupation and colonisation of the West Bank and Gaza Strip. The Palestinian people had suffered terrible privations for almost three decades, and yet Israel's negotiating stance during Oslo was that the sides approached the occupied territories as political and moral equals. Even on the left of Israeli politics, the fact of Israel's decimation of Palestinian society in the occupied territories was ignored: Amos Oz shrieked that the Palestinians had to deliver concessions in response to Israel's tiny withdrawal, but his demands ignored the huge losses already incurred by Palestinians to Israel. That the Palestinian people had been horribly wronged since 1967, let alone in the dispossession and expulsion of 1948–49, had fallen from history.[49]

Participation in Oslo thus bound the Palestinians to a renunciation of their historical and moral rights in return for limited territorial gain. Their automatic, internationally recognised right to the occupied territories was placed on the negotiating table and bargained away: if the sides could sign an argument ceding some of this territory to Israel, the former right would be forgotten. Israel's responsibility to atone for its crimes against the Palestinian people was dissolved in return for the limited empowerment of the Palestinian Authority. Although the Oslo process brought some limited, short-term gains to the Palestinians, they gave up their most powerful asset in the fight against occupation: ongoing and concerted resistance to Israel's violation of international law and annexation of their homeland.

As we have seen, Israel had an interest in limited Palestinian autonomy following its experiences in the intifada. In accepting agreements based solely on this model of self-rule, the Palestinian Authority actually advanced Israel's goals and began to work, inadvertently, in its employ. Resistance to Israel's occupation of 97% of the West Bank would now be directed not against the Israeli army, which had safely redeployed to the outskirts of the cities and fortified itself there; but against the Palestinian Authority and its police forces. The September 1996 clashes showed the terrible position in which the Palestinian police was placed: although some police officers chose to join the Palestinian people in fighting the Israeli army outside the towns, others were ordered to contain their own side so that Oslo negotiations could resume once more.[50] In accepting the responsibility to police themselves, but failing to win control over the most important influences on Palestinian existence, the Palestinian leadership allowed Israel to retreat to a safe distance and forced Palestinian resistance to collapse upon itself.

The concentration of power in Arafat's hands, and the besieged atmosphere of the Palestinian towns he now controlled, led inevitably to the fracturing of Palestinian unity and the encouragement of major divisions in the Palestinian struggle. Despite the various rivalries in the Palestinian resistance movement of the 1970s and 1980s, Palestinians were at least resolved that their chief opponent was the state of Israel. Under Oslo, however, with Arafat shaking hands with Rabin and Netanyahu whilst the annexation of the West Bank continued, Palestinian internal divisions became much more marked. Worse still, as Israel's appointed police chief in the occupied territories, Arafat himself was responsible for rounding up and incarcerating those opponents of Israel and Oslo considered (by Israel) to be militants and terrorists. The Israeli-built prisons in the big Palestinian cities were handed over to Arafat, who proceeded to arrest many of their former occupants under pressure from his peace partner. Arafat's acceptance of this policing responsibility contributed significantly both to the deterioration of the human rights situation in the occupied territories and the undermining of Palestinian unity.[51]

At the most general level, Palestinian participation in Oslo has enabled Israel to present itself as serious and generous in its desire for peace. Shamir, Rabin, Peres and Netanyahu have all exploited the existence of a peace process to imply that Israel had made progress towards conciliating the Palestinians of the occupied territories. In turn, the international community has tempered its earlier criticism of Israel's actions and strengthened Israel politically and economically.[52] In concluding a peace agreement with King Hussein of Jordan, Israel removed another major opponent and isolated the Palestinians once again. The support enjoyed by Palestinians in the 1980s, as well as the widespread recognition of their moral rights to the occupied territories and political freedom, was inevitably eroded by the impression that Israel was, via Oslo, treating them fairly. The facts of Israel's continuing occupation, and its effort to consolidate its presence permanently through settlements and roads, were obfuscated by diplomatic manoeuvring and the media's reluctance to distinguish between a 'peace process' and peace itself.

The international community

Israel does not operate in a political vacuum, but depends upon the support, or at least the apathy, of many other nations in the furthering of its aims. Given that Israel's treatment of the Palestinians has frequently attracted criticism from the international community, we might be surprised at the relative ease with which Israel has been able to deal with the rest of the world. Other nations condemned for their territorial acquisition – such as, in recent years, Iraq and Serbia – have felt the force of international sanctions and even multinational armed intervention in response to their military gains. Israel, by contrast, has faced little but strong words since its invasion of the West Bank and Gaza in 1967, and its invasion of Lebanon in 1982. As we will see, even this verbal condemnation has receded in the face of Oslo, despite Israel's ongoing retention (and annexation) of occupied territory.

Regional politics

Unsurprisingly, Israel has faced strongest opposition from its Arab neighbours. Those countries closest to Israel – Jordan, Lebanon, Syria, and Egypt – have all been engaged in war by their new neighbour and, in every case, have come off worst. Aside from the Palestinians, who lost the vast majority of their homeland in 1948–9, Jordan lost the West Bank (which it had been occupying) to Israel in 1967; Egypt lost Gaza and the Sinai desert to Israel in 1967; Syria lost the Golan Heights in 1967 and lost still more territory in 1973; and Lebanon lost a large section of its southern border to Israel in 1982, for the establishment of the so-called Israeli security zone. The legacy of these multiple defeats and losses has been an objection to Israel's aggressive expansionism, and a scepticism about the genuineness of Israel's desire for peace with its neighbours.

In consequence, these and other Arab states pooled their resources to bring concerted pressure to bear on Israel. In the 1950s and especially the 1960s, the charismatic Egyptian leader, Gamal Abdul-Nasser, sought to depict the Arabs as a single people with united goals. One of these was to defend the rights of exiled Palestinians, and so the notion of united, destructive Arab opposition to Israel was born. Israeli politicians justified their acquisition of extensive military hardware, up to and including nuclear weapons, by claiming that the Arabs sought to 'force Israel into the sea'. The Middle East became a zero-sum game: Israel had either to conquer its neighbours or be conquered by them.[53]

This rationale is at best debatable, especially after Israel's acquisition of an atomic capability in 1967.[54] Nasser's dream of 'pan-Arabism' began to crumble after Israel's successful assaults of 1967, and even the relative success of the Egyptian army in the Yom Kippur war of 1973, by which Egypt regained a little of its lost land, hardly convinced Israel's neighbours that they could reverse Israel's conquests. Instead of engaging in sabre-rattling with the Israelis, Arab leaders after 1967 came increasingly to speak of their desire to make peace, and the plans of Nasser (1970) and Sadat (1971) offered full recognition to Israel, on the condition that it would fully withdraw from the occupied territories. Restricting their pressure to the economic sphere, Arab states, especially Egypt, made a genuine effort to engage Israel in negotiations. This effort was consistently rebuffed.[55] In fact, peace talks only began when Anwar Sadat accepted the new US vision of peace, devised and put into place by a State Department headed by Henry Kissinger. Given that the US position had shifted from urging a full Israeli withdrawal from the occupied territories to envisaging only a partial one, this new orientation threw the Arab world into disarray; and Sadat's 'separate peace' with Israel destroyed the united front of Arab states which had previously exerted pressure. Egypt's acceptance of massive US aid, in return for making peace with Israel, provided a model for other Arab states in the future. If a nation was prepared to forego its commitment to a change in Israeli policy, the rewards were high.[56]

The Middle East has always been defined by various imperial and colonial influences, and the brief period of apparent solidarity between Arab nations soon came to an abrupt end. By the 1980s, external influences were once again the overriding determinant of internal policy: Egypt was receiving one of the largest US aid packages of any country; Iraq under Saddam Hussein was also the recipient of billions of US dollars ostensibly to prop up resistance to its neighbour, Iran, which had thrown out its US-backed leader, the Shah, in 1979; and Saudi Arabia, along with the other oil-producing nations of the region, had moved from active advocacy of the Palestinian cause to passive acquiescence in an American vision of the Middle East.[57]

These shifts in policy were crowned by the Gulf War, in which the last vestiges of pan-Arabism were triumphantly dashed before an enormous, worldwide television audience. Those who backed the 'wrong' side – including Jordan and the PLO – emerged in a weaker position after the conflict, and both parties were willing to let the US dictate the terms of their international rehabilitation. Hussein of Jordan was to make peace with Israel and to participate in its various economic plans; and the PLO was to accept the peace dictated at Oslo. Meanwhile, those Arab nations on the 'winning' side had little to boast about. Egypt had confirmed its place as a primary ally of the US and Israel, and had all but abdicated its former role as a supporter of Palestinian rights; Kuwait and Saudi Arabia had established the precedent of allowing massive US forces to inhabit their countries on a semi-permanent basis, while expelling the Palestinian diaspora communities they once housed.[58] Finally, Iraq itself was left under the charge of Saddam Hussein, a US client of the 1980s permitted to continue his work in the 1990s. Now espousing a policy of 'dual containment', the US designed crippling sanctions against Iraq with the aim of keeping both it and Iran in a state of virtual collapse.[59]

The Arab world therefore approaches Oslo in a condition of near-total dependence and weakness. The US, for all its pride in Israel as the 'only democracy in the Middle East', offers aid and military support to numerous Arab autocracies and dictatorships: Egypt, whose president, Hosni Mubarak, ruthlessly suppresses opposition parties and wilfully gerrymanders elections; Jordan, whose King is maintained in a toothless 'democracy' which privileges the views of Hussein over those of his people; Saudi Arabia, whose bloated ruling house suppresses its opponents with brutality comparable only to its corruption; and various other Gulf states which are committed more to the purchase of sophisticated military toys from the US than to the needs of their own people, let alone solidarity with the Palestinians.[60]

Those nations outside the US orbit are hardly a source of much Palestinian hope. Saddam Hussein, the most recent political saviour of Palestine, was as willing to toe an American line in the 1980s as any other US client. The Iranian government since 1979, although fiercely critical of Israel, has lacked the influence or the idiom to put the Palestinian case persuasively in the international arena; given the demonisation of the Islamic revolution there, an association between Iran and the Palestinian cause is usually reported pejoratively in the Western media. Syria, meanwhile, is neither democratic nor likely to exert serious pressure on Israel. Preoccupied with its own territorial losses in the Golan Heights, it can bring little to bear in pursuit of its own agenda, let alone a wider, Arab one. Its last attempt to recapture territory lost to Israel ended with even more extensive losses, so the claims of its elderly leader, Hafez al-Assad, to pose a serious challenge to the status quo are hardly credible.[61]

Oslo has seen the end of the Arab economic boycott of Israel, the effective incorporation of the Israeli economy into a regional system, and the deepening of Arab economic and political dependence on the US. The last decade has seen a decisive shift away from the language of Arab solidarity towards a political outlook conditioned by self-preservation: the US props up a number of corrupt and undemocratic regimes, which depend upon this external backing to offset the threat of their own people's disapproval. In the medium term, it is hard to see how this new orientation can be challenged, and so it is hard to imagine meaningful opposition to Oslo emanating from these same sources.

The European Union

European nations have, at least since 1967, expressed consistently their disapproval of Israeli actions, particularly the ongoing occupation and colonisation of the Palestinian territories. This stand has led many Palestinians to suggest that Europe be given a wider role in Oslo, particularly in the context of the centralisation of political and economic power in Europe during the 1990s. However, there are several obstacles to this development which make it unlikely that the European Union (EU) will play a significant role in the foreseeable future.

In the first instance, most of the large European states are enmeshed within various alliances and treaties with the United States. In spite of the recent moves towards centralisation in Europe, this partnership with the US is still a far from equal one. As the Gulf War demonstrated, America is adept at leading the international community in foreign policy initiatives, with the Europeans at best willing participants, at worst sidelined spectators. The war in Bosnia cast serious doubts on the ability of the EU to formulate coherent policy even on its doorstep, and the irony of a US-imposed solution to a European problem did not go unnoticed at the time. Although Europe's colonial heritage has ensured a lasting legacy in the Middle East, the US has effectively usurped European political authority in recent decades, leaving the European states simply to compete between themselves for some of the more bloated arms deals favoured by the region's autocrats and dictators.[62]

Recent evidence has suggested that Europe could play a more constructive role in the Middle East, particularly in brokering the Israeli–Palestinian dispute. European leaders have been noticeably tougher in their (verbal) support for international law than the US, and some high-profile visits to the region have presented a very different kind of diplomacy to the American standard. Malcolm Rifkind, the former British foreign secretary, declared on a visit to Israel in November 1996 that his government's policy had remained unchanged since 1967: every Israeli settlement in the occupied territories was illegal. Rifkind also spoke strongly earlier in the year for a Palestinian state in the occupied territories, reminding Israel that Britain viewed the Gaza Strip, the West Bank and also East Jerusalem as 'under military occupation'. Jacques Chirac, the French president, made an even greater impact on his visit to the occupied territories in October 1996, declaring his support for Palestinian rights but also showing open annoyance with attempts by the Israelis to control his impromptu walkabout in East Jerusalem. The sight of a major European leader losing his patience with Israeli soldiers and police in the occupied territories demonstrated the enormous gulf in thinking between Europe and America; it is impossible to imagine an American president issuing a similar rebuke.[63]

If American pressure and relative European weakness offer the EU states a strong incentive to keep out of the Israeli–Palestinian dispute, the lingering influence of the holocaust is perhaps decisive in ensuring their exclusion. From the debate over the foundation of Israel, until the present day, there has been an inextricable link between Middle Eastern politics and European history. As we have seen, European nations were forced to look more kindly on the possibility of a Jewish state because, given the logic of forced immigration to Palestine during and after the holocaust, European political developments had made a compelling argument for such a state. The former Axis powers, led by Germany, bore the majority of this appalling responsibility, but even those states that had fought Nazism faced accusations of collusion with Hitler in the 1930s or failure to shut down the death camps in the final years of the war. How could Europe muster political arguments, let alone moral ones, in the light of its own destruction of the Jewish people?

The holocaust has lived on in various forms, its influence felt directly or indirectly. Those nations which propounded fascism have found it hardest to escape from the crimes of their predecessors. Germany, the largest and, in some respects, the most progressive of the EU states, has hardly been able to lead a European drive to uphold international law in the Middle East. Materially, Germany paid reparations to Israel (including weapons) until well into the 1970s, while politically it remains unable to criticise Israel without raising the ghost of its own dreadful past. One German historian has spoken of the 'considerable pro-Israeli constituency' in German society which holds that, 'given the legacy of

Auschwitz, the Germans are the last people in the world to tell the Jewish state how to behave'.[64]

Aside from this direct guilt, a more pervasive constraint is the ongoing debate about anti-semitism in Europe, which serves to retain the memory of the holocaust but also to determine blame in the present period. The recent controversy over Daniel Goldhagen's *Hitler's Willing Executioners*, for example, has revived the debate over mass participation in the holocaust and, indirectly, has insulated the holocaust's progeny, the state of Israel, against European criticism. A more vivid example of the politicisation of the holocaust is the long-running dispute over Switzerland's complicity with the Nazi regime, and especially the alleged willingness of Swiss banks to deposit Nazi funds stolen from victims of the genocide. Although these actions took place over fifty years ago, the debate was raised to such a furious pitch that it claimed as high-ranking a casualty as the Swiss ambassador to the United States in 1997. With Israeli demands for reparations, and new accusations of anti-semitism in Europe on the part of the Swiss government or people, European nations were once again warned by Israel that their reserves of moral ammunition had been dangerously depleted since the 1940s.[65]

In sum, the EU nations find themselves caught between a past calamity and a current dependence in the context of Israel and Palestine. If European politicians succeed in escaping from an American sphere of influence, and articulate a strong policy line towards Israel, they will inevitably struggle to evade the legacy of the holocaust, particularly against an active Israeli lobby experienced at using the genocide of fifty years ago to secure political objectives in the present. Although many European nations share similar policy concerns with the US, there are also significant differences across the Atlantic divide. In the context of America as the sole international broker of Oslo, the absence of an active European overseer has undoubtedly impoverished the peace process.

The United States

The most significant external influence on the Middle East, and especially on the Israeli–Palestinian situation, remains the United States. As we have seen, the agency of the Arab countries and EU states has been heavily circumscribed by the US, which has used its political, economic and military power to advance its own interests in the region.

Broadly speaking, those interests have remained constant over many decades: the preservation of ready access to the oil reserves of the Middle East (if not for domestic use in the US, then for the sake of the profits of major British and American corporations); the containment of communism (at least up until 1989); and the happy progress of Israel. For virtually all of America's tenure as a superpower, these objectives have infused its policy making. However, this is not to say that they are internally consistent. In particular, support for Israel has been maintained at the cost of some Arab sympathy, even amongst those Arabs well-placed to deliver America's other priority, oil. Since at least 1956, the US has played off one interest against the other, trying hard to ignore their inherent incompatibility and to achieve all its objectives.[66]

For a time in the 1950s, the US backed Nasser as its man in the region, working on the assumption both that he could contain communism and that his pan-Arabist rhetoric, if it produced no concrete action, posed little threat to American interests. However, by the 1960s, it became apparent that the State Department was no longer prepared to depend upon him, particularly when he threatened the US-backed monarchy in oil-rich Saudi Arabia. American aid flowed instead, in enormous quantities, to Israel. For the next three decades, the US continued to pour money into Tel Aviv, doing its best to appease those Arab nations opposing Israel's expansion by throwing money at them as well.[67]

Although this policy scored some notable successes, especially Egypt, it hardly offered the US a secure footing in the region. US aid packages were directed towards specific regimes rather than populations, and the American money was rarely tied to pledges on democracy, human rights, or wealth creation for the poor. In consequence, America's friends in the Middle East were more often individuals than nations – the Shah in Iran, for example, whose spectacular fall from power left behind the most virulently anti-American regime in the world.[68] The billions of dollars which had reached the Shah had gone little further, and his people were more inclined to despise his banker than to thank the US for its gifts. The spectre of another population instigating another revolt hung over American Middle Eastern policy, encouraging such unlikely alliances as the one between Ronald Reagan and Saddam Hussein, which led to the US giving weapons to Iraq throughout the 1980s. If the Shah could be toppled, or Saddam could turn on his masters, it was obvious that US foreign policy in the region was seriously flawed.[69]

If we assume that, at least in part, American policy was undermined by the incompatibility of the three US motives for Middle Eastern involvement, it is easy to see the 1991 Gulf War as a spectacular success. For one thing, the conflict with Saddam confirmed the collapse of the

Soviet Union, and marked the end of the balance of power politics which had previously constrained unilateral US action in the region. The coalition forces marched united behind an enormous American army, with the Soviet Union, itself in an advanced stage of disintegration, permanently sidelined. More importantly, however, the war marked a split within the Arab world, opening up a gap which was quickly filled by US troops. Saudi Arabia had long been a discrete client of the US, its autocracy turning to the West for its luxuries and its advanced weapons systems with equal enthusiasm; but it would have been unthinkable in the 1970s or even in the 1980s for such an important Arab state to allow American soldiers to descend upon its soil. In the face of Saddam's army, however, and despite the tens of billions of dollars spent on US and European arms, the Saudi royal family allowed the US to use its territory as a base for an assault on an Arab neighbour.

The implications of this decision were made fully evident by the eventual war and its aftermath. The Arab world divided neatly, with Saudi Arabia and Egypt, the most oil-rich and the most significant of the Arab states respectively, choosing the American side. Iraq, which had previously been an unpredictable force for US policymakers, was left not only in a state of devastation but in circumstances which would preserve the weakness and suffering of its people indefinitely. To the surprise of those army commanders responsible for the coalition forces, the unimpeded American assault on Baghdad was broken off, and Saddam was reprieved to rule over an already brutalised population. In the name of 'dual containment', Iraq was subjected to a draconian sanctions regime which effectively prevented any recovery and led directly to the deaths of hundreds of thousands of Iraqi children.[70]

Meanwhile, the stage was set for the reconciliation of the two most antithetical US objectives: support for Arab states to preserve the supply of oil, and advocacy of Israel. Since the Israeli government had been persuaded not to intervene in the Gulf conflict, Israel appeared as another victim of Saddam's aggression. The sight of civilians in gas masks in both Riyadh and Tel Aviv may have horrified the viewers of CNN, but it must have excited those responsible for long-term American strategic planning. Saudi Arabia, the most oil-rich nation in the world, was united with Israel, in spite of the latter's actions in the occupied territories. It is little wonder that James Baker, then US Secretary of State, was so confident in his post-war pronouncements of a new peace process in the region; or that his boss, George Bush, should have prophesied a New World Order.[71]

America's desire for oil, and its espousal of strategies to guarantee its supply, is simple enough to understand. Its steadfast support of Israel as an end in itself, rather than the means to secure another objective, is not so immediately intelligible. Israel undoubtedly fits into a vision of 'stability' in the minds of US policymakers – which is to say, a geopolitical configuration which best advances American interests. It has been argued, along these lines, that Israel is a bulwark against communism in the region, America's only truly dependable ally; but it might equally be argued that Israel has deterred the encroachment of Arab nationalism, another US shibboleth. This second interpretation would place Israel squarely alongside the Shah's Iran and Saudi Arabia as a US client in the Middle East, and goes some way towards explaining how the US has been able to reconcile its support for Israel with its selective support for neighbouring Arab regimes.[72]

However, we cannot fully understand the relationship between America and Israel without taking into account a domestic factor within the United States: since its earliest days, Israel has benefited from an active and vociferous lobby in the US, which has used money in especially efficient and imaginative ways to influence the foreign policy of successive administrations. From Truman's advocacy of Israel's creation in 1948, in direct contravention of the advice of the State Department and with an eye fixed on possible Zionist backing for his ailing presidential campaign, to the unseemly efforts of both Democrats and Republicans to secure votes and funding in the election of 1996, the Israeli lobby in the US has been one of the most powerful.[73] More recently, the lobby has taken not simply to funding its supporters inside the American Congress, but to threatening those who oppose Israel's actions with direct opposition in their attempts to win re-election. A series of political action committees in the US has offered campaign finance to candidates prepared to run against those incumbents who have expressed the slightest concern at Israel's actions.[74] Given this threat, it is not surprising that so many American politicians decline to engage critically with Israel, and that the American Congress passes legislation in support of Israel that contravenes international law and would be unthinkable in Europe.[75]

The American electorate is often told that the enormous aid package to Israel is intended to bolster the country's democracy, and to protect a political achievement that is putatively rare in the Middle East. However, even if we accept that Israel is a democracy, a claim belied by its treatment of its Arab citizens and the captive Palestinians under occupation, it is hard to see evidence of American support of democracy elsewhere in the region. Egypt, recipient of the next largest aid package in the US budget, is governed undemocratically by Hosni Mubarak, who has ruthlessly imprisoned or killed opposition leaders and wilfully rigged the most recent 'democratic' elections. In Saudi Arabia, a monarchy is preserved without reference to human rights or suffrage, even though the ruling family imposes a legal system more draconian than that of Iran (which the US routinely decries). Even Palestinian 'democracy,' as we have seen, was specifically slanted to privilege the rule of the executive over the judiciary or the legislature. From these examples, it is clear that the establishment of democracy or the protection of human rights cannot be a part of the American agenda, even though these values play a large part in the presentation of Middle East foreign policy to the American people.[76]

In practical terms, the US provides Israel with around three billion dollars of aid each year, mostly in military equipment produced in the US and funded by the American taxpayer. In addition, the US regularly makes available larger sums as loan guarantees underwriting Israel's attempt to borrow more money from banks.[77] Politically, the American government is perfectly placed to disrupt the international consensus around the illegality of Israel's actions. As a permanent member of the UN Security Council, the US regularly vetos resolutions critical of Israel's conduct, thereby ensuring that the views of every other nation are overridden. At a frequency which is embarrassing, the US and Israel find themselves opposing every other nation in the General Assembly, which succeeds in passing resolutions condemning Israel but which, unlike the Security Council, has no real power. This political support, though less tangible than the aid package, is enormously helpful to Israel, confounding the possibility of concerted international action against its treatment of the Palestinians and offering Israel the substantial benefits of American moral approval. With US backing, Israel is not a pariah state but a plucky fighter, battling in a 'tough neighbourhood' for values which are at least American, if not universal.[78]

The Clinton administration has made much of its promotion of Oslo, but the American position as honest broker of the deal is extremely tenuous. Throughout the 1970s and 1980s, the US supported Israel militarily, politically and financially, even joining with Israel in many fora to condemn the PLO as a terrorist group, or to cast doubt on the rights of the Palestinians to the occupied territories. Even after Oslo, when the US has recognised the PLO and extended financial support to Arafat, it continues to give approximately ten times as much money to Israel, and to veto UN resolutions and international initiatives that every other nation supports. No one even casually acquainted with the facts could claim that the US is or has been equidistant between the Palestinians and the Israelis, and yet Oslo depends to a large extent on the impartiality and objectivity of its chief mediator. The latest US peace envoy, Dennis Ross, has himself been the cause of a breakdown in negotiations, the Palestinians claiming that his bias towards Israel offers them no room for manoeuvre.[79]

In some situations, American officials have seemed confused or even embarrassed by their own deference to Israel, and on several occasions it has appeared more that Israel is the superpower and the US is its client. State Department officials are used to presenting US foreign policy unequivocally. During the Gulf War, the various motives and subtleties for American intervention were sanitised and simplified for public consumption: Saddam was a monster who had to be stopped in Kuwait before he went on to seize other countries. On the subject of Israel, however, and its equally illegal invasion of the West Bank and Gaza, American officials have been less sure-footed. When asked for a clear statement on Yitzhak Rabin's settlement policy in the occupied territories in 1994, State Department spokeswoman Christine Shelly struggled to deliver:

> As to — you know, nothing has changed on that in terms of our position and, you know, I think it's — you know, I can refer you to, you know, to probably to previous statements by officials on that. But I don't have anything—you know, I mean, you know, our—I think — I don't have — you know, I — we — usually we try to have, you know, a little bit of something on that. I'm not sure that it's going to be, you know, specifically what you're looking for. You know, generally speaking, our position that on settlements that it's the Palestinians and Israelis have agreed that the final status negotiations will cover these issues and, you know, that's — that's also our view.[80]

Shelly's difficulty is an instructive one. Israel's actions are extremely difficult to explain, let alone to justify, a fact not lost on the rest of the international community in its regular criticism of the on-going occupation at the UN and elsewhere. Whatever credibility the US may have in international affairs is undoubtedly undermined by its zealous and, occasionally, improbable support for Israel's every gesture.

Although Bush's New World Order has certainly benefited the American vision of the Middle East in the short term, a policy based on blind support for Israel is highly unstable looking further ahead. The Israeli occupation has long rallied Arabs around a single issue, and the prevalence of Islamic resistance to US presence in the region does not augur well for America's long-term prospects. Recent attacks on American military bases in Saudi Arabia by the Islamist opposition were an especially graphic illustration of the resistance the US might face in a future Middle East.[82] As numerous commentators have pointed out, uncritical support for Israel is not compatible with American interests, since it encourages Israel to overestimate its regional importance and radicalises Arabs against both Israel and the US. Unfortunately, as long as the US continues to evade this fact by striking deals with the likes of Mubarak, King Hussein and Saddam, American policy in the Middle East will continue to defy a genuine peace.

Conclusion: 'a negotiation with ourselves'

Having considered the political landscape of Israel, the Palestinians and the international community, we can lay to rest some of the assumptions about Oslo that distract from the reality of the present situation, and prevent us from identifying the real obstacles to peace.

In the first instance, the Israelis and Palestinians did not enter the Oslo process as equals. Israel, the occupying power, was not forced to the negotiating table in 1991 but rather entered into peace talks from a position of great strength. The Palestinians had no political or military means to end Israel's occupation or halt its settlement programme, and Israel did not come under pressure from the international community to offer a peace deal in accordance with the dictates of international law. Yitzhak Rabin's massive expansion of the settlements was not opposed by the Bush or Clinton administrations, nor did any other external power intervene to hold Israel accountable for its political actions.

Secondly, the degree of debate and contention in Israel was far smaller than it appeared, with the 'yawning ideological chasm' of Shimon Peres's *Memoirs* amounting more to a difference of presentation than of policy. The triumph of Yitzhak Rabin's Labour party over Yitzhak Shamir's Likud was presented in the media as a victory of 'doves' over 'hawks', and yet, as we have seen, there was very little concrete difference in the two parties' views on settlement expansion, Jerusalem, or a future Palestinian state. Even to the left of Labour, in the peace movement with which Yitzhak Rabin was latterly associated, there was virtually no willingness to make the substantive concessions on settlements and Jerusalem that would be necessary for a stable two-state solution. If Israel was to be left to decide the terms of its peace agreement with the Palestinians, its political spectrum offered no hope that it would take the drastic action – including uprooting settlements and demythologising Jerusalem – which could lead to a sovereign Palestine.

Finally, the international community has experienced a particular paralysis regarding Israel which has prevented multilateral protest in defence of international law. Although nearly every member of the

United Nations has condemned Israel's occupation of the West Bank and Gaza Strip and its annexation of East Jerusalem, many factors have prevented substantive pressure being brought to bear. Arab states have been weakened by internal division and external reliance on the US, especially after the Gulf War; the European Union has struggled to emerge from an American shadow and the legacy of the holocaust; and the United States has continued to support Israel and legitimise its actions without hesitation. This last factor has proved especially destructive, weakening the resolve of every other nation to confront Israel and undermining any efforts to hold Israel morally accountable for its treatment of the Palestinians. As long as the American people continue to back politicians who privilege Israel to such an extent, and exempt it from the standards of international probity to which America so often holds other nations, the potential of the international community to make a positive contribution to Israeli–Palestinian peace will remain severely limited.

In the remaining chapters of this book, as we consider the effects of Oslo on the Palestinians and its likely course in the coming years, these political constraints upon the formation of the existing peace process should not be forgotten. Shimon Peres, in a 1994 speech, frankly conveyed the Palestinians' lack of agency in the Oslo process:

> From our point of view, it is really not a negotiation of give and take, because the PLO can give very little to Israel. They don't have land, they don't have authority, they don't have means. In many ways, it is a negotiation with ourselves, because what is driving us is the question: what sort of an Israel do we want to have in the future?[82]

The evidence of Rabin's and Peres's terms as prime minister suggest that the two 'doves' had a clear idea of the kind of Israel they wanted to see: a greater Israel, incorporating large areas of the West Bank and even the Gaza Strip, with an expanded Jerusalem at its heart. The settlements would stay, and the Palestinians would be crammed into reservations and forced to share a diluted sovereignty with Jordan. This vision of peace would be unfamiliar to anyone who had read of Rabin's 1992 'settlement freeze', or the obituaries of the former leader, or the editorials in the international media after Peres's defeat to Netanyahu in 1996. It was entirely familiar, however, to Dan Meridor, incoming finance minister in the new 1996 Likud cabinet, who even thanked his predecessors in a newspaper interview for keeping their shared dream alive while Likud had been out of office:

> In that regard, Yitzhak Rabin, may he rest in peace, and Shimon Peres deserve the highest praise for having increased the number of the Jews in

> Judea and Samaria [the West Bank] by 40% in the past four years. During their term of office many thousands of homes for Jews were built in Judea and Samaria, and their number rose from 100,000 to 140,000. But not only they deserve praise. Praise is also due to the Israeli left which did not say one word about that during the past four years, and to the American government which knew about it and did not interfere with it. Praise is especially due to the Palestinian Authority, that saw the construction and knew that massive building was going on, and which legitimised it by not stopping the continuation of the peace process.[83]

Meridor's effusive praise is a startling reminder that, when judged on their policies rather than their promises, Rabin and Peres had much more in common with their 'enemies' than outside observers would like to admit. Seen from this perspective, Oslo is an unbroken sweep of expanded Israeli control and diminishing Palestinian prospects. Meridor's commitment to settlement, under a Netanyahu government, is nothing less than a commitment to uphold an unassailable tradition in Israeli politics:

> It is obvious that in this area, we will not do less than the Labour party. I have already told the American ambassador that he can rest easy on one subject: we will not change the Labour government's real policy of massive settlement.

This image of Meridor, cabinet minister of the new, hawkish regime, informing the American ambassador of the new government's commitment to follow the 'real policy' of its predecessor, captures perfectly the dilemma into which the Oslo process has fallen. Its weaknesses and disasters are a direct result of the political climate in which it was produced, and we can expect little change in its implementation until this climate is altered. Since that would require a fundamental shift in Israeli thinking, and an about-turn in American policy, we should prepare ourselves for a deepening of the current crisis rather than its improvement.

Notes

1. For details of Peace Now's founding, see Mordechai Bar-On's *In Pursuit of Peace: A History of the Israeli Peace Movement* (Washington: US Institute of Peace Press, 1996), pp. 99–107. Bar-On dates Peace Now's first public protest to 1 April 1978. During the 1982 Lebanon invasion, Peace Now criticised Israel's actions sharply although, as Bar-On points out, the group's vacillation at the start of the assault left it open to criticism from within the peace movement itself; pp. 144–6.

2. 'Passage censored from the first edition', Yitzhak Rabin, *Memoirs* (Berkeley: University of California Press, 1996, expanded edition), pp. 383–4.

3. Rabin personally took charge of enforcing an 'iron fist' policy against Palestinians in the occupied territories after the intifada survived Israel's first efforts at suppression: McDowall, *Palestine and Israel: The Uprising and Beyond*, p. 7; F. Robert Hunter, *The Palestinian Uprising: A War By Other Means* (Berkeley: University of California Press, 1993), pp. 85–97; Don Peretz, *Intifada* (Boulder, Co.: Westview Press, 1990), pp. 44–5. At least 180 Palestinians were killed by live ammunition in the first year of the uprising, with still more deaths caused by plastic bullets and tear gas. Rabin himself told a rally in Beersheba on 8 October 1988 that more than 7,000 Palestinians had been injured during this period. See the report of human rights group Al-Haq, *Punishing a Nation* (Ramallah: Al-Haq, 1988), pp. 11–12. The intifada was far more brutally suppressed in its second year: by the end of 1989, at least 626 Palestinians had been killed, more than 37,000 injured, and almost 40,000 imprisoned. Hunter describes these casualty figures as 'staggering', given the Palestinians' reliance only on stones for their protests: *The Palestinian Uprising*, pp. 215–16.

4. This fact is conceded even by Rabin's eulogists. See, for example, the 'Afterword' to the expanded edition of Rabin's *Memoirs* by Yoram Peri, who notes that Rabin 'did not hesitate to employ an iron-fist policy to forcibly suppress Palestinians in the territories.' Peri sees Rabin as a consummate balance-of-power politician, who 'thought it was possible to use force to improve the state's political position.' Rabin's mentor in this thinking was, according to Peri, Henry Kissinger, who had extensive experience of the 'iron-fist policy' and, as a fellow Nobel Peace Prize winner, may also have been able to teach Rabin a valuable lesson about dovish self-presentation; *Memoirs*, pp. 346–7, 374.

5. For example, 43 Israeli soldiers and settlers had been killed by the end of 1989. Although the Palestinian death rate was 37 times higher, these Israeli casualties represented a sharp rise from the five deaths of 1987/1988. Hunter, p. 215.

6. For details of Rabin's acceptance of the bulk of Shamir's expansion plan, and his exemption of the entire 'greater Jerusalem' area from any freeze whatsoever, see 'Partial settlement freeze', *Middle East International*, 7 August 1992; and 'Rabin government inaugurates new era in settlement policy', *Report on Israeli Settlement*, Vol. 2, No. 5 (September 1992).

7. Rabin's biographer, Robert Slater, concedes that the new prime minister's 'freeze' was more of a 'cooling-off'. According to Slater, Rabin told James Baker that 'for legal reasons, it was not possible to undertake a greater building halt at this juncture.' *Rabin of Israel* (London: Robson Books, 1993), p. 426.

8. As late as January 1993, the Washington-based Foundation for Middle East Peace offered practical suggestions for cancelling the 11,000 West Bank apartments that Rabin had exempted from his 'freeze'. 'Is Rabin's figuring better than Shamir's?', *Report on Israeli Settlement*, Vol. 3, No. 1 (January 1993).

9. Meron Benvenisti points out that, in 1992, the Labour government in-

herited 137 settlements (excluding the new Jewish areas in East Jerusalem), and committed itself to their protection and expansion. *Intimate Enemies* (Berkeley: University of California Press, 1995), pp. 61–3.

10. According to Geoffrey Aronson, 'Rabin won for West Bank settlements a measure of recognition and permanence that no other Israeli leader managed to achieve'; see 'Israeli government adopts policy of accommodating settlers', *Report on Israeli Settlement*, Vol. 6, No. 1 (January 1996). See also supra Chapter 2, note 10.

11. Yitzhak Rabin, speech in the Israeli Knesset on ratification of the Israeli-Palestinian Interim Agreement ('Oslo II'), 5 October 1995. Note that Rabin not only declares that this enormous amount of occupied territory will remain under Israeli control in a final agreement, but also that these main changes are 'not all' of the territorial cessions to Israel which Rabin has in mind. Two years later, Binyamin Netanyahu reminded an American television audience of this awkward fact, in response to criticism of Likud's settlement plans: 'The late Yitzhak Rabin, who signed the Oslo accords, stood proudly before the Knesset when he presented the Oslo accords with the Palestinians. And he said we can build; there's no limitation, not in Jerusalem, not in the settlements. The Labour government refused to accept any contractual limits on building anywhere'; 'Interview with Binyamin Netanyahu', on The NewsHour with Jim Lehrer, 3 November 1997.

12. Rabin was especially fond of casting his dovishness in military terms: for example, his speech at the signing of the Israel–Jordan peace treaty in Washington on 26 July 1994: 'I, military ID number 30743, retired General in the Israel Defense Forces in the past, consider myself to be a soldier in the army of peace today.' Laqueur and Rubin (eds), p. 664. Robert Slater quietly reminds us, however, that Israelis were under no illusions when choosing Rabin in 1992: they chose Rabin for his military record, not for his dovishness, wanting a man who could 'stand up to the Arabs, if need be'; *Rabin of Israel*, p. 408.

13. See 'Faithful servant makes way for raffish hardman', *Sunday Telegraph*, 2 June 1996; and 'Peres backers and peace activists left in gloom', *New York Times*, 4 June 1996. Where there was divergence from this disappointment at Netanyahu's victory, it was inspired by an enthusiasm for Likud and its limited vision of peace, rather than a cynicism about Peres's dovish credentials. A.M. Rosenthal, claiming in a *New York Times* Editorial to be a 'maverick foreign journalist', praised the 55% of Israeli Jews who had supported Netanyahu, and castigated those US pundits who had backed Peres; 'That 55% of Jews', *New York Times*, 5 June 1996.

14. Shimon Peres, *Battling For Peace*, p. 231.

15. Shimon Peres, remarks at the opening of the winter session of the Knesset, 23 October 1995. We get little sense of a 'yawning ideological chasm' between Labour and Likud as we here witness Peres attempting to attack the Likud party's weakness in brokering the Camp David agreements, since these accords (unlike Oslo) obliged the government of Israel to dismantle a settle-

ment. If we are armed only with the simple vocabulary of 'hawks' and 'doves', Peres's remark is very hard to fathom.

16. Peres outlined his vision of 'eight industrial parks' along 'the dividing line between us and the Palestinians' in a speech to the 50th session of the UN General Assembly, 2 October 1995. Peres boasted, without any apparent embarrassment, that the new structure for geographical separation and economic vassalage would mean that 'the Palestinians will not have to cross the border and go through the checkposts of Israel but work will come to them and together we shall invest and together we shall develop'.

17. Peres's dream of advancement and justice was offered in the 2 October 1995 UN speech. The issues of closure and the failure of Peres's economic policy will be discussed in greater detail in Chapter 6.

18. 'Address to the 50th session of the UN General Assembly', 2 October 1995.

19. Shimon Peres, Knesset speech, 23 October 1995.

20. *Battling for Peace*, p. 322. Oddly, even though Peres refers at length to the drafting of the Gaza-Jericho agreement in 1994, he makes no reference whatsoever to either the 5,000 Jewish settlers living in Gaza or to the 65%–35% partition of the Strip which he and Rabin argued for in the light of the settlers' ongoing presence in the midst of around a million Palestinians, the vast majority of the latter in squalid refugee camps.

21. See *Battling for Peace*, p. 323, for Peres's bizarre nostalgia for his sea-trips with Gazan fishermen. Despite their 'endearing qualities', Peres banned the same fishermen from putting to sea at all in March 1996, eventually allowing them to cast their nets again in a still further limited area of the Gaza coastline than they are normally restricted to. Since more than a third of the Gaza coast has been given over to Jewish settlers, the initial ban and then heightened restrictions hit these fishermen and their families hard. 'The Gaza Strip: costs of the closure', *Middle East Economic Digest*, Vol. 40, No. 15 (12 April 1996); and 'Israeli Blockade Takes Toll', *New York Times*, 21 March 1996.

22. Amnesty International puts the figure of Lebanese dead at 'more than 250 civilians'; 'Israel's forgotten hostages: Lebanese detainees in Israel and Khiam Detention Centre' (London, July 1997), p. 3. Christian Aid estimated the number of refugees from 'Israeli bombing and shelling' at 'almost half a million': see the press release, 'Christian Aid appeals for funds as half a million Lebanese flee devastating Israeli bombardment', 19 April 1996.

23. The best account of the Qana shelling came from the victims themselves, whose appalling testimony was recorded by British journalist Robert Fisk: 'Seventeen minutes in Qana', *Independent on Sunday*, 19 May 1996. In Europe, the carnage encouraged a reassessment of Peres and a cynicism about his dovish claims: 'Not the least of the bitter ironies thrown up by Operation Grapes of Wrath is that Peres, the "dove", most at home in the chancelleries of the West, has turned into a fire-breathing man of action'; 'Carnage at Qana', *Sunday*

Times, 21 April 1996. The US press was far less ready to reach the same conclusion. Six weeks after the massacre at the UN compound, *New York Times* pundit William Safire appended the following, extraordinary suggestion to a piece on Shimon Peres's future after his defeat in the Israeli elections by Netanyahu: 'Now that the job of Secretary-General of the United Nations is coming up for grabs, how about an Israeli dove?'; 'Netanyahu's new way', *New York Times*, 3 June 1996.

24. Shimon Peres, address to the Knesset on the IDF operations in Lebanon, 22 April 1996.

25. The 'Report of the Secretary-General's Military Adviser' was published by the Council on 7 May 1996, with the personal endorsement of the Secretary-General, Boutros Boutros-Ghali. Boutros-Ghali himself repeated the report's most sensational conclusion, which was that 'the pattern of impacts in the Qana area makes it highly unlikely that the shelling of the United Nations compound was the result of technical and/or procedural errors.' The presence of helicopters and a remote-piloted Israeli drone aircraft directly above or adjacent to the UN compound was also established by the report, p. 6, and confirmed graphically in the videotape acquired by Robert Fisk from an anonymous UN officer in south Lebanon. 'Massacre film puts Israel in dock', *Independent*, 6 May 1996. Boutros-Ghali's refusal to suppress the UN report into the shelling was widely credited as the cause of his downfall later that year, when the US refused to support his re-election as Secretary-General. If William Safire had had his way, Boutros-Ghali would have been replaced with Shimon Peres, a crowning irony.

26. Shimon Peres, when asked to respond to the UN's report, dismissed it in the words of Israel's founder, David Ben-Gurion: 'It's not important what the goyim [non-Jews] say. It's important what the Jews do.' Israeli newspaper columnist Arieh Shavit summarised Peres's actions and self-righteousness in a despairing article in *Ha'aretz*: 'How easily we killed them without shedding a tear,' he wrote simply. See 'Anatomy of a tragedy', *Time*, Vol. 147, No. 21 (20 May 1996).

27. See, for example, 'A leader in the footsteps of Rabin: Barak takes up Labour struggle for peace', *Daily Telegraph*, 5 June 1997.

28. Ehud Barak, remarks before the International Press Institute, Jerusalem, 27 March 1996.

29. Ibid.

30. For the advocacy of this same plan by Israel's leading dove, see Shimon Peres's *Battling for Peace*, p. 352. Peres, the victim of an unusual form of transference, claims that 'the Palestinians probably still harboured hopes of taking over Jordan one day.'

31. Barak puts it brilliantly: 'If we will raise the ideas [of a Palestinian Jordan], it will appear to be a kind of patronising, or even better a kind of collusion or conspiracy. I believe it's very natural, in a more profound way

than the eye meets at first glance.' Given that the 'natural' co-existence of Jordanians and Palestinians was entirely due to Israel's expulsion of Palestinians to Jordan in 1948 and 1967, it is not surprising that Barak should tread carefully here.

32. Binyamin Netanyahu, *A Place Among the Nations: Israel and the World* (New York: Bantam Books, 1993), p. 343.

33. Mordechai Bar-On refers, in his study of the Israeli peace movement, to the efforts of the general public to depict Peace Now and Meretz 'as being on the fringes of Israeli society. Accusations of treason ... were voiced not just by the extreme right but occasionally by mainstream figures.' *In Pursuit of Peace*, pp. 322–4.

34. See the party's 1997 policy statement, 'Peace with the Palestinians'.

35. Moreover, Yossi Sarid, leader of Meretz and environment minister in Rabin's last Labour cabinet, actually presented an environmental award to Ma'ale Adumim, the largest settlement in the West Bank, in 1993. See 'Israeli settlements past, present and future', *Middle East International*, 10 June 1994.

36. The party's Jerusalem policy is expressed, in the 1997 policy statement above, in unequivocal terms: 'Jerusalem, the capital of Israel, will remain indivisible.' Sir Anthony Parsons, former British ambassador to the United Nations, wrote of Jerusalem in 1996 that 'even a Peace Now Israeli government would not agree to its redivision, or remove the ramparts of settlements now housing 200,000 people, or that it should not be Israel's "eternal" capital.' 'Reflections on the peace process and a durable settlement', *Journal of Palestine Studies*, Vol. XXVI, No. 1 (Autumn 1996), p. 17. See also Gideon Levy's Editorial 'Another nail in the coffin', *Ha'aretz*, 9 November 1997, written in response to Meretz's failure to include in its most recent platform a commitment to a Palestinian capital in East Jerusalem. According to Levy, Meretz's cowardice has left the party looking very like Labour, and means that the 'Israeli voter who thinks that real peace – not the peace of the candles in the square – will not be achieved without some kind of return to the 1967 lines, has no political home today'.

37. See Tanya Reinhart's 'Shooting and crying', *Yediot Aharonot*, 31 May 1995, in which the Israeli peace movement's relentless support for the Labour party, and championing of 'lesser evil-ism', is comprehensively critiqued.

38. 'A way to ease the pain of Hebron', *The Guardian*, 16 January 1996. Oz's own 'plea for peace', written after the suicide attacks in Tel Aviv and Jerusalem in February and March 1996, offers us a glimpse of the enormous distance between Israeli peaceniks and a genuinely conciliatory approach to the Palestinians. Oz's understanding of the Oslo agreements – 'we stop ruling over you and suppressing you' – is almost as fantastic as the claim that 'up until now we have delivered.' In the context of an Israeli withdrawal from 2.7% of the West Bank, Oz's warning to the Palestinians is remarkably shrill: 'Do any of you really think that you could possibly take without giving, or that Israel can give without taking?' 'Letter to a Palestinian friend', *The Guardian*, 5 March 1996.

39. 'It is a fact that the previous government that signed Oslo, the Labour government of Yitzhak Rabin, authorized under Oslo, and in accordance with Oslo, the Har Homa project.' Binyamin Netanyahu, press conference at the Madison Hotel, Washington, 7 April 1997. For details of the Peres government's approval of the Har Homa project, see the statement of Haim Ramon, interior minister of Israel, reported by Agence France Presse, 20 February 1996.

40. Bill Clinton neatly summarised the paucity of Palestinian options when asked to comment on the possibility of widespread rejection of Oslo on the Palestinian side after the Israelis had started construction of the Har Homa settlement at Jabal Abu Ghneim: it would be a 'terrible thing' for the Palestinians to oppose the bulldozers with force, because the lesson of the past was that 'they wind up losing'. 'US pledges support for 9% West Bank pullback', *Jerusalem Post*, 10 March 1997. See also Mahmoud Abbas, *Through Secret Channels*, p. 114, in which Arafat's deputy declares of the Oslo channel that 'there were no risks in it for us'. This statement more accurately refers to the PLO than to the Palestinian people at large, as subsequent events have shown.

41. See the speeches at the signing of Oslo in Washington, 13 September 1993. Yitzhak Rabin claimed that Palestinians and Israelis 'are destined to live together on the same soil in the same land', living 'side by side in dignity, in affinity, as human beings'. Bill Clinton was even more effusive: 'Uplifted by the spirit of the moment, refreshed in our hopes and guided by the wisdom of the Almighty, who has brought us to this joyous day, go in peace. Go as peacemakers.' Laqueur and Rubin (eds), pp. 612–13. Of course, the 'spirit' of the agreement was later to emerge more in the breach than in the observance.

42. For an assessment of the council's powers, see Ziad Abu-Amr, 'The Palestinian Legislative Council: a critical assessment', *Journal of Palestine Studies*, Vol. XXVI, No. 4 (Summer 1997), pp. 90–7. Abu-Amr, an elected member of the council, concludes sadly that it 'has been unable to ensure the executive's respect for the separation of powers.'

43. The report of Agence France Presse, 23 January 1996, notes that 40% of Palestinians according to one poll wanted the council to be more powerful than Arafat, the president, and 39% thought that it should be at least as powerful. Palestinian psephologist and political analyst Khalil Shikaki held out little hope of these wishes being realised: 'I expect the Council will be weak and Arafat will continue to be as authoritative as ever.' For details of Arafat's attempts to control, if not actually to rig the elections of January 1996, see, 'Arafat tinkers with polls', *The Guardian*, 2 January 1996; 'Arafat's bully-boys take the vote', *Sunday Telegraph*, 21 January 1996; and 'Autocrat Arafat's crown of thorns', *The Observer*, 21 January 1996. Norman Finkelstein argues that 'the real purpose of the January 1996 elections in the West Bank and Gaza was for the subject population to "democratically" ratify the annulment of its basic rights and to "democratically" install a Quisling leadership.' ('Whither the "Peace Process"?', p. 45.) It is ironic that the Legislative Council should only come to the fore in the summer of 1997 because of its attempts to prosecute those members of the Palestinian Authority accused of corruption.

44. Mohamed Heikal captures Arafat's dilemma in deciding whether to accept and promote Oslo: 'He could uphold the cause of Palestinian independence and remain an outcast at the head of a near-penniless movement, or he could accept the unacceptable and become a media prince of peace. ... The temptation to choose success and fame could not have been greater.' (*Secret Channels*, pp. 431–2.)

45. 'Shameless in Gaza', *The Guardian*, 21 April 1997.

46. 'Arafat puts off resignations', Agence France Presse, 2 August 1997.

47. For an account of the murder of land dealers, see Kol Israel, 11 and 19 May 1997; Arafat's response, in which he stressed the death penalty in Palestinian/Jordanian law against dealers who sold Palestinian land to Jews, was offered in an interview with Israeli tabloid *Yediot Aharonot*, 21 May 1997. In fairness to the PA, the headline figure for 'corruption', $329 million, included revenue opportunities missed due to mismanagement or possible malpractice. The actual figure for embezzlement was a fraction of this larger one. See the PA's Ministry of Planning and International Cooperation Report of 5 June 1997, presented in Washington to offset fears of donor countries that their money was not going to the places they had intended. The report makes clear that corruption accounted for a very small part of the total 'lost' amount.

48. Arafat's agreement with Israel to facilitate by-pass roads was discovered by accident; in a case against Israel in defence of a Palestinian landowner, the human rights group LAW was told by the Israeli attorney that the roads had gone ahead on the basis of an agreement between the PA and Israel. Arafat confirmed as much in a fax to LAW received on 6 August 1995. See LAW's report on the road programme, 'Bypass road construction in the West Bank: the end of the dream of Palestinian sovereignty', p. 17. Rumours of a deal linking Har Homa with the Gaza airport surfaced in March 1997, and were denied by chief Palestinian negotiator Nabil Sha'ath, and then again during August. See the BBC's translation of an Israeli Army Radio report, 19 March 1997.

49. 'Letter to a Palestinian friend', *The Guardian*, 5 March 1996.

50. For examples of this, see 'Palestinian police quell protestors', *Associated Press*, 29 September 1996, and 'The untold story of the Battle of Joseph's Tomb', *London Evening Standard*, 30 September 1996.

51. See Graham Usher's 'The politics of internal security in Palestine', *Middle East International*, 1 March 1996; and Amnesty's report 'Palestinian Authority: prolonged political detention, torture and unfair trials' (London, December 1996).

52. The economic benefits of Israel's participation in a peace process (or at least the semblance of one) were made clear by US Undersecretary of Commerce Stuart E. Eizenstat in an official address to the Israel–American Chamber of Commerce in Tel Aviv on 14 August 1996. Speaking of Israel's potential to become an 'Asian Tiger'-style economy post-Oslo, Eizenstat detailed the various economic successes of Israel since 1993 which amounted to a 'genuine peace

dividend', and insisted that the Oslo process be maintained by Netanyahu, for economic reasons as much as political: 'the peace process has accomplished much and we have a tremendous amount at stake in its continued progress'.

53. Rubin and Laqueur thoughtfully gather as many of Nasser's threats as possible in *The Israeli–Arab Reader*, pp. 117–20, concentrating on the period between 1960 and 1963. Although Nasser continues to espouse 'the liberation of Palestine', it is worth noting that he sees both Israel and Zionism not as Jewish phenomena but as the products of imperialism. This is a constant factor in Arab attacks on Israel up to and beyond 1967. Israel has tried hard to equate Arab nationalism with anti-semitism, but the rhetoric of Arab leaders, including Arafat, confirms that the destruction of Israel did not imply the murder of its population – instead, they would be a vital part of the new, secular state. See Arafat's 1968 interview, reprinted in Laqueur and Rubin (eds), pp. 224–8.

54. Israel's nuclear capacity was famously exposed by Seymour Hersh in *The Samson Option: Israel's Nuclear Arsenal and American Foreign Policy* (New York: Random House, 1991). It has never been formally admitted, however, even though Israel possesses an arsenal of around 200 warheads. Shimon Peres came closest to acknowledging the fact in the 1996 election, when he hoped that he might shrug off his image as feckless or weak by identifying himself with Israel's nuclear programme: 'Peres takes campaign to the heart of Israel's suspected nuclear arsenal', Agence France Presse, 23 May 1996.

55. See Noam Chomsky, *The Fateful Triangle: The United States, Israel and the Palestinians*, pp. 66–7. See also Robert D. Hormats, 'The politics and limitations of economic leverage', in *The Middle East in Global Perspective*, ed. Judith Kipper and Harold H. Saunders (Boulder, Co.: Westview Press, 1991), especially pp. 235–42.

56. Egypt currently receives around $2.2 billion annually in direct grants from the US, in return for keeping its peace with Israel. This amounts to the second highest direct grant from the US, after the $3 billion plus given to Israel itself. Donald Neff, 'Massive aid to Israel', *Middle East International*, 21 July 1995.

57. Hormats admits that 'the Arab moderates had both a political and an economic stake in their relations with the West, in particular with the US. Large portions of their funds were deposited in Western banks, Western technology was needed to develop their economies, and US arms were needed to reduce Soviet influence in the area.' (*The Middle East in Global Perspective*, p. 239.) As for Saudi Arabia, its retreat from active confrontation with Israel was linked to its new dependence on the US for arms ($34 billion between 1973 and 1980, compared with $1.2 billion between 1950 and 1972) and its fear of internal revolution after the US-backed Iranian Shah fell from power in 1979. See Bahgat Korany, 'Defending the faith amid change: the foreign policy of Saudi Arabia', in *The Foreign Policies of Arab States* (Boulder, Co.: Westview Press, 1991), pp. 337, 342–4. US aid to Iraq took on many forms between 1983 and 1990, including grants and loans to buy food and weapons. By 1988, Iraq

was the biggest recipient of US food aid to any country. See Amatzia Baram, 'US input into Iraqi decisionmaking 1988–1990', in David W. Lesch (ed.), *The Middle East and the United States: A Historical and Political Reassessment* (Boulder, Co.: Westview Press, 1996), p. 326.

58. Various pundits were lining up in 1991 to enthuse about the war's consequences, and the pages of *Foreign Affairs*, house magazine of the US policymaking establishment, were filled with upbeat assessments. See Peter W. Rodman, 'Middle East diplomacy after the Gulf War', *Foreign Affairs*, Vol. 70, No. 2 (Spring 1991), pp. 1–18, in which Hussein of Jordan's complete dependence on the US is spelled out; and Martin Indyk, 'Watershed in the Middle East', *Foreign Affairs*, Vol. 71, No. 1 (Summer 1992), pp. 78–93, which refers gleefully to Egypt's futile attempts 'to pick up the pieces of Arab unity'. For a less enthusiastic relation of the same events from outside Washington (Rodman was a member of the National Security Council, as was Indyk, before later serving as US ambassador to Israel), see the 'Afterword' to Noam Chomsky's *Deterring Democracy* (London: Vintage, 1992), pp. 407–40. On the expulsion of Palestinians from the Gulf states, see Nadim Jaber, 'Writing on the wall for Kuwait's Palestinians', *Middle East International*, 28 June 1991.

59. 'Dual containment', the policy of keeping Iran and Iraq weak by isolating them politically and economically, was fully theorised only under the Clinton administration. Anthony Lake, Clinton's national security advisor, described the policy in the terms of a mafioso: dual containment targeted 'the reality of recalcitrant and outlaw states that not only choose to remain outside the family but also assault its basic values'. 'Confronting backlash states', *Foreign Affairs*, Vol. 73, No. 2 (March/April 1994), pp. 45–55.

60. On Egypt's tradition of election-rigging under Mubarak, see 'Money calls the tune in Egyptian election', *Independent*, 30 November 1995; and 'Mubarak faces Islamic wave', *Newsday*, 21 December 1995. One of King Hussein's more recent intrusions into the 'democratic' political process of Jordan was his arbitrary dismissal of his prime minister, Abdul Karim al-Kabariti, in March 1997. Since Kabariti owed his position to Hussein's personal appointment, he cannot have been wholly surprised by his removal. 'Hussein fires Kabariti', Reuters, 19 March 1997. The Saudi royal family's crisis of legitimacy, exacerbated by its corruption, hypocrisy and collusion with the US, was admitted even in a recent article in *Foreign Affairs*: Milton Viorst, 'The storm and the citadel', Vol. 75, No. 1 (January/February 1996), pp. 93–107; 'it seems to me that the Sauds have not grasped the depth or breadth of the discontent simmering in their ordered land. Despite their apparent invulnerability, I suspect that they ignore it much longer at their peril.' The most recent arms purchases by the Gulf states, amounting to hundreds of airplanes and tens of billions of dollars, are listed in the special report of the *Middle East Economic Digest*, 'The United States and the Middle East', 26 September 1997.

61. Even though war with Syria has been talked up by Israel, which has even requested extra funds from the US to combat the 'threat', the sheer might of Israel's conventional and nuclear arsenal makes such a move on the Syrians'

part unlikely. 'Israel and foes race to upgrade arms', *Christian Science Monitor*, 30 July 1997.

62. According to Friedmann Buettner and Martin Landgraf, the EU 'missed its chance' in 1990/1991 to create a new role for itself in Middle East diplomacy: 'at no time in the course of the crisis did the [European] Community offer a viable alternative to the policy almost exclusively formulated in Washington and New York.' 'The EC's Middle Eastern policy', in Tareq Y. Ismael and Jacqueline S. Ismael (eds), *The Gulf War and the New World Order* (Gainesville: University Press of Florida, 1994), pp. 77–115. British historian Noel Malcolm, writing in *Foreign Affairs*, drew on the EU's Bosnian disaster to attack the concept of an integral European foreign policy and, with Bosnia in mind, to fête an American-led NATO: 'The case against Europe', *Foreign Affairs*, Vol. 74, No. 2 (March/April 1995), pp. 52–68. The same argument is taken up in the same issue from a more predictable source, Kissinger-manqué Richard Holbrooke: 'America, a European power', pp. 38–51. The United Kingdom has tried especially hard in the 1980s and 1990s to secure arms contracts in the Middle East, although its open and covert supplying of Iraq, and the suspicion of scandal surrounding an enormous Saudi Arabian arms deal in the last years of Margaret Thatcher's administration, led to legal and public recriminations. For an account of the policy from an insider, see Gerald James, *In the Public Interest* (London: Little, Brown, 1995).

63. Rifkind advocated a Palestinian state in an after-dinner speech in London in May 1996: 'Don't rule out Palestinian state, UK tells Israel', *Reuters*, 23 May 1996. Later in the year, Rifkind maintained this position even when visiting Israel: 'Rifkind tells Israel all settlements on Arab land illegal', *The Times*, 4 November 1996. Chirac's visit a fortnight earlier caused greater controversy: 'Chirac uses Israel visit to call for radical change in policy', *Agence France Presse*, 22 October 1996.

64. Thomas Risse-Kappen, 'Muddling through mined territory: German foreign policy-making and the Middle East', in Sharam Chubin (ed.), *Germany and the Middle East: Patterns and Prospects* (London: Pinter Publishers, 1992), p. 183.

65. The best treatment of Goldhagen's argument, and the political meaning of the book's ecstatic reception in the US and Europe, is Norman G. Finkelstein, 'Daniel Jonah Goldhagen's "crazy" thesis: a critique of *Hitler's Willing Executioners*', *New Left Review*, No. 224 (July/August 1997), pp. 39–88. The affair of the Swiss banks and 'Nazi gold' nearly claimed the Swiss economic minister in January 1997, when he referred to the efforts of Israeli and world Zionist groups to 'blackmail' the Swiss government into a hurried settlement of holocaust claims ('Swiss apologise to Jews', *Reuters*, 15 January 1997); the Swiss ambassador to the US, Carlo Jagmetti, was not so fortunate, forced to step down after referring to the propaganda 'war' which the Swiss government would have to wage if it was to stand up to concerted Israeli and American pressure: 'Swiss envoy to US resigns', *New York Times*, 28 January 1997. The

attack on Switzerland was coordinated entirely by Israeli and American Jewish groups, with major enquiries taking place under the auspicies of the Israeli Knesset. Given that not every Jew was in Israel or the United States, some commentators wondered aloud if some of the neediest victims of the holocaust, the survivors left over in Eastern Europe, would receive a fair deal amidst the demands of Jewish organisations located and operating in Israel and the US ('Brutal irony', *Jerusalem Post*, 25 May 1997).

66. Richard Falk has synthesised these three objectives in one imperative: 'US policy in the region was guided by the basic contention that radicalizing political tendencies of any sort would endanger the Western interest in favored access to cheap and abundant oil supplies, the very basis of post-World War II economic prosperity in the North.' 'US foreign policy in the Middle East: the tragedy of persistence', in Hooshang Amirahmadi (ed.), *The United States and the Middle East: A Search for New Perspectives* (New York: State University of New York Press, 1993), p. 67. Paul Findley, in *Deliberate Deceptions*, suggests to the contrary that US support for Israel is not compatible with its other interests, a position also held by a number of Washington figures who would accept uncritically the legitimacy of securing access to oil and fighting the 'communist threat'; Findley, pp. 218–24.

67. Malik Mufti, 'The United States and Nasserist pan-Arabism', in *The Middle East and the United States*, pp. 167–86.

68. For an account of America's dominant role in backing the Shah from 1954 onwards, and the subsequent fury of the Khomenist revolutionary regime, see Nikki R. Keddie, *Roots of Revolution: An Interpretive History of Modern Iran* (New Haven: Yale University Press, 1981), pp. 142ff.

69. US policy towards Iran has been marked by at least two disasters in terms of American interests in the past decades (there are many more disasters, of course, but their effects are limited to the civilians of the region): not only did the US back the Shah until his vertiginous fall, but the Reagan administration supplied arms covertly to Iran in a botched effort to win moderate support within the Khomeini regime. The errors of American policy since 1979 are captured by Mansour Farhang, 'US policy towards the Islamic Republic of Iran: A case of misperception and reactive behaviour', in *The United States and the Middle East*, pp. 151–75. Meanwhile, the most authoritative study thus far on US involvement with Iraq during the 1980s and 1990s concludes simply that 'the Western policy of arming and backing Iraq during the war with Iran, and of facilitating Iraq's massive rearmament programme thereafter, indirectly led to the August 1990 Iraqi invasion of Kuwait and the ensuing 1991 Gulf War'. See Mark Phythian, *Arming Iraq: How the US and Britain Secretly Built Saddam's War Machine* (Boston: Northeastern University Press, 1997), p. 291. This volume appears in 'The Northeastern Series in Transnational Crime'.

70. The conduct of the American-led coalition army at the end of the Gulf War surprised many, especially after Norman Schwarzkopf's admission that 'we had them [the Iraqis] completely routed': Norman Polmar (ed.), *War in the*

Gulf (Atlanta: Turner Publishing Inc., 1991), p. 214. Given that there was no operational constraint on the continuation of the coalition assault, and the apprehension of Saddam, it became obvious that American policymakers had decided to spare the errant leader. Laurence Friedman and Efraim Karsh make it clear in their history of the Gulf War that State Department officials sought a 'weakened' or a 'defanged' Saddam as their best hope for the maintenance of American interests in the future (*The Gulf Conflict: 1990–1991* (London: Faber and Faber, 1991), pp. 410–14); unfortunately, Saddam was not so weakened that he was prevented from massacring the large numbers of his own people who had risen up against him at the end of the war, with the tacit support of the US. See the Human Rights Watch Report *Endless Torment: The 1991 Uprising in Iraq and its Aftermath* (New York, 1992), pp. 38–43. The testimony of the resistance movement belies the US claim that only 'instability' would follow Saddam's fall: for a range of views from Iraqi resistance leaders, see *Iraq Since the Gulf War: Prospects for Democracy* (London: Zed Books, 1994), pp. 97–117. For the effects of the sanctions regime on Iraq's civilian population, see 'Counter-productive sanctions kill half a million Iraqi children', *The Guardian*, 1 December 1995; and 'UNICEF head says thousands of children are dying in Iraq', *New York Times*, 29 October 1996.

71. Bush first employed the phrase in a speech at the US Capitol on 29 January 1991: recent events (including the air attack on Iraq) had demonstrated 'the emergence of a new world order, one based on respect for the individual and for the rule of law, a new world order that can lead to the lasting peace we all seek'. 'White House briefing', *Federal News Service*, 30 January 1991.

72. Douglas Little has recently argued that, after 1945, 'US officials quickly came to regard secure access to Persian Gulf petroleum as their central objective in the Middle East'; and that, to achieve this objective, America sought to win over or to construct allies in the region. Little goes on to state that, by the early 1970s, 'America had lined up three pillars – Israel, Iran and Saudi Arabia – with whose help it hoped to keep the region's oil out of the hands of Arab radicals and their friends in the Kremlin'. ('Gideon's Band: America and the Middle East since 1945', *Diplomatic History*, Vol. 18, No. 4 (Fall 1994), pp. 513–40.) Noam Chomsky has also noted the American desire to keep these three countries within its sphere of influence; most recently in his *World Orders Old and New*, pp. 204–5.

73. The activities of the lobby from Truman onwards are recorded in Donald Neff's *Fallen Pillars: US Policy towards Palestine and Israel since 1945*. The frantic efforts of both Bob Dole and Bill Clinton to win Jewish support in the 1996 presidential campaign led both men to adopt increasingly hard-line positions in favour of Binyamin Netanyahu, a surprising move in Dole's case since the senator had been rigorous in his criticism of Israel earlier in his career. See Jonathan Freedland's article 'Jews to give Clinton early Hanukkah gift', *The Observer*, 20 October 1996. Freedland suggests that Dole's failure to make inroads into the Jewish vote was related to his earlier advocacy of policies more

critical of Israel; this should be a lesson to any younger politicians seeking advancement within the American political system.

74. Paul Findley, who lost his own congressional seat to an opponent funded by the Israeli lobby, criticises this tactic in *Deliberate Deceptions*, pp. 95–107.

75. For example, the 406–17 vote in the US House of Representatives in favour of moving the US embassy in Israel from Tel Aviv to Jerusalem, registered in June 1997 on the thirtieth anniversary of Israel's occupation of East Jerusalem (in contravention of international law). It is surprising that this measure could pass within a congressional chamber at all, let alone with virtual unanimity. Although the measure was not binding, and was intended largely for domestic consumption within the US, it led to greater anti-American feeling in the Middle East and sparked demonstrations in the occupied territories. 'How a House vote on Jerusalem backfired', *Chicago Tribune*, 18 June 1997.

76. Eric Davis states that 'a fundamental flaw of US foreign policy in the Middle East, and the Third World generally, lies in the propensity to support authoritarian rather than democratic regimes.' In the eyes of the people of the region, 'the US has become identified as standing against social change.' ('The Persian Gulf War: myths and realities', in *The United States and the Middle East*, p. 251. See also Richard Falk, 'Democracy died at the Gulf', in *The Gulf War and the New World Order*, pp. 536–48.

77. US aid amounted to around $3.5 billion in direct grants and $2 billion in loans during the 1996 fiscal year. *Washington Report on Middle Eastern Affairs*, Issue 14, No. 8 (April 1996), p. 49.

78. The 'tough neighbourhood' line, which is usually employed in Israel to justify actions contrary to international law and the norms of putatively 'democratic' states (such as assassinations, torture and the bombing of civilians), has become closely associated with Binyamin Netanyahu, who shrugged off any fear of Iraq during the Gulf War by deploying the phrase on CNN. 'Israel must make sense of Bibi talk', *The Guardian*, 26 May 1996.

79. See, for example, 'PLO official says US envoy can "go to hell"', Agence France Presse, 30 March 1997.

80. 'In the loop', *Washington Post*, 14 March 1994.

81. 'Saudi exile warns more attacks are planned', *New York Times*, 11 July 1996. US bases in Saudi Arabia were targeted, with considerable loss of life, in 1995 and 1996 by Islamist opposition forces. The immediate US reaction has been to retreat further into the desert, away from built-up areas, and to fortify its outposts even more strongly. 'US military in Saudi Arabia digs into the sand', *New York Times*, 9 November 1996.

82. Shimon Peres, Remarks to the 14th Mayor's Conference, Jerusalem, 15 March 1994.

83. Dan Meridor, interviewed by Ari Shavit, *Ha'aretz*, 19 July 1996.

4 *Life under Oslo*

With the inauguration of the Oslo process, the Palestinian people might reasonably hope not only for the return of land, but also for control over their everyday lives. As Israel's occupation was brought to an end, Palestinians would increasingly govern themselves and live in freedom from Israeli domination. The actual situation on the ground throughout the Oslo process, however, has presented a very different picture of this autonomy. Even after the creation of a Palestinian Authority and the 'liberation' of a small amount of Palestinian territory, Israel still defines the condition of Palestinian existence, and still discriminates against Palestinians in favour of Jewish aims and imperatives. As we shall see, this continuing Israeli influence has been a source of great distress to the population of the occupied territories, and has hardly inspired confidence in the Oslo process amongst ordinary Palestinians.

The permit system

Since Israel has conceded so little of the West Bank, and has sealed off the Gaza Strip from any outside power with the aid of fences and soldiers, the system of permits and identity cards which has marked the long occupation has continued to operate and to constrain Palestinian life. Permits and IDs have long been an effective tool by which Israel can control and subdue the Palestinian population. In the first instance, no Palestinian 'nationality' actually exists in the occupied territories; instead, the Israeli military authorities (euphemistically known as the 'Civil Administration') have divided the Palestinians into three different groups, each with a separate status and different rights of passage.[1] Jerusalemite Palestinians are the luckiest of all: their identification card enables them to move in and out of Jerusalem and to visit the various Palestinian areas. West Bank Palestinians are not so fortunate; they have relative freedom to move between the big towns, but they cannot enter Jerusalem or Israel without a separate permit. Given the particular emotional, religious and commercial significance of the capital, this has seriously affected many Palestinians who live just a few miles away from the Holy City. It has also undermined Israeli claims that the various shrines of Jerusalem would at last be open to all peoples – Jews, Christians and Muslims – under Israel's unification plan.

Palestinians from Gaza, meanwhile, have suffered most of all. Requiring documentation both to visit the West Bank and to reside there, Gazans have found the permit system to be an effective jail sentence. To be discovered at an Israeli checkpoint in the West Bank without a valid permit has meant 'deportation', a fine or even imprisonment. The difficulty for Gazans in moving around has of necessity made Gaza a more radical place, and has eroded a measure of the unity between the Gaza Strip and the West Bank.[2] In fact, Israel's entire permit system achieves this end. Although the Palestinians were given a guarantee as part of Oslo II that the territorial integrity of the West Bank and Gaza Strip would be maintained, the effect of the permit system has been exactly the opposite: families, friends and colleagues living in different Palestinian areas have been kept from one another, and the very idea of a single, sovereign Palestine has been undermined.[3] From the Palestinian Authority down to the lowliest commercial enterprise, the division of Palestinian identity into separate parts has made any unified Palestinian effort much more difficult and exacerbated existing economic and social problems.

The absence of formal Palestinian nationality has also made it more difficult for Palestinians to visit foreign countries, and has therefore constrained educational, political and economic opportunities. Although a permanent Palestinian passport has recently been introduced, there are no points of international entry or exit for holders of this document except those controlled by Israel, and Israel continues to restrict Palestinian movement around the occupied territories.[4] Thus, Palestinians can only travel abroad if they obtain the requisite permission from the Israeli authorities, by no means a formality. Even then, foreign trips bring with them the considerable risk that Israel will not allow the Palestinian to return to his or her home on the completion of their journey. This is especially true for those Palestinians who seek to study abroad or to be absent for a prolonged period, and for Palestinians seeking to return to Jerusalem, where Israel is most keen to thin out the Palestinian population. Ironically, foreigners enjoy many more rights in the Palestinian territories than do the Palestinians themselves. A passport and tourist visa ordinarily guarantee entry into all the Palestinian areas, a luxury envied by the actual inhabitants.

These travel constraints imposed upon Palestinians from Jerusalem, the West Bank and the Gaza Strip pale in comparison with the additional measures which constitute what is termed an Israeli 'closure' of the occupied territories. The meagre rights of a West Banker are reduced further in these situations, as Israel tries to seal off its 1949 territory from the lands occupied in 1967. This 'external' closure prevents Palestinians from the West Bank or Gaza Strip from visiting Jerusalem, even with a valid permit, and prevents or discourages Jerusalemites from venturing into the West Bank, lest their return is impeded. It might also impose similar constraints upon Gazans, whose inability to cross into Israel to work would in any case impoverish them such that travel would become unaffordable even if it were allowed. External closure, therefore, tightens the existing constraints upon Palestinians and makes their lives extremely arduous. Still worse, however, is 'internal' closure, the system of population control imposed on Palestinians after militant attacks inside Israel. Unlike an external closure, where movement between the Palestinian towns is at least technically possible, internal closure isolates each major Palestinian city from every other, and imposes a curfew on the entire Palestinian population. The effects of such a closure are devastating: the Palestinian economy collapses, with unemployment soaring to 60% or more and Palestinian life grinding to a standstill. The internal closures of March and April 1996, September and October 1996 and August and September 1997 each increased Palestinian hardship many times over, but failed conclusively to enhance Israeli security: after a closure was imposed in March 1996, militants still penetrated Israel to make two further, fatal attacks. The bombers continued their campaign, leaving the Palestinians collectively to suffer Israel's punishment.[5]

The permit system has ensured that Palestinians remain keenly aware of Israel's total control during the Oslo process, and has done little to encourage the growth of Palestinian society or to satisfy Palestinian national aspirations. The Palestinians have been living like foreigners in their own lands, with far fewer rights of passage than the tourists admitted by Israel into all parts of the occupied territories. The regular and devastating imposition of closures has further frustrated Palestinian society, and has been denounced by both Palestinians and international organisations as collective punishment, particularly in the light of ongoing terrorist attacks on Israel.[6] Whilst the rhetoric of Oslo has tended towards Palestinian independence and nationhood, the permit system and Israel's closure policy have contributed to a very different understanding of Oslo amongst ordinary Palestinians.

Detention and torture

After Israel's invasion of the West Bank and Gaza Strip in 1967, a state of martial law was declared to consolidate Israeli gains and effectively to police the Palestinian population. Very soon afterwards, the first Military Orders were issued, fiats from the Israeli army with the force of law. Thirty years later, these orders were still in place.[7] Regardless of the efforts of some Israelis to present the occupation as benign, it has always relied upon brute force and martial law for its perpetuation. In particular, the provisions of an open and accountable legal system have never been extended to the Palestinians: first, many of Israel's policy goals (such as the confiscation and control of Palestinian land and water supplies) could not be secured as quickly and certainly in an ordinary legal system; and second, Israel's occupation has always depended on levels of fear and coercion which can only be sustained by military law.[8]

Israel's ongoing extension of these Military Orders has ensured that every Palestinian lives in fear of arrest by the Israeli army or Shabak (secret police). Even if we disregard the evidence which suggests that Israeli agents operate inside Area A, supposedly liberated Palestinian territory, the scattered nature of these 'safe' areas ensures that all Palestinians have, sooner or later, to come into contact with Israeli soldiers at checkpoints or mobile patrols between the cities.[9] Moreover, those Palestinians living in areas B and C, where Israel retains full security control, can be arrested without any warning. After the bus bombs of February and March 1996, hundreds of students from Bir Zeit university near Jerusalem were arrested in an enormous dawn raid on their dormitories. Since Bir Zeit was in Area B, the students could do nothing whatsoever about this and, despite the transfer of 'civil' powers in the region to the Palestinian Authority, Palestinian police were powerless to intervene.[10]

Following an arrest, the Palestinians of the occupied territories face two terrible problems. The first is the nature of their confinement. Thanks to military law, Israel is not obliged to charge detainees or to release them; if it has cause to suspect them in any way, they can be kept in administrative detention virtually indefinitely. Thus, a Palestinian has very little recourse under military law, and can find himself or herself incarcerated on a false charge with no evidence or possibility of release. Orders for administrative detention can proceed without any judicial involvement whatsoever, providing that they are for less than six months' imprisonment; but they can also be renewed without limit, leading to many Palestinians spending years in Israeli prisons with no idea of the length of their future sentence, or the date of their possible release.[11] In the name of rounding up 'terrorists', Israel has regularly used this device to imprison politically active Palestinians, particularly those who have spoken out against Oslo, or to punish and intimidate particular groups (such as the Bir Zeit students).[12] Although Oslo II should have ensured that prisoners were held in Palestinian prisons under Palestinian jurisdiction, Israel has continued to arrest suspects in the West Bank and Gaza and to deport them to prisons inside Israel, a blatant violation of international law.[13]

At least as damaging as the arbitrary and unchecked system of administrative detention is the widespread use of torture inside Israeli cells. Israel is alone amongst Western nations in not only allowing torture to be practised but in codifying it within the Israeli legal system. Interrogators in Israeli jails and police stations are entitled to use 'moderate physical pressure' to extract information from their prisoners, even if the latter have not been charged with any crime. The rationale behind this extraordinary law is that the physical discomfort and injury caused to an individual in custody may be a worthwhile sacrifice for information leading to terrorists, or even to what the Israelis call the 'ticking bomb', a Palestinian who may possess information which could avert a future suicide attack.[14] In reality, torture has become another way by which the Israeli army can intimidate and control the Palestinian population living under occupation.[15] Palestinians are frequently arrested on suspicion of belonging to terror groups, and then tortured in the hope that they will yield the names of their 'colleagues'; the possibility that the 'terrorist' under torture may in fact be innocent does not delay the torturers. During the intifada years, torture was established as a standard feature in the lives of all detainees; sleep deprivation, exposure to extremes of temperature and beatings were all intended to break the spirit of the demonstrators and quell the entire uprising. More recently, Israel has provided more evidence of torture as collective punishment: the families of those deemed potential suicide bombers have been placed under 'moderate physical pressure' in the hope this might yield information about the whereabouts of an individual suspected of plotting a crime.[16]

Aside from its harsh treatment of Palestinians under military law, Israel also discriminates between the indigenous and settler populations in the occupied territories by supporting two separate legal systems for the two communities. Whilst the Palestinians face the prospect of Military Orders and army courts, Jewish settlers are tried under Israeli civilian law, and are not liable to the oppressive legal measures detailed above. If a settler kills a Palestinian, he or she is tried by a different court and under different conditions than if a Palestinian kills or otherwise harms a settler. In practical terms, this has led to many cases in which settler intransigence has been punished lightly, if at all. Palestinians can expect the opposite treatment from the army, frequently drawing lethal gunfire before an arrest for some infraction or another. Since the settlers are permitted to carry rifles around the West Bank with them, incidents of violence are commonplace and Palestinians are made to realise more fully their inferior status. There is no independent and fair method of arbitration between settlers and Palestinians, since the legal frameworks applicable to each have been designed specifically to preserve the disparity between the two.[17]

Although the Palestinians continue to suffer discrimination in the Israeli application of various legal systems to the occupied territories, Israel has tried to secure its own legal peace dividend at the expense of Palestinian rights and claims. In 1997, the Israeli Knesset gave a first reading to a bill designed to indemnify Israeli citizens and institutions against any Palestinian claims relating to army or police brutality during the Palestinian intifada. Given the enormous number of injuries caused by Defence Minister Rabin's 'iron-fist' response to the uprising, many Palestinian civilians have pursued the distant possibility of redress through the Israeli legal system in recent years. Now, however, given the new realities of Oslo and the supposed arrival of peace, Israel has attempted to write off these claims and to deny responsibility for its former activities. Again, the façade of Oslo offers Israel an opportunity to perpetuate its occupation in fact and yet to claim the benefits of a peacemaker before its own public and the international community.[18]

As international and regional human rights groups have noted, the Oslo process has introduced another element of fear into Palestinian existence: the judicial methods of the Palestinian Authority. To the surprise of many observers, conditions inside Palestinian cells and the procedures by which people are put there are little improvement on Israeli military rule.[19] Although this development has been used to suggest that Yasser Arafat is at least as responsible for the condition of his people as the Israeli occupiers, it is worth noting that the Palestinian police and legal systems were instituted as part of the Oslo process; and that Arafat's gross abuses of human rights derive in part from Oslo's agenda. Since Arafat's only responsibility under Oslo is to 'deal with Palestinian terror', he has succumbed to Israeli and American demands that he make sweeping arrests and apply his own pressure on the Palestinian population.[20]

A stark reminder of Arafat's reliance on US and Israeli guidance came in March 1995, when US Vice-President Al Gore visited Jericho. A meeting between Arafat and Gore was staged around a simple quid pro quo: Gore brought money and assistance from the US, whilst Arafat offered the US and Israel a new draconian system of military courts for trying those people whom Gore called 'the enemies of the peace process'.[21] These military courts had been roundly condemned by Israeli, Palestinian and international human rights groups as contrary to basic legal standards, and yet they were designed to appease the demands of the supposedly democratic governments of Israel and the United States. Christopher George, executive director of Human Rights Watch, wrote to Secretary of State Warren Christopher to protest against these courts, deploring Al Gore's endorsement of military 'justice' and insisting that 'the United States should not encourage the subordination of human rights to the battle against terrorism'.[22]

Since Gore's visit, little has changed. The US continues steadfastly to support Arafat's violation of due process and arbitrary detention of those it terms 'the enemies of peace'. Whenever Arafat rounds up terrorist suspects, his action is greeted with approval by the other Oslo players, even if the methods of arrest and detention he employs contravene international human rights standards. Israel and the United States are interested in results, such as the confessions of alleged suicide bombers or simply the incarceration of 'Islamic militants'; their respective governments appear to care far less about the means by which, for example, confessions are extracted, even though these must condition entirely the reliability of a suspect's testimony.[23]

Similarly, if Arafat releases a group of purported Hamas supporters whom he has been detaining without charge, reports in Israel and America suggest that he has gone soft on terror. In April 1997, after the bombing of the Apropos café in Tel Aviv, the US State Department and Israeli Ministry of Foreign Affairs gave numerous briefings to the press claiming that Arafat had given the green light to terror attacks.[24] In practice, this meant that Arafat had neglected to keep in administrative detention, without charge, some suspected supporters of Hamas or Islamic Jihad who could not be found guilty of a crime.[25] A similar soundbite was employed later in the summer of 1997, when Arafat was said to have shown the 'revolving door' to Hamas and Islamic Jihad activists, releasing them soon after he arrested them.[26] Once again, the truth behind this glib phrase has to do with human rights and the due process of law: if the 'revolving door' translates as a commitment to release those prisoners against whom no evidence exists, Arafat's apparent intransigence is in fact no more than the proper observance of human rights standards applicable in every civilised nation.

Arafat and the Palestinian Authority should have been encouraged to build an open and free society on the West Bank and in Gaza, on the assumption that radicalism and militancy would be diluted by a climate of liberal debate and political freedom; instead, Arafat has been fêted and rewarded inside Israel and in Washington whenever he acts to repress his own people. The connection between the number of detainees in Palestinian custody and the incidence of bombings inside Israel is clear: a terrorist operation leads to the instant arrest of hundreds of Palestinians, virtually all of whom have opposed the current peace process.[27] Thus Arafat is able to deal with his internal opposition; Israelis are given a false assurance that their security has been increased; and the Oslo process is further insulated from scrutiny by the suggestion that all of its opponents are terrorists and murderers, deserving of military courts, indefinite detention and the same 'moderate physical pressure' pioneered in the jails and detention centres of Israel. The powers given to Arafat by Oslo, and the American and Israeli conceptions of how Arafat might best deal with internal opposition, have ensured that Palestinians now fear unjust incarceration and torture from not only the Israeli forces but from fellow Palestinians.

Land confiscation

Although Israel conquered the West Bank and Gaza Strip in 1967, it has since sought to give legitimacy to its claims on the territory through various legal means. Whilst Israel has the sheer force to take and settle however much of the occupied territories it desires, successive governments have correctly surmised that such blatant confiscation will not enhance Israel's standing abroad, or satisfy more liberal elements in the domestic population. The state has therefore established a process in law whereby Palestinian land can be legally taken away from its owners and used to build Jewish roads or settlements. Thus Israel is seen to be acting with probity, even if the results of its actions seriously damage the indigenous population of the occupied territories.[28]

Israel's first step after 1967 was to take elements from the legal systems previously binding over Palestine, the Ottoman and the Jordanian laws, and to combine these in a procedure which best served Israeli interests. Since the occupation has continued for so long, and Oslo has given Palestinians legal control over such a tiny proportion of the territories, Israel's selective reimposition of these former systems has not been supplanted by a more modern, Palestinian code. The Ottoman and Jordanian laws offered Israel a concept of 'unused' land which was conducive to an extensive confiscation: these former laws allowed for land which had not been cultivated by individual owners to be taken and put to use for the good of the community as a whole. For Israel, this represented an opportunity to claim West Bank and Gaza land for the Israeli state, on the assumption that a case against the original owners and their neglect of their land could be made. Israel thus set about making cultivation of land as difficult to establish as possible, shifting the burden of proof onto the landholder rather than the usurper. In the Israeli understanding, only proof of cultivation of a piece of land for ten years in a row was sufficient for the Israeli government to honour the holdings of a landowner and to drop its own claim. A single year of non-cultivation would prove that a landowner was not putting the land to good use; and would enable the Israeli administrators of the West Bank or Gaza to declare an area 'State Land' and to transfer its ownership in perpetuity to the Jewish state. Aerial photographs of the occupied territories enabled Israel to monitor the land use patterns of particular areas, and to ensure that any failure to cultivate was recorded and used against the owners.[29]

These provisions have had a devastating effect on Palestinians. To begin with, they forced many landowners to grow crops which could be cultivated easily, but which were not necessarily profitable or useful to the Palestinian economy. Crops were grown simply to protect the land from confiscation, rather than to put it to best use. More generally, it was almost impossible to guarantee cultivation of crops for ten years in succession. The difficulty of the climate, the availability of water supplies and the agricultural traditions of the Palestinians could not satisfy the Israeli demand for consistent, unbroken planting and harvesting. Some Palestinians, especially the Bedouin, had based their livelihood on a mixed economy of crops and livestock, alternating between planting and tending their animals year by year on their holdings. Israel's reinterpretation of the old laws now threatened this way of life, if not the very land on which it was grounded.[30]

It is ironic that Israel should use a law, originally intended to return idle land to the Palestinians as a whole, to dispossess Palestinian landowners and transfer land to Jewish settlers. This system of expropriation is premised on the simple assumption that the people to whom unused land must be returned are Jewish rather than Palestinian. Perhaps unsurprisingly, this interpretation is supported right through the Israeli legal system to the Supreme Court itself. Although the court is obliged to ensure that Israeli procedures are correctly followed, the essentially discriminatory nature of the State Land apparatus is beyond its remit.[31] There is nowhere for Palestinians to go and argue the right of their case, since the Israeli legal hierarchy is constrained by the same exclusivist impulse as the Israeli state. Thus many Palestinians have tried to defend their land in person rather than through the courts, a decision which brought them into conflict with the Israeli army and which has had fatal consequences.[32]

Land confiscation harms Palestinians on the personal and the societal levels. Families which lose their land not only find themselves without a place to live but also sacrifice the livelihood of their following generations. A piece of land which has supported an extended family for decades cannot be removed without seriously threatening that family's continued existence. In a wider sense, the confiscations have dissected the agricultural areas of the West Bank such that their cultivation has become much more difficult. Agriculture is one of the largest sectors in the Palestinian economy, and offers at least some potential for independent development. However, the confiscations have upset the natural arrangement of the land, frequently dividing single areas of cultivation and making access to these fragmented fields more difficult. The by-pass road system, built on land confiscated during the Oslo process, has endangered the lives of Palestinians who have to cross the freeways to reach the various parts of their land; it has also consumed thousands of acres of prime, fertile soil which might have bettered the families of individual farmers and Palestinian society as a whole.

Land confiscation has continued throughout the Oslo process, in spite of its discriminatory nature and destructive effects. Many of the Palestinians who have opposed Oslo from its early stages were confirmed in their opposition by the experience of further Israeli expropriation in the middle of a putative peace process. To a large extent, the entire Israeli–Palestinian conflict revolves around land ownership, and for the Oslo process to permit continued dispossession via racist law and military force has been too much for many aggrieved Palestinians. This context enables us better to understand the debate in May 1997 about Palestinian land dealers and Yasser Arafat's supposed execution of the same. Some Palestinians who had been suspected of involvement with Jewish purchasers were found murdered around the West Bank, and Israel announced that they had been killed by Palestinian secret police, under Arafat's orders, for selling land to Jews. This prompted an international outcry not only against what was seen as Arafat's brutality but also his racism in attempting to exclude Jews from the land. In the US, calls were heard for the suspension of aid to the Palestinian Authority as a punishment for its anti-semitic and extra-judicial practices.[33]

Although this debate raised some valid questions about Arafat's security services and the absence of the rule of law in Palestine, its chief contribution was to mislead the American and European public, and further to disadvantage the Palestinians. If the Palestinian Authority's drive to make land sales to Jews a capital offence reeks of racism, it can only be properly understood in the context of the greater racism of Israeli land confiscation. Since the settlement programme began in 1967, huge areas of the West Bank and Gaza Strip have been taken from the Palestinian people for exclusively Jewish use. No Palestinians live in any of the Jewish settlements, just as no Palestinians are supposed to drive along the by-pass roads between them. Only in this light does the Palestinian impulse to curb land sales make sense: a possible 'Palestine' cannot afford to lose an inch of territory when it has been deprived of so many acres already. In addition, the state of Israel explicitly stipulates that the land inside Israel is to be held in perpetuity for the use of the Jewish people. Palestinians simply cannot own land in Israel, and Jews do not sell land back to Palestinians. The assumption that a free market exists, and that the Palestinians have tampered with it for racist reasons, completely ignores Israel's own exclusivist ideology and its practice of retaining land for solely Jewish use. A Palestinian who sells land to an Israeli Jew sells at the same time the right of any future Palestinian to live on, work on or even to cross that land. It is for this reason alone that the sale of occupied land to Jews has been accepted as a serious criminal offence by the overwhelming majority of Palestinians.[34]

House demolition

In addition to the gun, another vital Israeli tool for controlling the occupied territories is the bulldozer. In situations where Israel lays claim to land which supports existing structures, the army and Civil Administration can employ bulldozers to destroy buildings and clear the way for new Jewish settlement. Still more than in situations of land confiscation, this practice results in homelessness and despair for those Palestinians who block the path of increased Jewish presence in Palestinian areas.[35]

Before we examine house demolition as a means to facilitate settlement expansion, we must take account of the legal means by which bulldozers are employed to demolish Palestinian homes. Technically speaking, Israel is within its rights to destroy any home in the occupied territories which has been built without the proper documents and/or an Israeli permit. The Civil Administration on the West Bank and in Gaza is supposed to issue building permits on Palestinian request, and in accordance with town plans which specify land use and mark out residential, commercial and agricultural areas. However, as we shall see in the next chapter on Jerusalem, the process of permit granting and town planning is anything but fair. Since the Israeli occupying forces are responsible for deciding on the shape of the surrounding Palestinian communities, they have traditionally sought in their town planning to limit Palestinian development and preserve land for future Jewish use.

In effect, this means that Palestinians who can prove legal ownership of a piece of land are prohibited from building upon it. Even if a Palestinian area is miles away from a planned or actual settlement, the growth of that Palestinian area will be constrained by the Israeli planners.[36]

This practice of limiting Palestinian construction has left many Palestinians with no choice but to build illegally. With a Palestinian population expanding rapidly, and settlement confiscation reducing the land available to support this population, every available acre must be put to good use. However, the buildings which go up in these circumstances are always overshadowed by the possibility of demolition. If the occupying authorities need to demonstrate their mastery over the Palestinians, they can descend upon an illegally built house at any time and expel its inhabitants with impunity. When these demolitions are reported in the media, Israel distracts from the racist nature of the policy by claiming correctly that the bulldozers are merely enforcing the law. The problem, and the leap which many commentators and observers rarely make, is that the law is itself racist. Since the authorities typically give as little as 24 hours' notice of a demolition, this places thousands of families in a situation of constant fear and instability. LAW estimated that more than 1000 houses in the West Bank had outstanding demolition orders by August 1997, with Israel setting about the task of destroying them at the rate of fifty a month.[37]

Aside from those demolitions carried out to intimidate Palestinians or to assure them of Israel's control over the occupied territories, the bulk of bulldozing activity is directed against homes which have some value to Israel. As the settlements have expanded under the Oslo process, so the number of confrontations between the settlers (accompanied by the Israeli army) and the Palestinians of the neighbouring villages has multiplied. A plan to expand a particular Jewish settlement forces the Israeli authorities to consult their own development plans for the neighbouring Palestinian areas; and if there is a conflict between their proposals and the reality of a Palestinian house, a demolition order is brought to bear on the offending property. Since the demolition order confirms to the owners that Israel intends to enforce its own unfair law against their continued residence, the residents have few options but to leave their property; and so, the typical consequence of the bulldozer's work is the transfer of Palestinians from the area of the demolition.[38]

Under Oslo, demolitions have been given a shape and direction which was previously absent. Israel has retained full planning authority in Area C, comprising around 75% of the West Bank, and has enabled the Palestinian Authority to grant permits in areas A and B. This has given Israel a real incentive to demolish homes in Area C, on the understanding that the residents will be forced into areas A and B and will leave Area C with the smallest possible Palestinian population.[39] In late 1996 and early 1997, Israel began to 'deport' the Jahalin tribe of Palestinian Bedouins from their homes in Area C to a new site in Area B, cleaning out a section of land which was immediately used for the expansion of Ma'ale Adumim, the largest Jewish settlement in the occupied territories. The Jahalin homes were destroyed to enable not only the expansion of Ma'ale Adumim but also the more effective separation of Palestinians and Jewish settlers in the Territories. If Area C can be largely cleansed of non-Jews, the Israelis will find it easier in the later stages of the Oslo agreement to argue that Area C should remain in Israeli hands. Since a Palestinian presence in Area C is frequently evidenced by buildings as well as agriculture, house demolitions are essential to the successful completion of the settlement programme. This blatant policy of deleting the evidence of Palestinian presence, as well as scattering the residents of demolished houses into other areas, corresponds closely to the 'ethnic cleansing' which has marked other recent conflicts elsewhere in the world and which has been unequivocally condemned by the international community. It is worth noting that this cleansing is a direct consequence not of Israeli violations of Oslo but of the agreement as it has been drafted and signed.[40]

There is one further category of house demolitions which is not related to the settlements, or even to those buildings constructed without a permit. Since the intifada, Israel has also used demolition to punish particular Palestinians for various crimes against the Israeli state. It was common for Palestinian fighters in the uprising to face not only arrest but the demolition of their family homes.[41] Some of these houses, especially those in refugee camps, have never been rebuilt, and can still be seen in their demolished state today. More recently, Israel has targeted this policy against the families and associates of those suicide bombers who have attacked Jerusalem or Tel Aviv. After a bomber has been identified (with more or less certainty), the Israeli army locates his house, expels the inhabitants and then seals it off from the neighbourhood. Usually, the house will then be destroyed as a deterrent to other Palestinians who might think of attacking Israel. The fact that the family of a dead bomber is entirely innocent of his crime does not temper this policy or prevent the demolition. In March 1997, the house of Musa Ghanimat, alleged perpetrator of a fatal attack on a Tel Aviv café, was scheduled for demolition. Ghanimat's 21-year-old widow and four children, aged between one-and-a-half and eight years old, petitioned the Israeli Supreme Court against the demolition order, arguing that it would throw the family onto the street and compound their suffering. The court's president, Aharon Barak, a visiting professor at Yale Law School, claimed that the intention of the demolition order was not to punish Ghanimat's family but to deter further attacks, and that it was therefore justified whatever the consequences. In spite of a protest from one of the three judges, who agreed that the demolition represented collective punishment, the house of Musa Ghanimat was destroyed the next day and his young family was made homeless.[42]

Environmental and economic exploitation

Although much has been said and written about Zionism and the influence of ideology on the politics of the Israeli–Palestinian conflict, the importance of Jewish exclusivism should not distract from the plainly economic aspects and motives of Israel's continuing occupation. The West Bank and Gaza Strip are attractive to Israel for their putative historical or emotional significance in Jewish history, but they also offer two resources which Israel is especially keen to acquire: land and water. For all of the rhetoric about biblical or security priorities behind Jewish settlement, the Palestinians of the West Bank and Gaza most commonly associate Israeli encroachment on their lands with a simple motive: greed.

Israel has always presented its history as a spectacular experiment in nation-building under the most harsh circumstances. The myths of the early Zionist settlers suggested an epic endeavour to overcome every natural obstacle and to found a state. The early Israelis 'made the desert bloom' with their ingenuity and dedication, according to this story. The reality is very different. Israel has, for the past 30 years, been dependent upon the water resources of the West Bank and Gaza Strip to sustain its own population. With a constant stream of new immigrants encouraged to adopt a Western lifestyle in Israel, demand for water has steadily increased. To meet this demand, Israel has maintained across its entire occupation of the Palestinian territory several Military Orders dating from 1967 and 1968, giving full control over water supplies to the Israeli army. From 1967 onwards, all existing wells were placed under Israeli supervision, and no wells could be dug without express Israeli permission.[43]

The Oslo process was intended to reverse this pattern of total Israeli control and to establish the beginnings of a Palestinian water authority. However, the larger question of who actually owned the water tables beneath the West Bank and Gaza has gone unanswered, postponed until permanent status talks. Thus Palestinians have had to put up with the same water shortages during the Oslo period as throughout the occupation. During the summer months in particular, the lack of water for personal and agricultural use has been acute. The new settlements built during Oslo, of course, do not suffer from the same problem. The Israeli water authorities control both Jewish and Palestinian infrastructure, but are careful to prioritise existing supplies in favour of Jewish users. Palestinians are left to make do with what remains after every Jewish water requirement, however redundant or wasteful, has been satisfied.[44]

Israeli control of water supplies constitutes an entirely non-ideological aspect of its occupation, and has been touted by previous Israeli governments as a sound reason for retaining as much of the occupied territories as possible. Yitzhak Shamir's administration issued an unusual, full-page advertisement in the *Jerusalem Post* in 1990 which stated that:

> it is difficult to conceive of any political solution consistent with Israel's survival that does not involve complete, continued Israeli control of the water and sewerage systems [of the occupied territories], and of the associated infrastructure, including the power supply and road network.[45]

The advertisement went on to chastise 'those advocates of Israeli concessions' in any peace process, insisting that 'the claim to continued Israeli control over Judea and Samaria is not based on extremist fanaticism or religious mysticism but on a rational, healthy and reasonable survival instinct'. The same level-headed motivation lies behind the confiscation of land for settlements. As we have already seen, many of the settlements have been pitched towards Israelis who will respond favourably to economic inducements. Subsidised housing in the areas of the West Bank closest to Jerusalem has proved especially popular with young professionals, who can commute easily to work or return quickly to their homes after a night out in the city. The largest settlement outside East Jerusalem, Ma'ale Adumim, has been sold especially to such people, with an enormous infrastructural investment made by the Israeli government to improve communications between the settlement and the city centre.[46]

Elsewhere, settlements have been designed and built for wider economic aims, with land taken from Palestinians specifically to enrich Jewish Israelis. The new settlement of Har Homa, built on the Arab hill of Jabal Abu Ghneim, is a good example of this. Yitzhak Shamir, Yitzhak Rabin and Binyamin Netanyahu had all acted to further the Har Homa plan, but it was Netanyahu who ordered construction work to begin on 18 March 1997. In the immediate sense, Palestinians stood to lose yet more land to Israel, as the settlement was planned to cover Jabal Abu

Ghneim; however, the true reason for Israel's interest in the site was more than simply a desire to build more homes for Jews. Jabal Abu Ghneim occupies a beautiful spot between Jerusalem and Bethlehem, and was historically a stopping-off point for pilgrims journeying to the birthplace of Jesus Christ. A monastery and other ancient sites bore testament to the hill's significance and geographical importance. The plan for the new settlement of Har Homa understands and capitalises on this heritage in the most cynical fashion imaginable.

Even though Israel has controlled Bethlehem since 1967, the many pilgrims and tourists from around the world who visit the town have mostly encountered, and paid, Palestinian traders and guides rather than Israelis. The return of Bethlehem to Palestinian control in 1995 suggested that Palestinians could further consolidate their provisions for tourism and benefit economically from the new political reality. However, this hope has not been realised. For one thing, the creation of what is virtually a Palestinian bantustan in Bethlehem has given the Israelis many more opportunities to seal off the town than would have been possible, were the Israeli army still occupying central positions. Regular closures have hit the tourist market hard, making it much more difficult for Palestinian guides and shopkeepers to meet and interact with visitors.[47] Har Homa, however, is intended as a more permanent method of keeping tourist dollars away from the Palestinian economy. As part of an expanded and annexed East Jerusalem, Har Homa is intended as a massive 'visitors' centre' for Palestinian Bethlehem, which will head off tourists before they enter the Palestinian areas and ensure that their various purchases take place within Israel. Only a kilometre away from the holy sites of Bethlehem, Har Homa is perfectly situated to exploit the tourist opportunities of the Palestinian town. The settlement contains not only houses, but hotels and a number of 'themed areas' in which visitors can enjoy Bethlehem without venturing into the grubby reality of the Arab areas. Staying in relative luxury as guests of Israeli hoteliers, tourists will be able to steal into the churches of the real Bethlehem (under the supervision of Jewish tour guides, in Jewish buses) and escape again to the safety and comfort of 'Bethlehem, Israel': Har Homa.[48]

This new settlement will therefore cripple the already ailing Bethlehem economy, closing off another potential area for development. Bethlehem was subjected to an especially severe closure in August and September 1997 after the Jerusalem market bombing in July, even though the town was in no way responsible for the bomb blast. The Palestinian community was thereby offered a vision of its economic and political future: as construction continued unabated at the new rival centre, Har Homa, the traders of Bethlehem were prevented from meeting those tourists who were turned away by the Israeli army at access roads to the town. Upon the completion of 'Bethlehem, Israel', Palestinians in the real Bethlehem will have no chances to offer services and accommodation to Bethlehem visitors, and will most likely compete only for their charity. With Har Homa scheduled to be completed before 2000, the Israeli businessmen and women behind the plan, and the Israeli government which has carried it out, will be excellently placed to take advantage of the hundreds of thousands of visitors expected to descend upon Bethlehem for the bimillennial anniversary of Christ's birth. This scheme, with all its potentially disastrous implications for Palestinians, has been allowed to go ahead under Oslo, and the Israeli government has been able to claim that Har Homa is perfectly compatible with the various peace agreements.[49]

Living in Gaza

Any account of life under Oslo would be incomplete without special reference to the Gaza Strip, which differs in many important respects from the West Bank. The Strip is a very narrow area on the Mediterranean coast, home to more than a million Palestinians in one of the highest population densities in the world. Gaza suffered especially badly under occupation, and found itself ill-equipped to deal with the needs of an expanding population confined to substandard housing and refugee camps. According to one recent study, Israel's policies in Gaza were intended to de-develop the area: not simply to prevent it from achieving its economic potential, but to dismantle what little infrastructure and provisions had been left by the Egyptian administration before 1967 and to guarantee Gaza's perpetual backwardness. When the Strip was returned to Palestinian control in 1994 under the Oslo Accords, hopes were high amongst Gazans that the terrible legacy of Israel's occupation might quickly be overcome.[50]

The reality of liberated Gaza has not matched these hopes, principally because Israel's withdrawal from the Strip has been circumscribed by conditions.[51] The Palestinians have been offered only around 65% of the territory, with the rest remaining in Israeli hands. This has enabled Israel to maintain its tiny settler population on the Strip, in spite of the logistical and security difficulties this has caused. Only around 5,000 settlers live in Nezanim, Kefar Darom and Gush Katif, and yet Israel has retained about a third of the Strip's territory (including a prime coastal section) to support them. More than a million Palestinians are crowded into the remaining two thirds of the Strip, living in conditions that bear no resemblance to the comfort and luxury of the settlements.[52] Possibilities for commerce, agriculture and leisure, which the Palestinians of Gaza desperately require, are thus precluded by the Jewish settlers, established in Gaza, not out of economic necessity, but at the behest of their government.[53]

This tiny settler population brings with it the unwelcome presence of the Israeli army, which still patrols the streets of Gaza's towns near the many settlements. Aside from the historical grievances of Palestinians towards these soldiers, and more pressing anger at the Israeli government's ongoing suppression and dispossession of Palestinians under Oslo, the settlements themselves create new flashpoints for violent protest. The army is placed in the awkward position of having to defend 5,000 settlers living in comfort at the expense of a million unhappy Palestinians; the settlements and their guardians present an obvious and immediate target for Palestinian unrest. The refusal of the government to evacuate the settlers and return the land they have occupied is thus doubly unfortunate: the Palestinians are antagonised by the ongoing loss of their land, and they are presented with a clear and immediate object for their complaints.[54]

In addition to the land on which the settlements are built, Israel also controls a narrow band of territory running right around the three land borders of Gaza. This 'security zone' has been heavily fortified to ensure that Gaza is sealed off, not only from 1949-Israel but from Egypt. Although Gaza was supposedly liberated from Israeli control in 1994, its inhabitants remain confined within the Strip unless they can persuade the Israelis to let them leave. Apart from consuming even more precious land, these security measures contribute to the impression of some Gazans that the Strip has become a giant prison, with Palestinian warders, but with Israel holding the keys. As Gaza's population expands further, the belief that Gazans have been trapped rather than liberated will become increasingly prevalent among the Strip's inhabitants.

Since Gaza is isolated from the West Bank by part of 1949-Israel, it is more vulnerable to Israeli closures than the rest of the occupied territories. Whereas the Palestinian population can travel from town to town during an 'external' closure, any closing of the Gaza border prevents the entire Gaza population from visiting the other Palestinian areas. In addition, Israel has often created special restrictions for Gazans, on the assumption that they are more radical than their West Bank counterparts and therefore a bigger security risk. From the signing of the first Oslo agreement in 1993 to the present day, for example, Israel has imposed draconian travel restrictions on students from Gaza who are registered at universities in the West Bank. Since both of the Strip's own universities are heavily oversubscribed, thousands of Gazans have traditionally journeyed to the West Bank to study. In recent years, however, Israel has regularly cancelled their permits, causing enormous disruption to existing degree candidates and forcing many to drop out, or give up on the idea of a university education without even making an application.[55]

The plight of the Gaza students typifies the wider struggle of Gazan Palestinians to win their rights under Oslo. The Interim Agreement of 1995 was supposed to guarantee safe passage to the West Bank from Gaza, but it has been violated by Israel in pursuit of policies which can only be described as collective punishment. After the bus bombs of February and March 1996, for example, every Gaza student had his or her travel and residency permits cancelled, making a trip to the West Bank or continued residence there impossible. Without any process of application or screening, Israel decided to suspend (and in many cases to terminate) the education of thousands of innocent Palestinian students. Even students and academics inside Israel denounced this ruling as collective punishment, and urged the Israeli government to guarantee safe passage for Gaza students; but to no avail, as first Shimon Peres and then Binyamin Netanyahu refused to lift the ban for 'security' reasons.[56]

The students' difficulties have been experienced on an even greater scale by the tens of thousands of Gazans who try to cross over into Israel to work each day. Given the existence of the captive Gazan labour force, and the minimal industrial development within Gaza City, Israeli firms have not been slow to set up factories just inside the Israeli border. However, the regular and prolonged closures of this border, again in response to 'security concerns', have seriously affected the economic health of the entire Strip. Unemployment has soared to 60% or more during these periods of closure, raising the spectres of disease, malnutrition and even starvation amongst the powerless Palestinian population.[57] The experience of unemployment and poverty has convinced many Gazans that the Oslo process has not brought them closer to peace, particularly since no elements within the Strip seem to possess the agency to make living conditions and working opportunities any better. Combined with the decaying infrastructure and economic problems left behind by the Israelis, this new experience has contributed inevitably to Gazan discontent with Oslo and to the growth of radicalism.[58]

From this brief survey of Palestinian life under Oslo, it is clear that many of the most oppressive and damaging Israeli practices have remained a constant factor in Palestinians' lives even during a time of supposed 'peace'. The detail and extent of Israel's ongoing occupation and expropriation is often neglected by the media, since most of the issues above are absolutely commonplace and unremarkable. On those occasions when a bomb explodes in Tel Aviv or Jerusalem, the fact is widely reported and we are made fully aware of the price that Israel is paying for Oslo; but the enormous toll exacted of the entire Palestinian people by land confiscations, demolitions, closures, detention and the rest is rarely brought to our attention. Life under Oslo in Israel is marked by occasional and terrible trauma, but is otherwise normal: Israeli Jews move around freely, work and relax without interruption, and enjoy the benefits of resources which have been forcefully taken from another people. For Palestinians, the Oslo agreements define virtually every aspect of their existence: their jobs, homes and families are entirely governed by the few concessions Israel has made and the many more which it has refused to make. When so many aspects of Israel's long occupation seem still to survive in the Oslo process, disadvantaging Palestinians in such fundamental fashion, it is hardly surprising that support for Oslo amongst Palestinians has all but collapsed.

Notes

1. This summary of the permit system is based upon 'The politics of placelessness', a report by the Society of St Yves (Jerusalem, September 1996); and 'Life and travel coloured by pass laws', *The Guardian*, 20 November 1996.

2. The impact of particularly draconian restrictions upon the Gazan population is discussed by Sara Roy in *The Gaza Strip*, p. 309ff. See also 'Left to rot in a siege economy', *The Guardian*, 2 November 1996.

3. See the eighth clause of Article XXXI of the *Interim Agreement*, p. 28: 'The two Parties view the West Bank and the Gaza Strip as a single territorial unit, the integrity and status of which will be preserved during the interim period.'

4. A flurry of disinformation about the new Palestinian passport has been countered by the Alternative Information Centre, Bethlehem, which pointed out in its report 'Misleading information on Palestinian ID cards', 27 October 1997, that although Palestinian-printed ID cards may soon be a reality, they are still controlled by Israel (even down to the issuing of serial numbers), since Israel still controls the various checkpoints in the occupied territories.

5. See the *Middle East Economic Digest*, 'special report on Palestine', 22 August 1997, for a general account of Palestinian degradation under the effects of persistent closure. The various kinds of Israeli closure, including the most devastating, recent innovations in the form (culminating in 'internal' closure), are summarised in the *Report of the Director-General* of the United Nations'

International Labour Office, Appendix, 85th Session (Geneva, 1997), pp. 4ff. The enormous increase in unemployment during closure is referred to in paragraph 55, p. 23.

6. See 'Palestinian life blocked to make Israel more secure', *Washington Times*, 8 August 1997. The ILO, which strongly criticises the effects of the closure policy, states that 'there is no evidence of the effectiveness of such stringent measures against terrorism' (Appendix to the Report of the Director-General, 85th Session, paragraph 13, p. 5); in its conclusions, the report states that the 'obvious priority' for economic development and social stability should be 'the removal of hindrances to the movement of people and goods within and among the territories and across borders' (paragraph 70, p. 29). Meanwhile, the Director-General of the ILO, Michel Hansenne, told the *Chicago Tribune* that there was 'no evidence' to suggest that closure increased Israel's security; see, 'Israel cited for Arabs' job losses', 7 June 1997.

7. The standard work on military orders in the occupied territories is Raja Shehadeh's *Occupier's Law: Israel and the West Bank* (Washington: Institute for Palestine Studies, 1988, 2nd edition), pp. 76ff. See also Shehadeh's and Jonathan Kuttab's report for Law in the Service of Man, 'Civil Administration in the occupied West Bank' (Ramallah, January 1982), which challenges Israeli Military Order 947, the legal foundation for the establishment of the Civil Administration in 1981.

8. The Palestinian water supply was taken over by Israel in three Military Orders of 1967 and 1968: 92, 158 and 291. LAW has published a report outlining these three Orders and their perpetuation throughout the Oslo process: Shawqi Issa and Gert de Bruijne, 'Existing water laws and regulations in Palestinian territory' (Jerusalem, September 1995).

9. Israel makes little attempt to disguise its undercover operations inside supposedly sovereign Palestinian territory: see, for example, its murder of Yahya Ayyash, alleged Hamas bombmaker, in the Gaza Strip in January 1996; Derek Brown, in *The Guardian*, 6 January, noted that Israeli officials 'are generally happy to foster the image of an implacable power willing and able to track down its enemies – and eliminate them'.

10. 'One-tenth of our university is missing', Bir Zeit University statement, 30 March 1996. The statement warned that 'it is a negative and highly counter-productive signal to a whole generation of students and young people that their rights to education, to the due process of law and to freedom from arbitrary arrest are still in grave jeopardy'.

11. For a recent example, see LAW's press release, 'Three Palestinian prisoners, due to be released, given six month administrative detention orders', 17 July 1997. One of the three, Abdel Nasser Jamous, had reached the end of a twelve-year prison sentence only to be kept in administrative detention for at least another six months. His case is proof that even those sentenced to fixed prison terms cannot be sure of the duration of their incarceration.

12. Amnesty International's report on Israel and the occupied territories,

'Administrative detention: despair, uncertainty and lack of due process' (London, April 1997), outlines a number of trends in Israel's use of detention to hold Palestinians for prolonged periods. First, the few legal means afforded the detainee (such as the right to appeal a detention order) are entirely unsatisfactory and ineffectual, a fact borne out by the mass boycott of these appeal hearings by all Palestinian detainees since August 1996; second, Amnesty asserts that detention serves a 'punitive rather than preventative purpose', despite Israel's claims to the contrary; and finally, increasing numbers of detainees are not suspected of any military or terrorist activity, and are instead prisoners of conscience, incarcerated for political views which are overwhelmingly anti-Oslo.

13. For the illegality of this deportation and an overview of the deleterious effects of administrative detention, see the report of Israeli human rights group B'Tselem, 'Prisoners of peace: administrative detention during the Oslo process' (Jerusalem, July 1997). The report notes that administrative detention is permitted by international law, but only as an 'exceptional preventive measure', for short periods: 'Administrative detention in the Occupied Territories does not meet these requirements.'

14. The use of torture was upheld in an extraordinary decision by the Israeli Supreme Court on 15 November 1996. The court had been asked to approve an application from the Israeli Shabak for permission to use more extreme forms of torture against a Palestinian student, Muhammed Hamdan, who had been held in administrative detention without charge for four weeks. The court obliged, concurring with the secret police that Hamdan's torture was necessary to avert the loss of more lives. The so-called 'Hamdan decision' was the cause of a new wave of pressure from international human rights groups on Israel's institutionalised endorsement of torture. (See the report by LAW, 'Israeli High Court sanctions torture of Palestinian', 19 November 1996.)

15. An up-to-date guide to the practices and excuses of Israeli torturers and government ministers was offered by the United Nations Committee Against Torture, which after a lengthy investigation condemned Israel's actions and found it guilty of numerous violations of the 1987 UN Convention Against Torture, to which Israel is a signatory: 'Conclusions and recommendations of the Committee against Torture (295th and 296th meetings)', 7 May 1997. David Bar-Ilan, spokesman for Binyamin Netanyahu, claimed that the Committee's report 'sentences to death future innocent victims of terrorism', but none of the Israeli officials questioned could deny that at least eleven Palestinians had been killed under torture in Israeli cells since 1987, in addition to the hundreds who suffered serious physical and psychological injury. The report and various depositions were summarised in a Reuters article, 10 May 1997. See also the 'Oral statement to the United Nations Commission on Human Rights in the Israeli Occupied Territories' delivered by Amnesty International on 11 March 1997, which details the quasi-legal provisions underwriting the use of torture in Israel and dismisses Israel's 'ticking bomb' justification.

16. For example, seven relatives of Moheiddin Esharif, a suspected member

of Hamas, were arrested and tortured in February 1996 after the first bus bombings. *The Observer*, 18 February 1996.

17. *Occupier's Law*, pp. 91–100, discusses the entirely separate legal framework governing Israeli settlers in the occupied territories; Shehadeh describes the settlements as 'de facto extensions of Israel'. In fact, Israel's convenient application of some aspects of Jordanian and even Ottoman law in the case of land confiscation means that there are more than two unequal legal systems in play in the occupied territories. To accuse Israel of double standards is to underestimate the actuality.

18. See the Human Rights Watch report 'The Draft Law to halt Palestinian torture claims' (Washington, July 1997), and B'Tselem's urgent action report, 'Law denying Palestinians compensation passes first reading in Knesset', 31 July 1997.

19. Amnesty International's report, 'Palestinian Authority: prolonged political detention, torture and unfair trials' (London, December 1996), makes clear that, in numerous respects, the Palestinian security services have taken on exactly the same role formerly occupied by Israel. Some prisoners even found themselves spending time in the same prison under different regimes, having been detained by Israel and later by the PA in the same building.

20. The influence of 'external political pressure, in particular from Israel and the United States', is acknowledged in Amnesty's report as a factor encouraging the PA's human rights abuses: 'Time and time again wide-ranging measures to prevent violent attacks on Israeli targets have been a prerequisite for the implementation of what has been already agreed, or in order to progress to the next stage of the peace process. Such pressure has undoubtedly been a factor in encouraging the Palestinian Authority to carry out large-scale arbitrary arrests over the past two years', p. 1. See also Samih Muhsen's report for LAW, 'Freedom of press and opinion under the Palestinian Authority' (Jerusalem, June 1996), pp. 46–7.

21. Gore described the military courts as 'an important step forward in helping to build confidence in the peace process', even though human rights groups had already protested openly about the coercive and unfair nature of these courts. 'PLO crackdown: Arafat vows to squeeze saboteurs of peace', Newsday, 25 March 1995. Four months later, former Palestinian negotiator Hanan Ashrawi viewed the first abuses of these courts with dismay: 'I found it ironic that Al Gore congratulated Chairman Arafat on establishing the state security court which was viewed by the Palestinians as a major threat to their own civil rights and liberties.' ('PLO accused of human rights abuses in Gaza', Reuters, 2 July 1995.)

22. George's letter pointed out that Israel's own violations of human rights were at least as worthy of condemnation as 'Palestinian terror', particularly in the light of its collective punishment of the Palestinian people during the complete closure of February and March 1996: for George, the US 'should take the lead in condemning collective punishment, torture and ill-treatment, arbit-

rary arrests, and denial of fundamental due process rights by countries that purport to subscribe to the rule of law.' (Letter to Warren Christopher, Human Rights Watch press release, 3 April 1996.)

23. See *The New York Times* report on Madeleine Albright's visit to Israel and the occupied territories, 13 September 1997, for a typical encapsulation of US–Israeli demands that Arafat 'get tough with terror'. The exasperation of Palestinian officials at this repeated request is also recorded. Testimony gathered by Amnesty suggests that many of the 'confessions' obtained under torture are regarded by torturers not as sincere expressions of guilt, but as politically useful material which might mollify Israel: one detainee recalled the following explanation from his torturer: 'We want to show the Israelis we have caught the killer of the [murdered Jewish] settler. If you confess, your sentence will be very light, for ten years or so, and after a month we will release you.' ('Palestinian Authority' Amnesty Report, p. 20.)

24. Netanyahu's spokesman, Moshe Fogel, appears to have coined the 'green light' accusation in an interview given on the day of the Tel Aviv attack (AP, 21 March 1997). The phrase was then picked up by Netanyahu himself (Reuters, 23 March 1997) and contorted bizarrely by Madeleine Albright in an interview with the American CBS news show, Face the Nation, on 23 March: 'There is clearly a perception of the green light but no concrete evidence.' The mere possibility of a green light was enough to send the enormously pro-Israel American Congress into apoplexy, with Arlen Specter, head of the Senate Intelligence Committee, and Newt Gingrich demanding that aid to the Palestinian Authority be cut off until an American team could establish the colour of the light that Arafat had allegedly given (*Arutz 7* (Hebrew), 26 March 1997); the following day, *Arutz 7* reported that the US State Department had apologised in secret to Israel for not accepting the 'green light' accusations sooner.

25. In the language of Israel, of course, the released detainees become something immeasurably worse; in his 'green light' speech mentioned above, Moshe Fogel spoke of 'over a hundred hardened terrorists' leaving their cells over the course of ten days, no doubt bound for the pedestrian areas of Israel's cities.

26. See Madeleine Albright's interview with Margaret Warner on The News Hour with Jim Lehrer, PBS, 7 August 1997. Albright stated that the US wanted Arafat to 'make a 100 percent effort in terms of arresting people and keeping them arrested, not having a revolving door.' Secretary Albright did not elaborate on the judicial implications of 'keeping them arrested', a practice which usually involves the violation of international human rights standards rather than the fair application of law.

27. Amnesty's report on 'prolonged political detention, torture and unfair trials' under the PA makes clear that the greatest human rights abuses in PA areas follow close on the heels of violent attacks on Israel; Arafat rounded up some 1200 people after the bus bombs of February and March 1996 alone. With Israel detaining another 300 in the areas under its control, the combined

operation resembled Israel's mass arrests from the intifada days, when thousands of Palestinians were in administrative detention at any one time; under Oslo, however, the bulk of this work has been contracted out to the Palestinians themselves (see p. 11; see also, p. 2 of the April 1997 report on Israel, 'Administrative detention', for numbers of detainees during the intifada).

28. This summary is based on: Shehadeh's *Occupier's Law* and *The Law of the Land* (Jerusalem: PASSIA, 1993); the essays collected in Emma Playfair (ed.), *International Law and the Administration of Occupied Territories* (Oxford: Oxford University Press, 1992); Ian Lustick's 'Israel and the West Bank after Elon Moreh: the mechanics of de facto annexation', in Lustick (ed.), *Economic, Legal and Demographic Dimensions of Arab–Israeli Relations* (London: Garland Publishing, 1994); John Quigley, *Palestine and Israel: A Challenge to Justice* (Durham: Duke University Press, 1990), especially pp. 174–81; and Aronson, *Israel, Palestinians and the Intifada*, pp. 108–16.

29. State Land was the most important means of acquiring Palestinian territory, but by no means the only one. For a more detailed discussion of the issue, and a catalogue of the various Israeli techniques of expropriation, see Anthony Coon, *Town Planning under Military Occupation* (Aldershot, England: Dartmouth Publishing, 1992), pp. 158–67.

30. The Bedouin living near the Jewish settlement of Ma'ale Adumim, east of Jerusalem, were the victims of this particular policy, since their land had been alternately cultivated and used for grazing. They were eventually evicted by the Israeli army in late 1996 and early 1997; see, 'Israel evicts Bedouin to expand Jewish settlement', Reuters, 19 February 1997.

31. On the Supreme Court's acquiescence in unjust land confiscation, see Shehadeh, 'The legislative stages of Israeli military occupation', in *International Law and the Administration of Occupied Territories*, pp. 151–67. Ironically, it was the Supreme Court's ruling in the 1979 Elon Moreh case – finding illegal Israel's latest efforts to seize a large area of the West Bank for settlement building under the pretext of military necessity – that forced the Israeli government to adopt the State Land excuse instead. Since 1981, the Supreme Court has regularly defended this alternative means of stealing land. See: 'Israeli government speeds acquisition of disputed West Bank land', *Washington Post*, 10 February 1981; 'Israel changing face of West Bank', *New York Times*, 12 September 1982; and, for a detailed legal report into the working of the Supreme Court on state land cases, 'Acquiring state lands not prescriptive', *Jerusalem Post*, 4 May 1992.

32. See, for example, the fate of Atallah Amira, fatally wounded in the chest after being shot by the Israeli army whilst protesting peacefully at the confiscation of his land near the village of Na'alin and the new Israeli settlement of Kiryat Sefer: 'Dying for the land', *Newsday*, 25 November 1996.

33. Speaker of the House of Representatives Newt Gingrich, for example, attacked the 'Nazi-like' practices of the Palestinian Authority, calling for its grants from the US to be cut off. Without any apparent irony, he referred to the Palestinian actions as 'an egregious violation of human rights and of

international norms', a charge more usually levelled at Israel by the United Nations and international NGOs for its long and brutal occupation and colonisation of the West Bank and Gaza. ('Gingrich slams killings of land dealers', *Jerusalem Post*, 12 June 1997.)

34. This point is excellently made by LAW's press releases on the subject: 'LAW statement on the death penalty and land sales', 21 May 1997; and 'LAW's statement on the prohibition of the sale of Palestinian land to Jews', 7 June 1997. LAW condemns the use of the death penalty, but supports a legal system which considers Palestinian land sales to Israeli Jews as a serious crime.

35. An excellent overview of the demolition issue is provided by LAW's report 'Bulldozed into the cantons: Israel's policy of house demolition in the West Bank since Oslo' (Jerusalem, November 1997).

36. See Coon, pp. 107ff. LAW's report 'Bulldozed into the cantons' observes that Israeli planners have refused to grant permission for villages to expand beyond limits set in the early 1980s or before, so that new houses are all vulnerable to demolition. This is, of course, the perfect opposite of Israel's insistence that its own (illegally built) settlements should be given even more land for 'natural growth'.

37. After the demolition of nine houses in one day in August 1997, spokespeople from the Israeli Civil Administration and Jerusalem Municipality told the press that bulldozers had merely been 'enforcing building regulations' in areas 'not designated for housing' (BBC World Service News, 13 August 1997). For an extended discussion of the racist law by which Israel plans and demolishes in the occupied territories, see 'Bulldozed into the cantons'.

38. House demolitions increased alarmingly in August and September 1997, with some observers concluding that Israel sought to 'cleanse' Area C under cover of a full closure of the occupied territories, with the international community distracted and the Palestinians prevented by the internal curfew from mounting protests. See LAW's report 'The current closure' (Jerusalem, August 1997).

39. 'Israel seems to have understood its "legitimised" control of Area C, which was to be temporary, as a green light to prevent Palestinian expansion out of these enclaves [Areas A and B]. House demolitions play an important role in enforcing this.' ('Bulldozed into the cantons'.)

40. 'Israel evicts bedouin to expand Jewish settlement', Reuters, 17 January 1997. See also LAW's press release on the demolition of houses in Area C near Hebron: 'Ethnic cleansing campaign intensifies', 6 August 1997. LAW's 'Bulldozed into the cantons' report concludes: 'Israel's house demolition policy has no reasonable legal justification and can only be seen as a political act. It is part of a larger strategy to turn the West Bank into an Apartheid-like patchwork of disjointed Arab "self-rule" cantons surrounded by areas dominated by an Israeli settler and army presence that Israel can easily annex in any final settlement.'

41. Aronson, p. 338.

42. See: 'IDF destroys TA bomber's home', *Jerusalem Post*, 1 April 1997; and LAW's press release, 'Israeli High Court approves demolition of house of alleged bomber', 30 March 1997. President Barak argued that the demolition was not a form of collective punishment but rather a legitimate 'deterrent' against future attacks. This was too much even for one of his fellow judges. Despite Barak's regular interpretations of law as an instrument of collective punishment or torture, he continues to enjoy the hospitality of Yale Law School, which continues to send its finest students to clerk in Barak's Supreme Court in Israel, where they can learn about these legal verdicts from their author directly. Yale's record for rehabilitating such figures is worse than most US colleges; it also confers respectability on Eugene Rostow, whose eccentric interpretation of UN Resolution 242 as allowing Israel to expand its settlements indefinitely is routinely cited by the Israeli government to justify its illegal actions. (Chomsky, *Deterring Democracy*, pp. 428–9.)

43. See Sharif S. Elmusa, 'The Israeli–Palestinian water dispute can be resolved', *Palestine–Israel Journal*, Vol. 1, No. 3 (Summer 1994), pp. 18–26.

44. See LAW's report, 'Water quality in the West Bank: a scientific report on the status of West Bank groundwater' (Jerusalem, October 1996).

45. 'Israel – the land and its significance', *Jerusalem Post*, 10 August 1990. See also Noam Chomsky's *World Orders Old and New*, p. 211, which suggests that as much as 40% of Israel's water supply is derived from reserves captured in 1967, which would cost around $1 billion per year to replace. In the epilogue to the 1996 edition of the same book, pp. 284-6, the various inequities of Oslo II's water provisions are discussed.

46. See David Newman, *Population, Settlement and Conflict: Israel and the West Bank* (Cambridge: Cambridge University Press, 1991), esp. pp. 31 and 36–7, on settlers as commuters and settlements as suburbs.

47. For an example of the effects of closure on Bethlehem and its tourist economy, see 'After four weeks, Israel ends its blockade of Bethlehem', *International Herald Tribune*, 28 August 1997.

48. See 'Arafat says Israeli settlements pulverise peace', Reuters, 1 March 1997; and 'Israeli isolation squeezes the life and peace out of Bethlehem', *Independent*, 27 August 1997.

49. The Israeli government published a defence of its new settlement – 'Har Homa: legal aspects' – on 3 March 1997, maintaining that 'the approval of the Har Homa project and its implementation do not constitute any violation of these [Oslo] agreements'.

50. As Sara Roy points out, however, the notion of political independence for Gaza immediately concerned those who realised that Gaza had become completely dependent economically upon Israel. Separation was not the cure for Gaza's many ills. (See *The Gaza Strip*, p. 323 ff.)

51. See Uri Davis, 'Why Gaza is still under Israeli control', *Middle East International*, 21 October 1994. Davis notes the newly 'liberated' self-rule area 'remains under physical Israeli occupation'.

52. Roy observes that 'the disparities in land allocations between Jews and Arabs are mirrored almost surrealistically in the physical contrast between residential areas'. The settlements, with their swimming pools, 'carefully manicured lawns' and riding stables, are 'surrounded by electrified security fences or concertina wire, as if to insulate them from the sprawl and squalor of the rest of the Strip'. (*The Gaza Strip*, p. 176.)

53. Ibid., pp. 175–81.

54. Aside from the intifada, which began in the area immediately adjacent to one of the Jewish settlements in Gaza after the killing of four Palestinians by a truck driven by an Israeli soldier, the settlement of Gush Katif has been a persistent flashpoint throughout the Oslo process. See 'Government demands PA quell riots' (*Jerusalem Post*, 3 July 1997); and 'Gaza bombs latest in string of deadly blasts' (Reuters, 1 April 1997), for a catalogue of recent Gush Katif disturbances dating back to the Israeli army's 'withdrawal' from the Strip in 1994.

55. The best introduction to the Gaza students problem is Bir Zeit University's 'Background guide to the issues confronting Gaza students' (Bir Zeit, November 1996). The campaign to guarantee academic freedom for Gaza students won the backing of Israeli groups (such as B'Tselem) as well as international organisations (such as Human Rights Watch).

56. The Israeli policy of total closure was upheld, even after protests from academics and students from all over the world, including Israel; on the day that an international petition was submitted to Israeli embassies across the world condemning the policy of collective punishment, a spokesperson for Binyamin Netanyahu told the BBC that not a single Gaza student could be allowed to study in the West Bank, since the students 'meet the profile of terrorists'. (BBC World Service News, 4 March 1997.)

57. See supra note 5.

58. On the special circumstances of Gaza's economic deprivation under Oslo, see the *Report of the Director-General* of the ILO, pp. 22ff.

5 *Jerusalem*

Jerusalem is literally and figuratively at the centre of the Israeli–Palestinian dispute. In the literal sense, the city lies between the West Bank and 1949-Israel and was the location of fierce fighting in 1967 as Israel took over the Palestinian territories. In the abstract, Jerusalem's religious and historical heritage has confirmed its importance for both peoples, persuading the respective leaderships that their states could only be run from Jerusalem. Recent events have proved that Jerusalem's disputed status remains a source of conflict; from the bombings that have regularly disrupted its Jewish areas, to the violence of September 1996 which killed scores of Palestinian civilians, the lack of an equitable agreement between Israelis and Palestinians has been obvious to even the most casual observer.

Given the unresolved nature of the political arrangement in Jerusalem, which, for the last thirty years, has been administered exclusively by Israel, it is surprising that the city does not form an essential part of the current Oslo agreements. Jerusalem is another 'permanent status' issue, postponed until the final round of talks and currently not covered by any of the Oslo Accords.[1] The reason for this exclusion is that Israel does not recognise its occupation of Arab East Jerusalem as a temporary one, which at least it has done in some parts of the West Bank and Gaza Strip. As we will see, even the most liberal of mainstream Israeli politicians have insisted on retaining control of all of Jerusalem, regardless of Palestinian claims or the edicts of the international community. If we take these politicians at their word, and look carefully at the huge numbers of Jewish neighbourhoods built since 1967 on occupied Palestinian land in Jerusalem, it is impossible to see an agenda for discussion at the permanent status talks. Jerusalem's fate is already decided in the minds of its rulers and by the houses of its newly built suburbs.

The purpose of this chapter is twofold: first, to consider Jerusalem as an example of Israel's wider policies toward the Palestinians, especially where Israeli Jews and Palestinians live in close proximity; and second, to consider the resolved fate of Jerusalem – with Palestinians living in difficult circumstances under complete Israeli control – as a model for the eventual arrangement for the entire occupied territories. Since one of the contentions thus far in this book has been that Oslo's course has prejudiced any permanent agreement on the issues of greatest import, Jerusalem provides a glimpse of the situation after Oslo with which Palestinians will have to contend. From the examples that follow, it is hard to conclude that a post-Oslo situation will be any more equitable or stable than the present one.

Building Jerusalem

As we have already seen, the Israeli generals and politicians who invaded the Palestinian territories in June 1967 resolved very quickly to make the occupation of Jerusalem a permanent one. However, the Israeli public was to a large extent taken by surprise when this decision became evident, even if popular opinion in Israel quickly fell behind those pioneers who took their first steps in the Arab Old City early in June.[2] Despite Jerusalem's religious significance and its centrality to ancient Jewish history, the city had not seemed essential to the Zionist project. Aside from his willingness to consider sites for a Jewish state outside the Middle East altogether, Theodor Herzl, the founder of the modern Zionist movement, rarely mentioned Jerusalem in his writings and speeches.[3] Accounts of the 1967 war and its aftermath suggest that enthusiasm for a single 'unified' Jerusalem was manufactured only after the eastern half of the city was captured, the daring of the operation itself contributing to a new notion of Jerusalem's centrality in Jewish life and indivisibility.[4]

However, a clear problem blocked the way to successful absorption of Jerusalem into Israel: the indigenous Palestinian population. In 1967, the newly unified city contained around 200,000 Jews and at least 70,000 Palestinians, with still more in the large towns of Ramallah and Bethlehem just a few miles from Jerusalem's Old City.[5] If the Palestinians were driven from the city en masse, Israel's occupation of Jerusalem would seem still less legitimate, and the international community might act firmly to reverse the territorial gains. However, if the Palestinians were allowed to stay, they would threaten the Jewish majority in the city, endangering plans to govern it principally for Jewish gain and making a powerful case for a Palestinian political presence as well as a Jewish one. The imperative of Jewish exclusivism did not easily combine with Israel's expansion plans, forcing politicians to make compromises and special arrangements in the wake of the unambiguous military victory.

Israel's solution was based on two general approaches to Jerusalem:

the first concerning the political status of Palestinians, the second affecting the territorial extent of the city. By the end of 1967, it became apparent that Israel would not succeed in a discrete deportation of Palestinians, even though it provided regular and free transportation to Jordan for those Jerusalemites who could be persuaded to leave.[6] Instead, Israel extended jurisdiction of the Jewish town council, the municipality, to the Palestinian half of the city and invited the Palestinians to become citizens of Jewish Jerusalem, if not of the Jewish state. Although this offer of Israeli citizenship seems contrary to the course of Jewish exclusivism that we have plotted thus far, the special circumstances of Jerusalem explain the inconsistency. In 1967, it was most important for Israel to confirm its hold over the city, against competing Jordanian and Palestinian claims; the religious/ethnic purity of Israel could be dealt with later. If Palestinians could be persuaded to accept Israeli citizenship, Israel could easily point to their new status as evidence of the benign nature of Israeli rule; the Palestinians might even be described as 'liberated' from Jordanian domination. Most importantly, the argument for a Palestinian capital would be effectively trumped by the enfranchisement of Palestinians in the Jewish state, and the permanence of Israel's action would be confirmed.[7]

The second part of Israel's plan for control over Jerusalem involved a redrawing of the city boundaries. If the Palestinians of East Jerusalem took up Israel's offer of citizenship, or even if they merely stayed in Jerusalem as stateless residents, their numbers would challenge the Jewish majority necessary to preserve 'democratic' exclusivism. The Labour government therefore announced in December 1967 that 'unified' Jerusalem would be considerably larger than the combined Israeli and Jordanian-administered sectors prior to 1967. Israel's cartographers drew the new boundaries with enormous care and prescience, excluding centres of Palestinian population in the West Bank but including Palestinian agricultural land. Declaring that this new Jerusalem was now the perpetual possession of the Jewish people, Israel soon began erecting settlements in the eastern 'half' of the city, which had formerly been the West Bank. For the exclusive use of Jews alone, these new 'neighbourhoods' ('settlement' was soon to drop from the vocabulary of Jerusalem's planners) would guarantee the Jewish majority and constrain Palestinian expansion.[8]

Although the groundwork was laid in 1967 and 1968, Israel did its best to conceal the extent of its plans until 1980, when a law formalising and completing the process of annexation begun in June 1967 was approved by the Israeli parliament.[9] The international community has responded to every Israeli move with disapproval, evidenced by numerous resolutions passed by the Security Council and General Assembly of the United Nations. Israel's annexation of East Jerusalem has, in the terms of these resolutions, 'no legal validity'; Israel's putative capital is 'under military occupation'; the Israeli government must 'desist in particular from transferring parts of its own population into the occupied Arab territories.'[10] Although this strong criticism has at least thwarted Israel's hope that the world will recognize Jerusalem as the 'eternal' capital of the Jewish state, these words of condemnation have not brought a single acre of occupied land back into Palestinian control, or even pushed the occupation of East Jerusalem onto the Oslo agenda. In pursuit of its general plan to create 'facts on the ground', Israel has for thirty years concentrated on the practical business of annexing Jerusalem, content for the international community to protest and complain whilst a *fait accompli* is engineered.[11]

As for the Palestinians of Jerusalem, they have witnessed a massive increase in the city's Jewish population alongside a stagnation in their own growth. With Jewish expansion remaining the priority of the national government and the Jewish municipality, Palestinian population figures have remained dormant to such an extent that, in 1993, the Jewish population outnumbered the Palestinian population even in East Jerusalem.[12] Meanwhile, Palestinian Jerusalemites have been hamstrung in their efforts to better their situation politically by their reluctance to legitimise Israeli rule. Few Palestinians have accepted the offer of Israeli citizenship, seeing it as a recognition of Israel's intransigence and the renunciation of their rights in a possible Palestine of the future. Similarly, few have taken up the opportunity to vote in elections for Jerusalem's municipality, refusing to accede to absolute Israeli control. This has left the Palestinian population in a vulnerable position, and has enabled Israel at both national and local level to promote exclusively Jewish interests with impunity.[13] Although the mere presence of the Jerusalemite Palestinians is contrary to Israel's guiding philosophy and founding objectives, the greater Jerusalem that has been built around the original residents of East Jerusalem has effectively contained them and suppressed their political potential. With its control over these Palestinians firmly established, Israel has set about implementing its exclusivist policies throughout its new, 'undivided capital'.

Town planning

Israel's occupation of the West Bank in 1967 ensured its military jurisdiction over Palestinian territory, but more significant was its annexation of Jerusalem in the same year which granted planning control to the Jewish state. According to international law, Israel could not tamper with the Palestinian communities of the occupied territories, or attempt to supplant them with its own population; but if Israel could create the impression that parts of the West Bank were actually within Israel, the scope for 'creating facts' would be greatly increased.[14] In a 'unified' Jerusalem, local government would take responsibility for planning and zoning all the areas under its jurisdiction, a practice which offered rich possibilities to those committed to engineering Jewish domination in formerly Arab areas.

For thirty years, the Jerusalem municipality has used its wide-ranging powers to plan new neighbourhoods for Jews and to prevent existing Palestinian areas from growing bigger. Given the refusal of Palestinians to vote for the municipality's representatives, this process has been implemented with very little dissent and with astonishing success.[15] The process starts from the assumption that the city's government should oversee all aspects of the city's development. Claiming that only a carefully planned development could adequately serve the city's needs, the municipality insisted that no building could exist without the explicit permission of a Town Planning Scheme (TPS) which would strive to balance residential, commercial and leisure priorities with the need for effective infrastructure (especially transport) and respect for the environment. Jerusalem would not be allowed to develop organically, but would rather benefit from careful and state-engineered planning in the common interest.[16]

On the face of it, this planning requirement does not seem unreasonable. Given Jerusalem's special qualities, a methodical approach to its expansion would act as a check to unbridled development and short-term demands. However, such an arrangement places enormous power into the hands of town planners, and conveys the trust of local residents that no special interests will be allowed to crowd out the general welfare. In the case of Jerusalem, the planners were directed to expand Jewish areas and to thin out Palestinian ones, an outcome which was well within their power to effect. Since the town plans were rigorously policed on the ground, Palestinian landowners could easily lose the right to build on their land, and even lose their land to a road or similar 'public' scheme.[17]

In the first instance, no construction work of any kind can take place in Jerusalem without a permit, and a permit can only be issued in conjunction with a completed TPS. For a Palestinian to build on his or her land, therefore, requires not simply an individual request but an enormous local effort on the part of the municipality. The planners must be called upon to produce a TPS, often at the expense not only of the city but of the individual landowners. The planners next take a map of an Arab neighbourhood and 'zone' it; that is, they decide which sections of the map should be used for which purposes. Areas for housing and commerce are laid down, as are requirements for civic buildings, roads and 'green areas' in which the beauty of a particular district is preserved. When the TPS has been approved by all relevant sections of the municipality, permits for building may be issued in strict accordance with its stipulations for land use. There is no standardised appeal system or easy avenue of redress.[18]

If we can see in this procedure the foundations of a responsible planning system, we can also see enormous potential for discrimination and gerrymandering – and so it has turned out in Jerusalem. Thanks in part to the efforts of former municipality workers to expose the racism of the planning procedures, the systematic discrimination which underlies the creation of a TPS can now be traced. It is true that Jewish and Palestinian neighborhoods are planned under the same system, but there the similarities end. The Jewish areas which have grown most rapidly in the last 30 years are those in the occupied east of the city which were built on confiscated land. Because those areas were now claimed by the state of Israel, the Jerusalem municipality has paid in full for the various planning schemes essential to their development. Within a particular TPS, only Jewish housing is provided: the municipality does not plan for 'mixed areas', let alone imagine the possibility of Jews and Palestinians in the same apartment building. Thus a generous TPS in a specific Jewish area guarantees Jewish growth. Planners will concentrate upon residential zoning, ensuring a high proportion of houses by cutting back on commercial or industrial activity. Some 'green areas' may be provided to beautify apartment blocks, but respect for the local environment is not the planners' top priority. Housing will be encouraged vertically as well as horizontally, with multi-storey buildings ensuring the largest possible Jewish population in a limited area. All of this takes place with no effort whatsoever from the eventual resident, who only emerges at the very last stage and simply pays rent or the price of an apartment. The municipality strives to make the business of living in a Jewish suburb as easy and carefree as possible, a consideration which goes some way towards explaining the expansion of Jerusalem's Jewish areas after 1967.[19]

Although the planners approach Palestinian areas with the same degree of care and detail, they are guided in this by the contrary objective: to house as few Palestinians as possible. Armed with a map detailing land ownership in a neighbourhood, the planners set out to minimise the growth of the community through aggressive and destructive zoning. Thus, in Palestinian areas, the proportion of residential land in a TPS is substantially smaller than in Jewish areas; and accompanying restrictions on vertical development prevent Palestinians from building the same apartment blocks that cover Jewish neighbourhoods.[20] Instead of approving more housing, the planners give the go-ahead to roads or civic buildings or, most common of all, they create spurious or temporary 'green areas'. Planners defend their approach to Palestinian areas by pointing to proposals for new roads or new schools and claiming to have planned for the good of communities rather than individuals; and yet the roads or civic buildings they propose are either unnecessary and covered by existing provisions, or unviable, given the municipality's spending plans. Planners have advocated more roads or schools in full knowledge of the fact that these will not be built, and that the land thus designated will simply stand idle whilst the municipality fails to act. Even though the land would be open, the TPS would rule out any use except for the specified one, and any 'illegal' construction, even on the legally owned land, would be terminated.[21]

Whilst a TPS specifying road building can become an embarrassment when the road has not been built several years after the plan's 'implementation', the creation of 'green areas' in a neighborhood effectively ends Palestinian development without incurring obligations on the part of the municipality. It is unsurprising, therefore, that 'green areas' have been one of the most popular zoning tactics to limit population in the Palestinian planning schemes. Although guidelines suggest that the 'green areas' should protect sites of natural beauty and preserve the character of an area, in practice they are used to ring residential areas and to deny Palestinian landowners the chance to build on their land. In some cases, the spuriousness of the measure is obvious; in others, the full extent of the planners' forward-thinking only becomes evident at a later date. The Palestinian owners of Jabal Abu Ghneim, for example, have been prevented from building on the hill for decades because of its forested 'green area'; and yet with the approval of the TPS for the Jewish settlement of Har Homa, to be built on the same hill, the 'green areas' have been destroyed by Israeli bulldozers to make way for Jewish housing and commerce. The only conclusion to be drawn from this is that zoning in Jerusalem is entirely political, dedicated not to the service of all Jerusalem residents but to the privileging of Jews over Palestinians.[22]

Town plans for Palestinian areas are effective in their final provisions, if we are to understand them as serving only the Jewish community, but also contribute to exclusivist aims before they are agreed upon and published. As we have seen, Palestinian landowners cannot build upon their land until a TPS has been issued; and so the municipality has done all in its power, at various bureaucratic levels, to delay the passage of schemes for Palestinian areas. Whilst it is uncommon for Jewish neighbourhoods, even those created from scratch, to wait more than 3 years for a TPS, virtually every Palestinian area has had to wait for at least 5, with many frozen for 10 or even 15 years as a scheme is bounced from one part of the municipality to another. This has further delayed Palestinian growth, and prevented many landowners from realising the potential of their land. Since there is no guarantee that a landowner who contributes to the cost of a TPS will, many years later, benefit from its provisions, it is easy to see why many Palestinians eschew the 'legal' avenue and erect structures without permits. Israel has no difficulty in crushing such structures, even pointing to the law and claiming that right is on the side of the bulldozers.[23]

When Israeli spokespeople justify house demolitions, they perenially refer to the requirements of the law, and the equal application of the same to Jewish areas of the city. What this position disguises is the extent of discrimination endemic to the laws and procedures which govern building in Jerusalem. Palestinians are disadvantaged at every stage of the process, which forces many to resort to illegal building where the legal path is entirely impassable. Contrary to these Israeli claims, a racist planning system cannot be equally enforced since inequality is its guiding principle.[24]

Quality of life

These restrictions on house building for Palestinians have had a dramatic impact on Palestinian life in Jerusalem. Many families have been forced to leave the city because of the chronic housing shortage, estimated by one former municipality planner at around 20,000 units (about 80,000 to 100,000 people).[25] Those families that have remained have been forced to live in ever more cramped surroundings; while Jewish families are housed in Jerusalem at rates of approximately 1.1 person per room, the corresponding Palestinian figure is 2.2.[26] In some Palestinian areas where no TPS has been approved, and where the shortage is therefore especially acute, the density is even higher. Thus the natural increase in the Palestinian population is effectively channeled outside of Jerusalem, as families are forced to leave their homes rather than to expand them. This has enabled Israel to peg the Palestinian population of Jerusalem at around 25%, in spite of the demographic advantage of the Palestinians.[27]

Palestinians are hardly encouraged to remain by the infrastructure and services surrounding their homes. Israel assumed control over municipal affairs when it formalised its annexation in 1967 but it has never sought to develop Jewish and Arab areas equally. In the Hebrew press at least, this policy can be openly conceded. Teddy Kollek, mayor of Jerusalem for 25 years after its 'unification' in 1967, and with a reputation in Israeli circles and abroad for his liberal policies towards Palestinians, put his actions into the proper context in an interview with *Ma'ariv* newspaper in 1990:

> For Jewish Jerusalem I did something in the past twenty-five years. For East Jerusalem? Nothing! What did I do? Nothing! Sidewalks? Nothing. Cultural institutions? Not one. Yes, we installed a sewerage system for them and improved the water supply. Do you know why? Do you think it was for their good, for their welfare? Forget it! There were some cases of cholera there, and Jews were afraid that they would catch it, so we installed sewerage and a water system against cholera.[28]

Because of the proximity of Jews and Palestinians in Jerusalem, it has been necessary for the municipality to carry out some vital maintenance on the eastern side, but the purpose of this work has been simply to prevent a public health calamity or some other disaster which might threaten Jews. Although the municipality has not allowed Palestinian life to collapse completely, it has taken care to encourage a state of continual decline.

Practically, this means that conditions in Palestinian areas do not bear comparison with the western side. Roads are poorly paved, if covered at all; street lighting is inadequate where it is even evident; the water and sewerage systems, despite Kollek's papering of the cracks, require urgent and massive investment.[29] Educational provision is desperately underfunded, resulting in large class sizes, ineffective teaching and enormous drop-out rates. Even though Jerusalem's Palestinians pay taxes to the municipality for exactly these services, they receive a fraction of their entitlement: the Jerusalem-based Alternative Information Centre estimated in 1994 that Palestinians paid 26% of the cost of municipal services through taxes, but received in return just 5% of these services.[30] As Kollek's quote makes clear, this discriminatory treatment is hardly taboo in Israel: it is instead the logical conclusion of an exclusivist ideology.[31]

The Jerusalem municipality announced on 3 March 1997, with great ceremony, that an extra $39 million was to be poured into Arab East Jerusalem during 1997 and 1998 to address some of the needs outlined above. But it seems highly unlikely that such a small sum can go very far towards addressing the accumulated needs of a Palestinian community which has been systematically disadvantaged for 30 years.[32] This plan was announced to distract from Israel's destruction of the green area atop the Palestinian hill of Jabal Abu Ghneim, site of the 'Har Homa' settlement which Binyamin Netanyahu would only approve, his spokespeople maintained, in the knowledge that Palestinian houses elsewhere in East Jerusalem would be built. However, an examination of the projects side-by-side reveals the emptiness of any claim of parity between the measures. Palestinian landowners at Jabal Abu Ghneim stood to lose their land without compensation as Israel built an enormous, Jewish-only neighbourhood with state funds. The eventual inhabitants of Har Homa would have only to move into the high-rise blocks which had been laid out for them. By contrast, the approval of '3000 housing units' in the municipality press release committed Israel only to offering 3000 permits for sale (each costing thousands of dollars) to Palestinians, who would then have to build these neighborhoods from their own funds, without state assistance. As a condition to the granting of permits, Israel would implement the various TPS provisions and drive new roads across Palestinian land, thereby constraining Palestinian development and reducing drastically the property of some Palestinian landowners. Assuming that Israel kept its promise to sell 3000 permits, it is extremely unlikely that Palestinian landowners would be left, after the Israeli road-building schemes and payment of planning and other fees, with enough land or money to construct anywhere near 3000 new houses. Thus the Palestinian community, in spite of Israeli press releases promising more houses or better infrastructure, has experienced no real improvement in its quality of life from the actions of the Jerusalem municipality or the national government.[33] Moreover, with the election of the right-wing Ehud Olmert as Jerusalem's new mayor, still harsher policies can be expected. It was Olmert who drove through the plans for the tunnel opening in the Old City which led to the violence of September 1996, and who advocated the implementation of the Har Homa settlement project in early 1997. Although Olmert had commissioned reports on Palestinian infrastructure when he took office, his latest plans to channel funds to East Jerusalem will do little more than scratch the surface of the problem.[34] Meanwhile, Olmert displayed the extent of his goodwill in July 1997 by encouraging the construction of another Jewish neighbourhood in the Palestinian area of Ras el-Amud, a plan so provocative that even Netanyahu had to oppose it. Under Olmert's leadership, it is highly unlikely that the material conditions of Palestinian existence in East Jerusalem will improve.[35]

Permits and the 'quiet deportation'

Although Israel has found many indirect ways to control the number of Palestinians in Jerusalem, it has also made use of the most direct method: the permit system. Amidst all the talk of 'unified' and 'undivided' Jerusalem in 1967, little was said about the new relationship between Jerusalem and the West Bank. Before 1967, Israelis used to travel freely from, say, Tel Aviv to West Jerusalem, but could not cross over into the East; similarly, Palestinians could journey from Jericho or Ramallah to the east of the city, but could not enter the West. The 1967 victory did not remove this barrier and allow both peoples to mingle freely, but rather created the conditions in which Palestinians could visit neither East nor West Jerusalem unless they resided in the city. Israel's annexation simply pushed its border out into the West Bank, dividing the Palestinian territory and creating a new boundary which Palestinians could not easily cross. Restrictions on Palestinians passing into the 'undivided' city have been a consistent feature of the years since 1967, with a complete ban on entry, except for special permit-holders, in force from March 1993 to the present day.

As for those Palestinians who live inside Jerusalem, Israel conceded in 1967 that they would, in the main, be allowed to stay in their homes; but the offer of Israeli citizenship, intended to efface Palestinian political claims on the city, has not been widely taken up. Thus, Palestinians in Jerusalem have been living as resident aliens inside Israel, denied most of the benefits of citizenship but afforded a few rights and at least permitted to stay in the city. Although these Palestinians have certainly lived as second-class citizens inside the Israeli state, their condition compares favorably with the third- or fourth-class status of their fellow Palestinians in the West Bank and Gaza Strip. If Israel hoped that inferior conditions and systematic discrimination would soon rid Jerusalem of its Palestinian population, it has not yet obtained its wish.[36]

However, the permit system gives some scope for more proactive Israeli efforts to 'cleanse' its would-be capital. In 1967, a census was quickly taken of current residents to establish citizenship rights in Jerusalem. From that moment onwards, Palestinians have battled with Israeli definitions of residency qualifications in search of a particular ID, especially a Jerusalem ID. Those out of the city in 1967, but who could prove their long-standing connection with Jerusalem, have fought a long and mostly unsuccessful campaign against classification as West Bank or Gaza Strip residents, rather than as Jerusalemites. As Israel has increased the levels of security around the 'undivided' city, and sealed it off from the West Bank with enormous resolve, so the quest for a

Jerusalem ID has become more desperate. Business people cannot afford to work in Jerusalem without a Jerusalem ID, since they can find themselves completely cut off from their shops and offices in the event of a closure, and always at the mercy of the permit system even if they live on the outskirts of the city. Families who depend upon each other cannot rely on free access to Jerusalem from the West Bank, and must either reside together in Jerusalem or, if permit problems or housing shortages dictate, must move out to the West Bank. For all these people – the genuine inhabitants of Jersualem – Israel's efforts to break the natural contiguity between East Jerusalem and the West Bank have made Jerusalem seem more a divided than a united place.[37]

Given that Israel's policies towards East Jerusalem and the West Bank made Jerusalem citizenship still more desirable or necessary for Palestinians, the hoped-for Palestinian exodus was slow in appearing. This prompted Israel to rethink its strategy on Jerusalem residency rights, and to adopt an even less tolerant approach to Jerusalemite Palestinians. After twenty years in which Jerusalem IDs were given routinely to family members of the 1967 residents, Israel changed its permit policy fundamentally in the late 1980s, insisting that any significant stay away from the city would lead to the loss of a Jerusalem ID. This ruling was intended to cap the non-Jewish population and to give existing Palestinian Jerusalemites every encouragement to move out of the city altogether. Since Israeli citizenship has proved so unpopular, successive governments of the last decade have sought to close the net on those they term 'resident aliens' living in Jerusalem who refuse formally to recognise themselves as citizens of the state of Israel.

Since 1996, therefore, Israel has been pursuing a policy of permit revocation and cancellation which has been dubbed 'the quiet deportation' by Israeli human rights groups. Taking advantage of Jerusalemites who have left the city temporarily to work abroad or in the West Bank, Israel has begun to challenge its own conception of 'permanent' Jerusalem citizenship by insisting that all permit-holders live in the city. These expulsions take place through various quasi-legal channels, such as the application process for families to be reunited in one location. Jerusalemites who have been living outside the city with their spouses not only have had their permit requests for their spouses denied, but have seen their own Jerusalem ID cancelled at the same time. The estimated 60,000 Jerusalemites forced out of the city by housing shortages and permit problems since 1967 have found it increasingly difficult to return, since their forced absence has been claimed by Israel as a voluntary renunciation of their links with Jerusalem.[38]

This policy represents a deliberate attempt on the part of the Peres and Netanyahu governments to consolidate Israel's grasp on Jerusalem ahead of permanent status talks, where any notion of a shared capital will be undermined by a diminished Palestinian citizenship in the city. Israel's interior minister, Eli Suissa, confirmed as much in an interview in May 1997: according to Suissa, the denial of permits was intended 'to prevent a flooding of Jerusalem' by Palestinians, and to effect 'a rise in the Jewish population'. Pointing out the integrated package of discriminatory measures at the disposal of the Jerusalem municipality, Suissa warned that the Israeli government would 'fight with all our power in the war over Jerusalem, whether through this law or through the building and planning law or another law. It does not matter what means I or other ministers use.'[39] Thus the Palestinians of Jerusalem face the immediate prospect of expulsion from the city, a fate met by at least 1,000 residents in the first year of the policy's operation. As with the planning laws, the Palestinian population will be affected much more quietly than if Israel decided once again to provide free buses for the one-way trip out of the city; but the results of both approaches are the same. If the present Israeli policies continue, the 'quiet deportation' will permanently cleanse Jerusalem of thousands more Palestinians and cement Jewish claims over the entire city.

From settlements to suburbs

Although settlements were established across the West Bank soon after the 1967 victory, from the earliest stage it became apparent that occupied East Jerusalem was to be given a special status and priority in plans for Jewish expansion. When deciding on the boundaries of the new, expanded and 'united' Jerusalem in 1967, the Israeli government carefully included areas of open land which could become Jewish settlements in the future. The policy of successive governments of the last 30 years has been to rise to the challenge of the 1967 vision of Jerusalem, filling in the blank (i.e., Palestinian-owned) spaces inside Jerusalem's new boundaries with exclusively Jewish neighbourhoods. Given that the annexed area in the West Bank was three times the size of the Jordanian conception of East Jerusalem, the 1967 vision has presented many opportunities to the housing and infrastructure ministries of recent decades, and the plan for an overwhelmingly Jewish East (as well as West) Jerusalem is only now coming to fruition.[40]

Unlike many of the settlements on the West Bank, whose isolation from and disparity with surrounding towns makes their foreignness more distinct, Jerusalem's Jewish settlements have been carefully styled as natural extensions to an already Jewish town. The new Jewish areas occupy exactly the same status under international law as the most far-flung settlements in Gaza or the Jordan Valley, and yet their appearance has been so harmonised with the existing structures of West Jerusalem that it is less easy to point them out or cut them off from other Jewish areas.[41] The green line which demarcated the Palestinian and Jewish lands before 1967 has been buried, appropriately enough under roads and new Jewish houses. Israel has tried desperately to present the new Jewish areas of French Hill, Gilo or Ne've Yaacov as suburbs rather than settlements, and it has in large measure succeeded in this aim. The idea of separating these 'suburbs' from the rest of Jerusalem, or evacuating them to make way for renewed Palestinian ownership, has become harder to imagine; and so Israel has once again created 'facts' which define the political reality and constrain alternatives to the present situation.[42]

Israel's motives for the settlement programme in Jerusalem are many and varied, although all are guided by the principles of Jewish exclusivism and the need to isolate the Palestinians. Most obviously, the suburbs of East Jerusalem confirm Israel's hold over the city and support its claims to sole sovereignty over the entire area. In demographic terms, this means that Israel must maintain a high ratio of Jews to Palestinians in the city; the proportion of three to one was established in the early 1970s and has been adhered to ever since. The new settlement-suburbs provide an easy way of counter-balancing any increase in the Palestinian population, since they not only house Jews but prevent the construction of houses for Palestinians on Palestinian-owned land. An entirely Jewish Jerusalem is also promoted by the geography of the expanded city. The Palestinians of East Jerusalem have been effectively surrounded by new belts of settlement, from Kalandia in the north to Har Homa and Gilo in the south, and the former contiguity between the Palestinians in the city and the West Bank has been severed. Those who have argued for a Palestinian capital in Jerusalem have now to contend with an Arab city centre itself boxed in by Jewish neighbourhoods. Israel has been careful to prevent the growth of Palestinian East Jerusalem and to isolate it further, strengthening its own claims and insulating its preferred capital against non-Jewish influence.

Although Jerusalem's separation from the Palestinian West Bank has served a vital Israeli interest, the true relation between the expanded city and the rest of the occupied territories is more sophisticated than it first appears. Just as Jerusalem was originally expanded in 1967 to include possible sites for new Jewish settlements, and to exclude Palestinian areas, so the West Bank settlements outside the annexed boundaries form part of an even greater Jerusalem foreseen by Likud and Labour politicians including the late Yitzhak Rabin. Since Israel has succeeded in presenting the 'undivided' city as other than occupied territory, politicians have dreamed of expanding the boundaries further to pull in those Jewish settlements that would be threatened by an Israeli withdrawal on the West Bank. If Israel could succeed in annexing the largest West Bank settlement, Ma'ale Adumim, it could further guarantee that any eventual agreement would not lead to a wide-scale disbandment of settlements. The Jerusalem marque might help Israel to turn some of its biggest West Bank colonies into 'suburbs', conferring legitimacy upon its illegal actions and further confounding the possibility of a Palestinian state.

For Palestinians, these measures will be catastrophic. If more of the occupied territory of East Jerusalem is confiscated by Israel, the existing housing shortage will be worsened beyond remedy. Conditions for Jerusalemite Palestinians will decline further, and the city's Arab community will continue to dwindle in numbers. Meanwhile, the expansion of Jewish Jerusalem will have drastic effects on the West Bank. The agricultural lands near Jerusalem will be destroyed by confiscations, houses and Jewish infrastructure; the tourism possibilities of the West Bank (especially Bethlehem) will be lost, with no ready access to the many foreign visitors in Jerusalem; and the political goal of a separate Palestinian state administered from Jerusalem will remain a dream, with the Palestinian 'half' of the city buried beneath layers of Jewish settlements in a new, expanded Israel. The West Bank has already been cut in half by Jewish expansion around Ma'ale Adumim, and Israel has recently built an enormous, winding by-pass road to convey Palestinians from Ramallah to Bethlehem on a route that runs many miles to the east of Jerusalem, tripling journey times and keeping non-Jews well clear of the newly Judaised city. Palestinians can expect similar restrictions and inconveniences in the years ahead, as the leaders of the 'undivided' Jewish capital do everything possible to exclude non-Jews from its environs.

Sympathy and symbolism

It is no coincidence that Jerusalem has been the location for two of Israel's more spectacular celebrations in recent years. The year 1996 was declared, somewhat arbitrarily, to be 'Jerusalem 3000' year, when Jews would celebrate the founding of the Jewish city by King David and, by implication, the historical sanction for a new Jewish domination over the city. No matter that the date could hardly be established with accuracy, or that Jews had been absent from Jerusalem for more than two thirds of those three millennia; the celebration could only help Israel in its modern efforts to claim the city, and lavish provisions for festivals, firework displays and merchandise were put into place.[43] Some astute observers did point out the absurdity of the celebration, even venturing to remind the authorities that the Israeli government had staged a previous 'Jerusalem 3000' event in 1954; but the pageant went ahead regardless.[44]

Buoyed by the success of its '3000' campaign, the Jerusalem municipality decided to celebrate a more recent and even more dubious anniversary in 1997: 'Jerusalem 30' commemorated the Six-Day War and Israel's glorious 'reunification' of the city. The high profile given to the event tells us a great deal about Israel's self-belief and regard for outside opinion: one might expect that the anniversary of June 1967 would be allowed to slip past quietly in Israel, since the entire international community has never recognised Israel's invasion and annexation, and has repeatedly stressed its condemnation in the Security Council and General Assembly of United Nations. The organisers of 'Jerusalem 30' decided that the best way to meet this disapproval was to go on the offensive, and the banners that decked the streets of the city in the summer of 1997 proclaimed Israel's pride in its achievements and its intention to hold onto its gains.[45]

These two events give some idea of the ways in which Israel has packaged its occupation of East Jerusalem, and of its confidence that a proud defence of its actions can reduce international pressure to reverse its course. The Jerusalem which Israel seeks to export is a city under the sensitive guidance of a democratic, Western people, familiar and intelligible to Europeans and North Americans. As Western tourists can testify, Jerusalem is kept open to everyone, its central area no longer divided by fortifications and opposing front lines. The Jewish people will tend the holy sites with care, calling upon their own heritage and their 'Western' qualities of tolerance and cultural sensitivity to preserve even those areas which are anathema to their religious beliefs. Meanwhile, Christians can feel especially satisfied with the return of Jews to Jerusalem, not only because of a shared belief in the same biblical texts but because of the apocalyptic predictions of the New Testament, which anticipate a Jewish 'return' before Christ's second coming. Christian Zionists in the United States and elsewhere have even raised funds for Israeli settlement in Jerusalem, buoyed up by the spectacle of a renewed Jewish community and looking heavenward for the next stage in God's plan.[46]

Somehow, Israel has managed to persuade many non-Jews, especially in the United States, that an exclusively Israeli capital is a safer, better place than the divided Jerusalem of 1967, or some future shared capital. Over the years, the Israeli government has sought recognition from foreign countries that Jerusalem, rather than Tel Aviv, is its capital; and yet virtually all the international embassies remain in Tel Aviv, and Israel's capture of 'united' Jerusalem goes unrecognised.[47] However, the US has been brought to the verge of this recognition, a move which would surely lead to a large-scale shift on the part of other nations. The American–Israel Public Affairs Committee (AIPAC) has been lobbying politicians for years on this issue, and is finally showing results. Bob Dole, previously critical of Israeli policies on settlements, was a surprising convert to the cause of a 'united' Jerusalem in the 1996 presidential campaign, attacking Bill Clinton for the latter's failure to move the embassy from Tel Aviv; meanwhile, the House of Representatives overwhelmingly approved a measure to transfer the US embassy to Jerusalem in May 1997, with virtually no representatives speaking out against the plan and its obvious disregard for international law.[48] Only President Clinton, the most uncritical supporter of Israel amongst recent American leaders, remains to be convinced. If these latest American developments are anything to go by, the momentum for proper recognition of what Israel has achieved in Jerusalem seems irresistible.

What is forgotten in the rush to praise Israel is the human cost of its efforts to judaise Jerusalem. The tourists who admire the Western conditions of the city and the well-kept holy sites fail to notice, however, that the resident Christian community in the area has been decimated by discriminatory policies. Those Christians, who happen to be Palestinian, have been systematically oppressed by the same municipality which welcomes foreign pilgrims and boasts of the glories of its undivided city. For Muslims also, the city is far more welcoming and open to its visitors than to the Islamic section of its population. Behind every Jewish success lies Palestinian failure, the vitality of Jerusalem's rulers and rhetoric belying the utter despair of its unwanted, indigenous population.

If we look beyond the slogans of 'undivided' and 'eternal' Jerusalem we see division and contingency on every side, for Palestinians at least: they are given a separate infrastructure, are treated differently from Jews in their attempts to build homes on their land, and are increasingly isolated from their fellow people on the West Bank and in the Gaza Strip. Perhaps it is not surprising, then, that Israel should be so eager to detach the Palestinians from Jerusalem altogether, a measure which would radically improve Israel's chances of matching its rhetoric to the reality of the city. As long as Palestinians remain, they will be certain of discrimination and coercion in a Jerusalem dedicated to Jewish indivisibility. The lesson of Jerusalem 3000, for those willing to read it, is that an Israeli Jerusalem seeks to unify itself in and with the past rather than the present. Palestinian residency is an anachronism in that former scheme, and Israel's eagerness to bind itself to an entirely Jewish Jerusalem will not be curtailed by the claims and needs of the non-Jewish population that blocks its way.

Notes

1. See Chapter 5, Article XXXI, paragraph 5 of the *Interim Agreement*, p. 27.

2. See Avishai, pp. 244 ff.

3. Herzl famously argued in *The Jewish State* (p. 95) that 'Palestine or Argentine' would satisfy Jewish national aspirations: 'we shall take what is given us.' Even when Herzl began to favour Palestine, he maintained that Jerusalem was not his goal. In his notebook, he recorded a meeting with the Pope in Rome in January 1904 in which, responding to the Pope's anxiety about the territorial ambitions of Zionism, Herzl maintained that 'we are not asking for Jerusalem, but for Palestine, only the profane part of the country.' *Excerpts from His Diaries*, ed. Mordecai Newman (New York: Scopus Publishing Company, 1941), p. 120.

4. See Leshem's *Israel Alone*: the war 'led to the discovery of new dimensions of geographic space and geopolitical strength.... Jerusalem would never again be a divided city. Indeed, it would now be an even more eternal [sic] capital of Israel than when that claim was made for the western half of the city alone'; pp. 172–3.

5. These figures are taken from an Israeli census of September 1967, cited in Dumper, p. 74. The Palestinian total does not include the many thousands who had already fled the city after the June war.

6. Dumper refers both to a 'steady trickle' of deportations from September 1967 onwards and to the initial flood of refugees, maybe as many as 15,000 or 20,000; p. 74. See also Donald Neff, *Warriors for Jerusalem* (New York: Linden Press/Simon and Schuster, 1984), pp. 289–90, 323–4. Nur Masalha's *A Land without a People* is the best account of Israel's transfer policy in East Jerusalem following the Six-Day War; Masalha refers to the range of Israel's deportation options, from a 'voluntary' bus service to Jordan to forcible eviction by the army, pp. 61 ff. The late Chaim Herzog, internationally renowned statesman and former president of Israel, admitted in 1991 that he had coordinated the transfer efforts in East Jerusalem and the West Bank in 1967. The buses under Herzog's charge were 'waiting near Damascus Gate [in east Jerusalem] to transport any Arab wishing to depart to Jordan, on condition that each departing Arab sign a statement to the effect that he was leaving voluntarily'. *A Land without a People*, p. 85.

7. See Teddy Kollek's praise for Meron Benvenisti's efforts (as an assistant to the mayor in 1967) to give Palestinians as much equality with Israeli Jews as

possible: 'Meron's quick action in initiating the process of creating equal conditions for the Arabs was mistakenly – or deliberately – portrayed by his critics as "pro-Arab", though this is obviously the most intelligent pro-Israel and pro-Jewish attitude one can take.' (Teddy and Amos Kollek, *For Jerusalem*, New York: Random House, 1978, p. 207.)

8. Meron Benvenisti later admitted that 'when the city's boundaries were marked out, Arab-populated neighborhoods were excluded in order to ensure an overwhelming Jewish majority.' ('Warriors for Jerusalem', p. 317.) See also Jan de Jong, 'Israel's "Greater Jerusalem" engulfs the West Bank's core', in 'A Jerusalem primer', a report of the Foundation for Middle East Peace (Washington, 1994).

9. Originally, in 1967, the Knesset extended Israeli law to the entire area of 'greater' Jerusalem; the law was not a formal, explicit act of annexation. This was to follow in 1980, when the Knesset endorsed legislation recognising 'Greater Jerusalem', including the areas taken from Jordan in 1967, as the undivided capital of the state of Israel. For details, and a discussion of the various meanings of 'annexation' in the debate over Jerusalem, see Moshe Hirsch, Deborah Housen-Couriel and Ruth Lapidoth (eds), *Whither Jerusalem? Proposals and Positions Concerning the Future of Jerusalem* (The Hague: Martinus Nijhoff, 1995), pp. 145–6. The annexation of 1980 is breathlessly recalled in Eliyahu Tal's *Whose Jerusalem?* (Jerusalem, International Forum for a United Jerusalem, 1994), pp. 114–15. The book's title misleadingly suggests that its content will pose the question of the ownership of Jerusalem. For Tal, however, the answer is never in doubt.

10. These words are taken from UN Security Council Resolutions 271 (15 September 1969) and 446 (22 March 1979). See also Resolutions 252 (21 May 1968), 465 (1 March 1980) and especially 468 (20 August 1980), which explicitly condemns Israel's formalisation of the annexation process through the passing of the Basic Law recognising Jerusalem as Israel's capital.

11. The General Assembly has, since 1981, passed annual resolutions reaffirming Security Council Resolution 478 and condemning the formal annexation of Jerusalem in 1980. For a recent example, see General Assembly Resolution 51/27, 11 February 1997.

12. The Foundation for Middle East Peace dates the emergence of the Jewish majority to 1993 at the latest. It records the city's population for this year as 168,000 Israeli Jews and 154,000 Palestinians. ('A Jerusalem primer'.)

13. Dumper, p. 48, estimates that less than 1% of the Palestinians in east Jerusalem accepted Israel's citizenship offer, and no more than 20% of Jerusalemite Palestinians have voted in elections for the Jewish municipality; according to Dumper, these people have sought not to 'confer legitimacy upon Israeli rule in the occupied areas'.

14. 'Warriors for Jerusalem', p. 312. This policy of fact creation was praised by Moshe Dayan, who championed the fait accompli of immediate annexation; see Kollek, p. 200.

15. The summary of town planning practices which follows draws upon former municipality planner Sarah Kaminker's 'East Jerusalem: a case study in political planning', in *Palestine–Israel Journal of Politics, Economics and Culture*, Vol. II, No. 2 (1995); and Dumper, *The Politics of Jerusalem Since 1967*; and B'Tselem's report, 'A policy of discrimination – Land expropriation, planning and building in East Jerusalem' (Jerusalem, January 1996). See also Sarah Kaminker's article 'For Arabs Only: building restrictions in East Jerusalem', *Journal of Palestine Studies*, Vol. XXVI, No. 4 (Summer 1997), pp. 5–16.

16. Dumper, p. 97. 'The very concept of an enlarged Jerusalem as the capital of a Jewish state imposes planning priorities of necessity inimical to a third of its inhabitants, the Palestinian Arabs.'

17. Kaminker, p. 60. See also Dumper, p. 98, on 'strategic planning'.

18. Kaminker, p. 60. 'A policy of discrimination', pp. 71–91.

19. Dumper relates the inducements offered to would-be settlers in East Jerusalem, as well as the element of state planning upon which the entire enterprise depends; pp. 109 ff., especially p. 119.

20. For example, the town plan for the Ras el-Amud area of East Jerusalem, a controversial site of proposed Jewish settlement, is for Jewish homes in a high-density pattern, built up to four storeys high; the Palestinian homes nearby are limited to low-density and only two storeys. (Kaminker, p. 61.)

21. The village of al Issawiya, within the borders of the expanded Greater Jerusalem, offers a good example of the restrictions on land use which the municipality imposes unilaterally; see LAW's report 'House demolition and the control of Jerusalem' (Jerusalem, June 1995), p. 6. See also 'A policy of discrimination', pp. 79–82.

22. Kaminker, pp. 61–3. The practice of designating Palestinian land as 'green areas' and then levelling the same land for Jewish settlement building is common in Jerusalem. The residents of Shufaat, for example, lost 500 acres of their land in 1967 after the creation of an enormous 'green area', only to see the same land taken formally by Israel in 1994 and the construction of 2500 housing units for the new Jewish settlement of Reches Shufaat. See 'Eastern Gate swallows up Shufaat', in the *Jerusalem Times*, 5 July 1996. Kaminker refers to a minuted version of a meeting of the municipality's finance committee in 1991 in which Kollek explained the purpose of the 'greening' of Shufaat: 'Mr Kollek stated that the green paint was originally applied to the map of Reches Shufaat in order to prevent Palestinian construction on the land until the time was ripe to build a new neighborhood for Jews.' (Kaminker, pp. 62–3.) See also Dumper, p. 123.

23. In 1975, the 19 Palestinian areas of East Jerusalem were without a TPS, which meant that any building was illegal. Twenty years later, in 1995, only 7 had received a planning scheme. Aside from the many plots within these 7 schemes which could not be built upon (for 'green' reason, etc.), any building whatsoever in the remaining 12 areas was illegal. (Kaminker, p. 65.) For

Dumper, since the Palestinians 'have very little chance of obtaining the necessary permits' for building, they have 'no choice' but to build illegally; pp. 125–6. See also 'A policy of discrimination', pp. 87–90.

24. This conclusion has been drawn by the Israeli human rights organisation B'Tselem, which has identified the town planning process as 'an additional means – legal and efficient – to limit development, reduce the areas designated for Palestinian building, and strengthen Jewish control in every part of the city'; 'Building a Jewish neighborhood on Har Homa' (Jerusalem, February 1997).

25. Dumper, p. 126.

26. See B'Tselem's report, 'The truth about the "unification of Jerusalem"' (Jerusalem, June 1997), for the current Palestinian population density and the needs of the Palestinian community in the future. See also Dumper, p. 109. According to B'Tselem, the gap has doubled since 1967; 'A policy of discrimination', p. 39.

27. Dumper states that this ratio has 'long been common knowledge', but that his research revealed evidence that quotas for Palestinian residence in 'Arab sectors' have been cited in municipality documents; p. 121.

28. Interview with *Ma'ariv*, 10 October 1990.

29. See, for example, the admission of Amir Heshin, advisor on Arab affairs to the mayor of Jerusalem: 'In half the [Palestinian] neighbourhoods there is no original sewerage system and other parts are in severe need of repair. Half of the [water] system needs to be replaced.' *Ha'aretz*, 4 May 1994.

30. AIC report, 'Urgent issues of Palestinian residency in Jerusalem' (Jerusalem, 1994).

31. For an overview of infrastructural discrimination, see Dumper, Chapter 5, 'Servicing the city', pp. 128–59.

32. 'Building and infrastructure development in East Jerusalem – plans for immediate implementation', Jerusalem municipality press release, 3 March 1997.

33. See the report of B'Tselem, 'Building a Jewish neighborhood on "Har Homa"' (Jerusalem, February 1997); and Patrick Cockburn's 'Another sting in the tale of the city of scorpions', *The Independent*, 4 March 1997. For Cockburn, Netanyahu's supposedly 'even-handed gesture' was only a 'marketing gimmick'; the prime minister 'has no plans to build new homes for Palestinians.' See also 'Netanyahu wins first round of battle for Jerusalem', *Report on Israeli Settlement*, Vol. 7, No. 3 (May–June 1997).

34. 'Struggle for Jerusalem's land and soul', *Christian Science Monitor*, 27 November 1996.

35. 'Netanyahu opposes Jerusalem housing plan', *New York Times*, 25 July 1997. As we have seen, Netanyahu's opposition was short-lived. For Ehud Olmert's relationship with Irving Moscowitz, and the duo's plan after Ras el-Amud to 'press on with a host of similar projects elsewhere in East Jerusalem',

see 'The mayor and the millionaire', *Jerusalem Report*, 16 October 1997. According to the article, if these new settlements 'discomfit Prime Minister Netanyahu, so much the better for Olmert's hopes of replacing him.'

36. Dumper, pp. 48–9.

37. See the report of B'Tselem, 'The quiet deportation: Israeli residency policy in East Jerusalem' (Jerusalem, April 1997); and, for a human demonstration of Israel's policy, Thomas Friedman's 'If I forget thee, O Jerusalem', *New York Times*, 22 September 1997. Friedman speaks of Israel's 'systematic attempt to squeeze Palestinians ... out of Jerusalem'. See also the criticism of Naomi Chazan, Israeli Knesset member, 'Israel has no right to play games with the rights of Palestinian Jerusalemites', *Jerusalem Post*, 4 June 1997.

38. Masalha, *A Land without a People*, p. 230.

39. 'Israel chips away East Jerusalem Arabs', *Washington Post*, 5 May 1997.

40. For an overview of the Israeli plan, see the report of the Applied Research Institute Jerusalem, 'The status of Jerusalem reconsidered' (Bethlehem, August 1997).

41. In *Whose Jerusalem?*, coffee-table propagandist Eliyahu Tal offers a glossy account of how the new Jewish suburbs 'sprang up' in the late 1960s and early 1970s. Dumper, pp. 75ff., offers a more sober narrative of the suburb-settlement drive.

42. In his autobiography, *For Jerusalem*, Teddy Kollek cleverly dismissed the international outcry over the construction of settlement-suburbs by saying that, unlike the Old City, development elsewhere in 'Jerusalem' (i.e., the West Bank) was 'purely an internal matter to be decided by the citizens of Jerusalem alone' (p. 222). The fact that the expansion of Jerusalem into the West Bank had always been led by the Israeli government, or that the Palestinians of East Jerusalem rejected Israeli elections and therefore played no role in the expansion, is omitted from Kollek's account.

43. See 'Fireworks over a birthday bash', *Time*, 18 September 1995; 'Jerusalem celebrates "birth-date"', *Los Angeles Times*, 5 September 1995.

44. A.N. Wilson, writing in the London *Evening Standard*, 22 September 1995, was unimpressed by the celebrations: 'Mr Rabin's claim that East Jerusalem belongs to the Jews has as much moral validity as would a claim to our city by the Italian government because Julius Caesar built the Tower of London.' Criticism also came from Israeli Jews, who saw the celebrations as either inflammatory towards Arabs or simply impolitic, given that the effort to stress 'united' Jerusalem was in fact revealing its deep divisions. See David Gauron, 'Would King David have approved?', *Palestine–Israel Journal*, Vol. II, No. 2 (Spring 1995), pp. 73–6; and 'Bad timing', *Jerusalem Post*, 11 September 1995. 'Jerusalem 3000' had an earlier incarnation in 1953–54, when Israel's hold over the western half of the city (in contravention of the 1947 UN partition plan) was far from secure, at least in the minds of international observers. Featuring a new opera by Milhaud and, in its American programme of events, a concert starring Frank

Sinatra, this was a high-profile celebration; although conveniently ignored in most of the 1995–96 reportage. See Martin Gilbert, *Jerusalem in the Twentieth Century* (London: Chatto and Windus, 1996), pp. 257, 358. By this reckoning, we can expect another 'Jerusalem 3000' in the early 2040s.

45. See 'Israel marks anniversary of Six-Day War', Associated Press, 4 June 1997; and 'Israel is gripped by the curse of '67', *Independent*, 6 June 1997.

46. The most prominent Christian Zionist group is the millenarian International Christian Embassy in Jerusalem (ICEJ), which channels funds to Zionist projects and convenes conferences in Jerusalem on the assumption that the progress of Israel implies the imminent return of Jesus Christ. For their most recent conference, see 'Israel's Christian supporters say God works for Israel', *Jerusalem Post*, 21 October 1997. The Israeli Communications Minister, Limor Livnat, put the case plainly to the assembled gathering: 'We all know that the Lord blesses those who bless Israel and curses those who curse Israel.' *Arutz 7*, 27 October 1997. Although the ICEJ's theological vision is anathema to Judaism, Israeli leaders have gone out of their way to court the organisation. In 1995, their Jerusalem conference was addressed not only by Yitzhak Rabin, but also by Ehud Olmert and Binyamin Netanyahu. 'Rabin addresses Christian Embassy assembly', *Jerusalem Post*, 10 October 1995.

47. Eliyahu Tal offers a recent formulation of Israel's demand: 'If primacy, persistence and predominance were put on the scales of justice, the Jewish case would certainly tip the balance', *Whose Jerusalem?*, p. 122. As yet, the international community has not given in to 'persistence and predominance', even though Israel boasts formidable reserves of both.

48. See supra, Chapter 3, note 73 and accompanying text.

6 *The 'permanent status' of Palestine*

Completing the Oslo process

Aside from its material failures and the continuation of violence on both sides, the Oslo agreement has been seriously delayed in many of its most important provisions. Withdrawal from the West Bank cities, scheduled to take place in 1995, was consistently put back for 'security' reasons and was not completed until the middle of 1996. Hebron was a special case: the partition map was signed by Rabin in September 1995, but neither he nor Peres pushed through the redeployment, which Netanyahu successfully stalled until January 1997. The troop redeployments from Areas A and B of the West Bank were also delayed, with serious consequences. By August 1997, the date by which Oslo II had promised the Palestinians complete control over all the areas of the West Bank (excluding the 'settlements and military areas' of C), Israeli withdrawal from B and C had not even begun and Arafat was still in control of only around 3% of the territory. The final stages of negotiations, the so-called 'permanent status' talks, were due to start no later than 4 May 1996; but they did not in fact take place until February 1997, and were then suspended almost immediately. The Oslo timetable was put back at virtually every stage of the process.[1]

Binyamin Netanyahu's announcement in March 1997 that he sought accelerated permanent status talks was therefore surprising in several respects. Netanyahu declared that instead of the original plan for two years of negotiations, he wanted to conclude the process in six months of 'intensive' talks. Media speculation even extended to the possibility of a Camp David-style peace summit, in which Israeli and Palestinian leaders would negotiate without interruption in one location until a solution was reached. Given all the delays thus far in the process, Netanyahu's offer seemed surprising: if Israel had wanted to speed up Oslo, why had it not adhered to the original timetable for troop withdrawal? And what of the principle that a permanent settlement depended on the good will of the two sides, fostered over their years of co-operation as negotiating partners? There was little evidence to suggest that this prerequisite was safely in place by March 1997, or in September 1997, when the offer surfaced once more.[2]

In retrospect, it seems that Israel must originally have embraced the concept of a drawn-out peace process for one reason in particular: the longer the period before a final agreement was signed, the more opportunities open to Israel to create more 'facts on the ground' and to prejudice that agreement. Ensuring that the Oslo Accords made no specific reference to settlements, the successive governments of Rabin, Peres and Netanyahu continued to colonise and effectively to annex the West Bank even as they spoke of Israeli withdrawal and Palestinian self-rule. By March 1997, this process of fact creation was virtually complete. East Jerusalem had been almost entirely ringed by Jewish housing projects; the central West Bank settlements had been expanded beyond the point where they might feasibly be dismantled; and the road network confirming the primacy of Jewish presence in the occupied territories was already in use by settlers. Netanyahu's offer was not made from some desire to make up for lost time, but rather out of embarrassment at the degree of permanence Israel's settlement actions had already stamped on the process.[3]

Netanyahu carefully offered not only to accelerate the talks but to dissolve the Interim Agreement of October 1995 in favour of a permanent solution. The abandonment of Oslo II was a deliberate tactic. The agreement committed Israel to leave Areas A and B completely and to hand back everything in Area C except for those lands Israel decided, unilaterally, to retain. Having confirmed in the January 1997 negotiations over Hebron that the US would uphold this unilateral right, Netanyahu was at liberty to hold on to all of Area C, amounting to more than 70% of the West Bank. In his offer of accelerated talks, he offered Arafat control over Area B, on the tacit understanding that no Israeli withdrawals from Area C would take place. Oslo II had become an embarrassment because it implied that there would be a substantive Israeli withdrawal from Area C; Netanyahu had decided rather that Israel should retain all of Area C as the basis of its claims for a permanent settlement, and so the Oslo II agreement had outlived its usefulness. Instead of offering a tiny redeployment of Area C as an Israeli concession, Netanyahu sought to dissolve Oslo II and to commence talks on the final extent of Israel's annexation of the occupied territories.[4]

The 'permanent status' issues

Many Palestinians had been suspicious of Oslo's grand timetable from the start, particularly so as it became clear that Jewish construction in the occupied territories would continue unabated. 'Permanent status' talks were regarded with cynicism, if not despair; people began to speak of the 'final solution' which Israel had in store for the Palestinians.[5] As Oslo has unravelled, and Israeli actions have conditioned the possibilities of a permanent agreement, it has become easier to plot the outcome of this peace process. Based on the trajectory of negotiations since 1991, and the facts created since then on the ground, we can predict with some confidence the outcome of permanent status talks on the most important issues: borders and settlements, Jerusalem, Palestinian refugees and the nature of Palestinian statehood.

Borders and settlements

As early as July 1967, the Israeli government drew up a plan for permanent annexation of most of the West Bank and Gaza Strip, alongside limited Palestinian self-rule. Submitted by Deputy Prime Minister Yigal Allon, the plan provided for the Gaza Strip to become 'an integral part of the state of Israel' and the West Bank to be divided between partial Palestinian autonomy and Israeli annexation. The northern West Bank, with the exception of a fifteen kilometre strip to be retained by Israel, was to remain in Palestinian hands; but much of the rest of the West Bank would be claimed and settled by Israel. Allon carefully considered absorbing all of the territory (an option he rejected for fear of enfranchising the non-Jewish population) or none of it (a wasted opportunity and a security risk), resolving instead to take as much as possible for Israel whilst excluding the Palestinians from the Jewish state.[6]

The detail of this document belies those who have tried to present Israel in 1967 as an accidental and innocent occupier of territory. Allon's plan demonstrates that the Israeli government was either extraordinarily quick to exploit the potential of the June 1967 victory or had made plans for the West Bank and Gaza Strip even before the Six-Day War. Still more deleterious to the image of Israel as unwitting in its early occupation is the recent revival of the same Allon plan as a basis for negotiations to conclude the Oslo peace process. Netanyahu himself encouraged speculation about the so-called 'Allon Plus' plan, a restatement of the original intention to exclude Palestinians but absorb Palestinian land into Israel. In the 1997 version, the Palestinian self-rule area was substantially reduced, whilst the annexed territory was commensurately increased – hence the 'plus'. Following Netanyahu's Hebron agreement and his offer of intensive talks, various plans were presented as alternatives to Allon, but each made the same effort to exclude citizens and include land, absorbing no Palestinians into Israel but annexing around 60% or more of the West Bank.[7]

Given Israel's twin commitments to security and settlements, we can conjecture with some authority the extent of a Palestinian state and its borders. From Allon to the present day, no Israeli politician has been able to countenance the return of the Jordan Valley to the Palestinians.[8] Regardless of the good relations which might exist between Israel and Jordan after a final agreement, the valley has become central to ideas about Israel's secure boundaries and its proper relations with the Arab world. If this rationale should waver even slightly, the extensive water resources in the area act to steady the mind and reaffirm Israel's permanent presence. Meanwhile, a commitment to every existing Israeli settlement involves the absorption of a huge proportion of the West Bank and a disproportionate segment of Gaza. Even the most exposed setttlements have received affirmation from Oslo: in Hebron, the zealous knot of settlers at the heart of the city have forced a partition of the entire area, a guarantee of constant tension and continuing conflict; meanwhile, in the Gaza Strip's biggest settlement, Gush Katif, the American hotel chain, Days Inn, has announced a new outlet which will confirm the permanence of the Jewish presence there, again surrounded immediately by tens of thousands of aggrieved Palestinians.[9]

With the settlements protected and expanded under Rabin, it is difficult to conceive of an Israeli plan, from the Right or the Left, to remove them. The principles both of their continued existence and their 'natural' growth were established by Rabin and have been an integral part of the Oslo process. The eventual carve-up of the occupied territories must therefore cede to Israel not only the settlements but the lands around them which will facilitate future development. By this reckoning, between 50% and 70% of the West Bank will eventually be annexed to Israel, leaving a patchwork of Palestinian areas, the majority of which will not be connected to each other. The Palestinian areas will be constrained from expansion by Israel's annexation, and the natural Palestinian majority on the West Bank will decrease over time as existing Jewish settlements are expanded into towns and cities. In Gaza, the settlements will continue to enjoy a drastically inequitable share of scarce resources, and the Israeli army will maintain a substantial presence in the midst of more than a million Palestinian residents.[10]

Jerusalem

The Palestinians had long focused on Jerusalem as the symbol of their struggle with Israel, and so hopes were high that the Oslo process might lead to the transformation of the occupied eastern sector into a Palestinian capital. Israel, however, had resolved on the fate of Jerusalem 30 years before the permanent status talks began. Although Oslo pays lip service to Jerusalem as an issue of contention between the sides, on the evidence of mainstream political debate inside Israel, the Israeli government will be no more willing to negotiate on its capital than on land within 1949-Israel. As Yitzhak Rabin confirmed just a few weeks before his death, in a speech to the Israeli Knesset proposing acceptance of the Oslo II agreement, Jerusalem was the 'eternal and undivided' capital of the Jewish state.[11]

Since Oslo began, Israel has specifically forbidden all Palestinian political activity in Jerusalem and has continued its project to thin out the city's Palestinian population. Although Yasser Arafat has insisted in speech after speech on the centrality of Jerusalem to the Palestinian conception of peace, organisations affiliated to the Palestinian Authority, or simply working for Palestinian rights, have been harassed or forced to leave the city.[12] Meanwhile, as the previous chapter has shown, the Palestinian citizens of Jerusalem have found it increasingly difficult to defend their rights from Jewish encroachment. Town planning schemes which limit population growth have been used in tandem with house demolitions to ensure that the Palestinian presence is not allowed to develop at the same rate as the Jewish neighbourhoods. Jerusalemites have been forced to live in cramped surroundings and to refrain from building on their land, even when they can prove their legal ownership.

The Jewish settlement suburbs of East Jerusalem now form a crescent from Kalandia in the north to Gilo in the south, isolating the Palestinian community in the eastern half of the city and dissecting Palestinian sovereignty in the West Bank. Money from Israeli and foreign sources has gone towards the purchase of some of this occupied land, the original owners forced to sell by Israel or giving up their holdings in unscrupulous land deals. In February and March 1997 the planned settlement of Har Homa, to be built on the occupied Palestinian hill Jabal Abu Ghneim, was said to be sited on 'Jewish' land – which may have been sold illegally to Israelis after 1967 but which remains occupied under international law. In July 1997 a similar claim of Jewish ownership was made for Ras el-Amud, a district deep inside Palestinian East Jerusalem, which had been acquired by the Jewish American bingo-hall magnate, Irving Moskowitz. This process of confiscation and compulsory purchase has enabled Israel to consolidate its grasp on Jerusalem, and to claim that various dubious 'ownership' rights, acquired by Jews, override the central fact of Israel's continuing, illegal occupation.[13]

The judaisation of East Jerusalem has had many disastrous consequences for Palestinians. Those living in the city have seen the quality of their lives gradually diminish, and those living on the West Bank and Gaza have faced terrible difficulties in travelling to Jerusalem to work, to see relations or to pray at the holy sites. As for a Palestinian capital, Israel has brushed away suggestions that Jerusalem might be shared between an Israeli and Palestinian state, with a municipality controlled by a Jewish and an Arab mayor. Instead, Israeli government officials have talked up the possibility of converting Abu Dis, a small Palestinian area between Jerusalem and Ma'ale Adumim, into the political and administrative centre of the new Palestinian state. Abu Dis would be excluded from the 'eternal and undivided' Jewish capital, and its residents would have no a priori rights to visit East Jerusalem. Even the village's natural contiguity with the Palestinian areas of East Jerusalem is threatened by the development of new Jewish settlement in Ras el-Amud, which will effectively block any access to the holy sites of the Old City. Given the Jewish settlements which already ring Abu Dis, it is hard to see how the village could develop into a capital in anything but name; and given the emphasis placed by Palestinians on the importance of Jerusalem to a lasting peace, this 'solution' will fail in every way to address the religious, political and economic claims of the Palestinian people.[14]

Refugees

The Jewish state was founded on the principle that all Jews around the world were would-be citizens of Israel, and could 'return' at any point to reclaim the rights of their ancestors. The Law of Return provided for Jews to enter Israeli society as full and equal members, if they could satisfy the authorities that they were truly Jewish. The Palestinians, however, fell outside this definition of belonging in Israel. Those who had been living before 1948 in what became Israel, and were forced out after the first Arab–Israeli war, lost their homes and their right to live on their land. Still more Palestinians fled during the 1967 Israeli invasion of the West Bank and Gaza Strip, leaving behind their right to reside in these areas.[15]

The Palestinian refugee problem has an internal and an external dimension. 'Internal' refugees are those forced into camps in the West Bank or Gaza by the offensives of 1948 and 1967. Some refugees even lost their homes twice, fleeing after 1948 to areas that were 'cleansed' in the aftermath of Israel's 1967 victory. These refugees are still in the camps established for them up to 50 years ago, sprawling concrete towns like Balatta in Nablus and Jabalya in Gaza City. During permanent status negotiations, Israel may offer these people a cursory compensation deal, but in return they will have to renounce finally their claims on land now in Israel. Some families have kept alive these claims for generations, and will not look favourably on a Palestinian leadership which signs them away. In practical terms, these refugee populations will most keenly suffer the inevitable social and economic adversities following Oslo. Since most are already in the poorest sectors of Palestinian society, they will find the general weakness of an 'independent' Palestine will little advance their lot. The refugee camps will continue to exist, since the Oslo agreements will liberate too little of the occupied territories to provide for the rehousing of so many homeless people; and the camps will remain the fulcrum of unrest and opposition to Israel, as the refugee population gains no benefit from Israel's conception of a permanent peace.[16]

The creation and expansion of Israel also drove Palestinians outside the occupied territories into the neighbouring countries and beyond: hundreds of thousands of Palestinians were pushed north into Lebanon or east into Jordan, and those countries have for at least 30 years contained a substantial and ailing refugee population, estimated to be at least two and a half million people.[17] The fate of these people after permanent status talks seems clear. As with their 'internal' counterparts, there is no chance of these people returning to their original homes in Israel, which will continue to guard zealously its Jewish character and to exclude non-Jews from its citizenry. The hopes that these Palestinians may have cherished that they might return to an independent Palestine, however, seem highly unlikely to be fulfilled. Israel has so far refused to allow Palestinians to administer their own port or airport, partly out of fear that they might attempt to repatriate these refugees; and Israel has made this repatriation even more difficult by depressing the material conditions of the new Palestine such that a large-scale reabsorption will be impossible. Oslo has given the Palestinians too small a homeland to support their existing population; it is simply not feasible for an additional two million or more to inhabit these scattered areas. Israel can only repeat its previous insistences that the Arab countries of the region accept their 'fellow Arabs', and that the former Palestinian residents forego their homeland permanently.[18] Of course, Israel's Law of Return, allowing any Jew from any part of the world to take up citizenship in Israel at any time, has survived the Oslo process unchallenged. Jews from Europe and North America who have never been to the Middle East will continue to be guaranteed a home and a vote in Israel, whilst those forced out of their homes by Israel in 1948 and

1967 will remain in Jordan or Lebanon, without a place to live or a nation to call their own.

Palestinian statehood

Since the beginning of the Oslo process, the status of the Palestinian governing authority and the extent of the land it will finally control have been subjects of great speculation. Although Arafat has done everything possible to assure his people that Palestine now exists and is set fair to meet their national aspirations, the Israeli government has been scrupulous in its insistence that no formal declaration of statehood be made. Foreign diplomatic missions to the Palestinian Authority are not 'embassies' but 'representative offices'. Arafat heads a 'National Authority', but not a nation. A complaint was even made by the Israeli government to the International Olympic Committee in 1996 after the Palestinian team bound for the Atlanta Olympic Games was registered as representing Palestine. The issue of how exactly to describe the Palestinian entity has become important at the symbolic and material levels.[19]

Binyamin Netanyahu has been less sanguine than his predecessors about the possibility of a Palestinian state. Whereas Rabin and Peres kept open the option of a neighbouring nation, Netanyahu ruled this out definitively, and began publicly to explore attenuated alternatives and to offer some analogies to the Palestinian situation.[20] When in November 1996 he suggested that the tiny European nation of Andorra offered a model for limited Palestinian sovereignty, he received an official protest from the Andorran government, which did not take kindly to his comparing their rights and conditions to those envisaged by Netanyahu for the Palestinians.[21] The Andorran objection is an instructive reminder that the title given to a particular area is in many respects less important than the material conditions of that area. Although Israel and the Palestinian Authority will presumably agree on a classification to bestow upon the Palestinian territories after permanent status talks, we would do better to look beyond language to the quality of statehood visible on the ground in any projected Palestine.

Since 1967, Israel has been adamant that the Arabs of the West Bank and Gaza Strip should not be permitted to move freely amongst Arabs of neighbouring countries, even where there is a natural contiguity between the two. The original Allon plan sought carefully to insulate Palestinians with a layer of Israeli military control both along the Jordan Valley and throughout the Gaza Strip. Since 1967, settlements have been established in these areas and elsewhere in the occupied territories, and a permanent agreement based on their retention will inevitably lead to a Palestine consisting of isolated reservations, or bantustans. Since none of these bantustans will border upon a neighbouring country apart from Israel, the Palestinians will find that their lives are still totally constrained by Israel. The reservations will be tiny islands in a sea of Israeli sovereignty, with restricted access between the Palestinian areas and total dependence on Israel for productive relations with neighbouring countries.[22]

Given the inordinate length of Israel's occupation, the West Bank and Gaza Strip are by now totally dependent on Israeli infrastructure and services. The water, electricity and telecommunications networks which serve the Palestinian areas are extensions of Israel's own systems, and were designed and put into place to consolidate the occupied territories as a part of Israel. An enormous investment would be necessary to uproot these systems and begin afresh, an ambition further complicated by the piecemeal nature of Palestinian sovereignty. To build new networks between the Palestinian cities would require open access to those parts of Area C which almost certainly will be ceded to Israel in a permanent agreement. It is much more practicable for Israel to continue as the provider of services and resources (even if it has originally taken those resources from Palestinian areas), and its retention of this role will enhance its control over the new Palestine and further reduce the agency of the would-be state.[23]

Arafat and the PLO had long declared their intention to establish a Palestine over the smallest portion of land ceded by Israel, on the assumption that the fact of a state in name would eventually force Israel to make the state viable on the ground.[24] This strategy was an interesting inversion of Moshe Dayan's 'facts on the ground' thesis. For Dayan, Israel should speak softly and colonise as much land as possible, on the assumption that the lack of legitimacy adhering to the settlement programme would be overcome by its incontrovertible, material completion. Dayan understood that, in time, might would make right, and Israel's unscrupulous gains would be accepted as a regrettable but irreversible circumstance. Israel has not made the mistake of quibbling over what to call its settlements, or how to define their legal relation to 1949-Israel; it has merely got on with the business of expanding and fortifying them. The Palestinian claim, which does not have might at its disposal, has failed to prevent Israel from colonising the bulk of Palestinian territory and now stands on the verge of cancellation by the international community as a consequence of Oslo's final agreement. If Arafat's strategy for establishing a Palestinian state has depended on Israel's eventual concession of its inevitability, he should surely recognise by now that no such concession is likely to be made, and that Israel is capable of envisaging a permanent status for Palestinians which falls well short of independence.

Palestine after permanent status

To understand fully the implications of Oslo, we must extrapolate from the recent years of negotiations and agreements the shape of a future Palestine and the condition of its people. Let us assume that a permanent status agreement has been signed. The majority of the West Bank and a significant minority of Gaza must remain in Israel's hands, as a prerequisite for the ongoing maintenance of the settlements. The agreement has been presented as a compromise between Israel's historical or moral hold on the occupied territories and the Palestinians' claims. Since, given this presentation, both sides could reasonably hope for all of the territories, this 'compromise' whereby Israel is given a little more than 50% of the land in perpetuity can be made to seem fair enough. The international community, which has long paid at least lip service to the illegality of Israel's occupation under international law, will interpret the agreement as a cancellation of the Palestinians' legal claim to the entire occupied territories. Let us also assume that Israel concedes full statehood to the Palestinian entity, under international pressure. What will this new Palestine resemble? What opportunities will it offer to its newly liberated inhabitants?[25]

On the social level, Palestinians will face many of the problems they have faced for the last three decades. Although they will enjoy freedom from direct Israeli control in the cities, the dislocation of Palestinian sovereignty, because of the bantustan nature of the new 'state', will make them dependent on Israel for movement between one part of Palestine and another. An agreement on freedom of movement will perhaps be signed between Israel and the Palestinians but, as with previous travel agreements within the Oslo process, it can and will be revoked should Israel deem Palestinian movement a 'security risk'. Oslo II was supposed to guarantee free access, under Israeli supervision, between the Gaza Strip and the Palestinian-controlled parts of the West Bank; and yet Gaza has suffered enormously from regular closures for Israeli security reasons. Assuming that at least some militant Palestinians are not satisfied with the conclusion of Oslo, and that terror attacks inside Israel continue, it is highly likely that Israel will respond by closing off the Palestinian areas and imposing an effective curfew on Palestinian existence in the supposedly sovereign areas. Even if Israel does allow Palestinians to move from one area to the next, a system of passes and permits will continue to overshadow Palestinian independence. Israel will retain the right to select the criteria by which Palestinians can move around, and so the agency of the Palestinian government will be seriously circumscribed by an external, sovereign power.

Within the bantustans, it is hard to imagine anything other than discontent with the permanent solution, and subsequent unrest. The big cities are already crowded beyond capacity, a pressure raised further by the expanding Palestinian population and the territorial constraints imposed by any final agreement. The existing refugees will not be rehoused in Israel and the options for siting them somewhere else in Palestine will be limited seriously by the large-scale annexation of the West Bank to Israel. Population density, already at dangerous levels in Gaza City and elsewhere, will continue to rise without hope of amelioration. Crime and protests will increase in proportion to the decreasing likelihood of a change for the better. During Oslo, Palestinians have been encouraged by their leadership to control their suspicions and fears about the extent of Israel's control, keeping their eyes on the prize of an eventual withdrawal from the occupied territories and a sovereign Palestinian state. Should this dream be firmly established as a fantasy, as is likely, it is hard to see how the same Palestinian leadership will control the anger and disappointment that will ensue. If the international community also recognises a final agreement which fractures and subdues the Palestinians of the occupied territories, the dignified and patient elements within the Palestinian struggle will be eclipsed entirely by more militant groups, pointing with some justice at the failure of a peaceful approach to win meaningful rights for Palestinians.

These social consequences will be underpinned and amplified by the economic condition of Palestine after permanent status. Looking at the population and resources of the entire West Bank and Gaza Strip, it is possible to view Palestinian economic development with some optimism. Yasser Arafat has spoken of the Asian tiger economies as a possible model, in which small populations and limited land areas have achieved economic success with effective government control. The post-permanent-status Palestine, however, would face significant obstacles on its road to similar development. In the first instance, the resources of the occupied territories would be retained or controlled largely by Israel after a permanent agreement, with land and water at best regulated by the external power, more likely transferred to that power. Palestine would be dependent on Israel for a steady supply of water and also for those other essentials that have been channelled into the occupied territories through Israeli infrastructure, especially electricity. If the

Palestinians could attain a measure of economic success, Israel would find it easy to adjust the terms of these infrastructural provisions to control the extent of Palestinian growth.[26]

Even in the unlikely event that a resource base could be guaranteed, Palestine would find itself with no avenue of import or export except Israel. The Israeli position since 1967 has been to surround the Palestinians with an army acting in Israel's 'security' interests, and the formal annexation of these areas will leave Palestine stranded in the middle of Israel. Trade with other Arab countries will be dependent on Israeli goodwill, and the internal movement of raw materials, manufactures and personnel will also depend on Israel allowing its borders to be open. Should Israel choose to tighten these crossing points, in response to an attack, the threat of an attack or any other reason, the economy of 'sovereign' Palestine would be thrown into chaos. A factory in Gaza dependent on raw materials or imports from the West Bank would be forced to a standstill. A business in one area of Palestine dependent on workers from another would be unable to operate as long as they were confined by a closure. This process of economic strangulation has already defined the status of the Palestinian territories during the Oslo period, and any permanent agreement based on the cantonisation of the occupied territories would of necessity preserve this destructive arrangement indefinitely.[27]

The relationship between conditions inside the bantustans and Israel's closure policy would be symbiotic. If we imagine that the final agreement would leave a sizable proportion of Palestinian society with a lingering anger towards Oslo and its supporters, we can see the roots of a continuing terror campaign inside Israel. From numerous instances in the recent past, we can predict with confidence the Israeli response. The entire Palestinian population would be punished with full border closures, even if, as in February and March 1996, these closures failed to prevent further attacks. Closure would cripple Palestine's already fragile economy, cutting off Palestinians from jobs in Israel or in another of the bantustans. Unemployment and deprivation would increase, giving rise to more anger; which might push militant groups towards further attacks, which would strengthen the closure. Repression and violence would continue without hope of remission, at the cost of some Israeli lives and the economic well-being of the entire Palestinian population.

Arafat's ambition to convert a liberated Palestine into a tiger economy is dependent on true Palestinian sovereignty and massive international investment. As we have seen, the former will not follow from a permanent status arrangement which corresponds to the priorities and standards of the Oslo process. As for external investment, the constraints described above make it highly unlikely that companies would see Palestine as a good prospect, even given considerable inducement by the Palestinian Authority and the World Bank. The very nature of a fragmentary state would raise questions of access and free movement for a would-be investor, even without Israel's long history of border closure and restriction of Palestinian travel. If Israel could be persuaded to sign an agreement guaranteeing free movement, it is hard to see how it could be forced to keep to this agreement, should it argue that overriding security concerns had necessitated non-compliance. The Palestinians would hardly be in a position to threaten Israel, or to withhold from Israelis some commensurate right which would cripple the Israeli economy; whilst the international community would find it difficult to exert pressure or to query the security rationale.[28]

It is most likely, therefore, that multinational companies and foreign investors would give Palestine a wide berth, with grave reservations about its lack of territorial integrity and its ongoing dependence upon the goodwill of Israel. With the international component removed, Arafat's dream of a Middle Eastern Singapore dissolves to leave only local investment and the efforts of organisations like the World Bank to forge some regional understanding. Industrial estates allowing Palestinians to work at least for other Palestinians would be promoted, but the success of these would also depend on some Israeli guarantee of safe passage.[29] As closures become a commonplace even in an 'independent' Palestine, and the energy and commitment which now attend the search for an economic solution begin to fade, economic logic would dictate its own role for the Palestinians. Since the fragmented territorial arrangement and the limited resource base would deter indigenous economic activity, the Palestinians might be left merely with their value as labourers, just as with the residents of the South African bantustans. Labour inside Israel has for decades been a cornerstone of the Palestinian economy; under a final Oslo agreement, it is more likely that this relationship will be confirmed than overturned. It may be possible for the occupied territories' economic potential to be realised, but this process will be conducted by and for Israel in the areas it has formally annexed. The Palestinians' contribution will be merely to expedite this arrangement, their efforts rewarded with meagre wages whilst Israel takes the lion's share of the profit.[30]

This picture of Israeli exploitation and Palestinian subservience is entirely compatible with the Oslo agreements thus far. It is also a blueprint for Grand Apartheid, bearing a striking resemblance to the system imposed on the blacks by the white South African government. However, it is worth noting some of the differences between the South African example and the Israeli situation, if we are fully to understand the predicament in which the Palestinians have been placed. The most obvious difference is one of size: South Africa covered a huge area, which made separation policies more effective. The homelands could be divided from the white areas by large buffer zones, and both blacks and whites could be kept from witnessing the full extent of the disparity. Although many blacks were drawn to the cities as cheap labour, the sheer distance of this journey was itself a dispiriting and exhausting influence. Israel does not have such a huge territory to play with. From the Mediterranean to the River Jordan is a distance of only forty miles; any part of the West Bank and Gaza is just a few miles from the Israeli border, with Jerusalem as a gateway between the peoples. The size and location of the Palestinian bantustans cannot offer Israel the same opportunities for separation and selective exploitation as were available to the white South African government.

In addition, a long history of violent relations between the Israelis and the Palestinians might affect the arrangement of final status with which Israel could be comfortable. Given the ongoing hardships in the Palestinian areas, would Israel be able to trust a Palestinian labour force to cross its borders, offer its services and return happily to its own collapsing country? The proximity of the Palestinian areas would allow for the easy movement of Palestinians into Israeli factories and their return to their own homes at the end of the day to avoid extended residence in Israel; but it would also create an opening which militant groups might take advantage of.[31] As long as some Palestinians had cause and conviction to strike at Israel, any Palestinian presence would create a security risk; and since the system of political balkanisation and economic exploitation would give Palestinians every reason to hate Israel, it is likely that the attacks on Israeli soldiers and civilians inside Israel would continue. This element of political instability has not been removed but worsened by Oslo and so there is no secure basis on which to employ large numbers of Palestinians as a cheap resource in the Israeli economy. Owners of factories and farms in Israel would have to prepare themselves to be without their workforce during extended periods of closure, a prospect which would ensure that Israeli businesses employed fewer Palestinians in the first place.

We can see more clearly the Palestinian dilemma if we consider the remarks made by former Deputy Foreign Minister Yossi Beilin, architect of the Oslo process, at a meeting of the Jerusaelm Economic Forum in January 1995. Beilin's assessment of Palestinian economic potential represents the mainstream position of the Labour party, and is especially close to the public statements of Shimon Peres:

> I believe in the idea of separation. I believe that in the next few years, we will have to make every effort to reduce the number of Palestinians working in Israel. This cannot be accomplished by simply dismissing them, because we also bear responsibility for the Palestinian economy. In both the West Bank and Gaza, we must establish industrial parks. I believe that the true economic interest of both sides lies in the establishment of such parks – because, ultimately, both we and the Palestinians have a direct interest in the regional economy, until the Gazan economy will receive outside investments.[32]

Under a Labour government, supposedly the most dovish mainstream Israeli political force, the Palestinians cannot expect to work inside Israel but must instead look towards industrial parks on a new, expanded border. Israel, meanwhile, will refashion its economy to exclude Palestinian labour, with the Palestinians relying more heavily on outside investments. What Oslo has actually achieved is the accomplishment of one of these objectives – the relative disengagement of the Israeli economy from a dependency on Palestinians – and the complete failure of the other: the establishment of a viable, indigenous Palestinian economy with the aid of outside investment. The minimal territorial concessions offered in the various Oslo agreements have deterred any foreign investment, as the Palestinians have been trapped in their bantustans by the ongoing coercion of Israel's army; and the jobs of many Palestinians crossing over into Israel have been lost after persistent and debilitating border closures. The new industrial parks have failed to emerge, as organisations like the World Bank have struggled to attract international investment for Palestinian development. Israel retains a stranglehold over the Palestinian economy, but denies responsibility for the ongoing difficulties and seeks effective separation from a problem of its own making.

Thus the true picture of Palestine after final status is of a fragmented state and a depressed people, crammed into overcrowded bantustans and unable to move freely from one place to the next. Prevented by these constraints from creating their own economic apparatus, they would be forced to extend their dependence on Israel. However, given the deteriorating conditions and morale of the Palestinians, Israel would be more and more reluctant to depend upon them economically. We are left with the vision of a Palestine in economic and social freefall, walled in by Israel and without hope of improvement. This is the

Palestine which the Oslo process, in practice, has inexorably encouraged, and its fundamental instabilities do nothing to suggest that Oslo's legacy will be a durable peace.

Final solutions

The two scenarios outlined above may result from Oslo's final phase: a Palestine of economic dependence, with its workforce engaged in cheap labour inside a greater Israel, or a Palestine of absolute economic collapse, its territory sealed off completely by the Israeli army and its workers languishing in unemployment and poverty. The momentum of Oslo is more towards realisation of the second scenario, not least because Israel has already begun to replace its Palestinian labour force with immigrants from outside the Middle East. Tens of thousands of East European and Asian workers have been brought into the Israeli economy as resident aliens, taking jobs that were previously held by Palestinians. These labourers live inside Israel, receive virtually no benefits and do not bring with them the baggage of a claim on land which Israel currently occupies. Since they pose no security risk, the immigrants present an attractive alternative to the indigenous Palestinian labour force, and allow Israel more effectively to execute its plan of separation.[33]

The exclusion of the Palestinian workforce and the sealing off of the bantustans still leaves Israel searching for a permanent solution to the Palestinian problem. In the scenario outlined, as the reservations descend inevitably into unrest and violence, Israel's respectability and security will be endangered.[34] In a post-Oslo context of Palestinian protest and militant attacks, the latter virtually guaranteed by the proximity of Palestinian areas to the new greater Israel, the only solution that offers a certain outcome is the one on which Israel was founded: the transfer of the Palestinians from lands which Israel seeks to acquire. The simplest and most direct form of apartheid, transfer entails a comprehensive removal of the indigenous population away from its territories to make way for non-indigenous settlement. In South Africa, the whites found a relatively stable method to dispossess the indigenous population and to keep them nearby for ongoing exploitation. In North America during the 18th and 19th centuries, the indigenous population was not amenable to such exploitation and was simply transferred westward, some tribes being forced off their lands on more than one occasion.[35]

Israel faces a modern corollary of the European colonists' problem in America: with military might at its disposal, how can a settler population most effectively annex the lands of the native people?[36] As recent scholars have pointed out, Israel has believed throughout its history that a large-scale transfer of the Palestinians to Egypt or Jordan is the only lasting answer to the exclusivist challenge of Zionism. Given the desire of Zionists to build a state exclusively for Jews, and given the prominence of expansionist ideology within modern Israel, the presence of Palestinians in the West Bank and Gaza (let alone in Haifa or Nazareth, within 1949-Israel) has become increasingly undesirable. After Oslo, as long as the reservations corrode Israeli security and tarnish Israel's international reputation, the option of transfer will remain attractive.[37] Of course, there would be difficulties. An international outcry would surely follow, and Israel would have to find some way to deal with its own significant Palestinian citizenry, if it were truly to lay the problem to rest. International criticism could be offset to a great extent by the successful presentation of a 'threat to Israel's existence', the excuse used formerly to justify mass transfer in 1948/9 and 1967.[38] The worsening of terror attacks inside Israel, or even a war with Syria, could be presented in such a way as to make Israel's continuation seem dependent on Palestine's demise. Since Israel would certainly depict itself as the honest actor in any conflict, it is hard to see how the international community could defend Palestine if the latter's survival threatened to destroy Israel.[39] As for those Palestinians still living in Israel as full citizens, they could yet find themselves as a bargaining chip in a final Oslo agreement. Speculation has been intense that the 'little triangle' area of 1949-Israel, which contains the majority of Palestinian Israelis, might become one of the Palestinian reservations after the final status talks: such an arrangement might appeal to a Palestinian leadership still blindly bound to an attenuated two-state solution, and would enable Israel to jettison a sizeable proportion of its Arab minority in exchange for a minimal territorial concession.[40]

Perhaps the most powerful argument which Israel could make for transfer would be that it represented the last remaining option for peace. With the Oslo process complete, the inclination of observers will be to conclude that ongoing discontent in the new Palestine will reflect ingratitude, envy or blind hatred of Israel. If Palestinian militants continue to draw Israeli blood, perhaps the only reasonable response would be to deport the Palestinians to a place where they can be more securely contained. This was exactly the conclusion reached by American journalist Thomas Friedman in his award-winning *From Beirut to Jerusalem*. Friedman asserted that the Palestinians should be given a chance to make a full peace with Israel but, in the event on their ongoing unruliness, they should be 'thrown over the Jordan river' to solve the problem for good.[41]

Friedman's analysis was offered before Oslo, but it alerts us to the dangers which Palestinians will soon face.[42] If the Oslo process is accepted as a genuine example of constructive peacemaking, the Palesinians are at risk of being blamed for its destructive consequences. Should Israel finally try to transfer the Palestinians out of their homeland altogether, it will point to the Oslo process for proof that the Palestinians have failed the cause of peace. Oslo's inadequacies and its promotion of apartheid prove that the opposite is the case: 'peace', at least in its Oslo form, has failed the Palestinians. Only a wide recognition of Oslo's failure in these terms can offer a true understanding of the Palestinians' dilemma, and protect them from an even greater injustice in the future.

Notes

1. On delays in the latest redeployment schedule, see 'West Bank troop withdrawal on hold', *Financial Times*, 1 September 1997. See also 'Delays that made history repeat itself', *Independent*, 3 January 1997, which blames Israel's slow progress for increased Palestinian radicalism; and 'Israel's peace clock drags', *Christian Science Monitor*, 6 January 1995.

2. Netanyahu's offer was reported in the *Jerusalem Post*, 20 March 1997. Bill Clinton welcomed the proposal in March ('Washington says Israel talks proposal useful', *Reuters*, 20 March 1997), and Secretary of State Madeleine Albright embraced it in September 1997 ('Albright gets down to work', *Middle East Economic Digest*, 19 September 1997).

3. For an inadvertent confirmation of this view, see Charles Krauthammer's brutish assessment of Oslo, 'Final status, final peace', *Jerusalem Post*, 8 April 1997. Krauthammer argues that 'Oslo is dead', and that President Clinton should bring Arafat and Netanyahu to the US, 'lock 'em up' and 'not let them out' until they produce 'the real deal'. In the 20 March 1997 *Jerusalem Post* article referred to above, Netanyahu denied that his offer was a 'ruse' to distract either from the construction of Har Homa, which had begun just days earlier, or from the further redeployments in the West Bank, which the Palestinians were already decrying as paltry and tokenistic.

4. When Netanyahu announced in March 1997 that the next phase of redeployment from the West Bank would cover only around 9% of the territory, with not even that 9% being transferred fully to Palestinian control (some of the land would move from C to B status, i.e. total to partial Israeli control, rather than from C to A), his offer was rejected; and so no further redeployment actually took place. See 'Palestinians refuse Israeli pullback', *Agence France Presse*, 9 March 1997; and 'Israel, Palestinians plunge into crisis over redeployment', *Reuters*, 10 March 1997.

5. See 'Arafat's nation', in *The Guardian*, 24 February 1996. 'Final solution' was, at least to begin with, an inadvertent English translation from Arabic of 'permanent status agreement'.

6. The Allon plan is reprinted in full in *Can Israel Survive a Palestinian State?*

7. 'Allon Plus' was mooted around the time of the Hebron redeployment, but was formally adopted by Netanyahu only in June 1997. The Palestinian 'state', which would emerge from this plan would consist of only around 40% of the West Bank. See 'Netanyahu proposing West Bank partition', *The Washington Post*, 16 June 1997. Breathless praise for Netanyahu's 'extraordinary' plan came from Martin Peretz, editor-in-chief of the *New Republic*, who feared that the plan would come to grief only because 'the Palestinians remain fixated on imaginary maps that can never be.' 'Off the map', *The New Republic*, 7 July 1997.

8. Israel's leading 'dove' after Rabin's and Peres's departure from the political scene, Yossi Beilin, signed an agreement of shared principles in 1997 with Labour and Likud politicians which assured the future of Israel's Jordan Valley settlements. Although Beilin criticised Netanyahu's approach to the Palestinians, his plan was remarkably similar to that of the prime minister in almost every important area. 'Likud, Labor MKs sign plan for final status', *Jerusalem Post*, 27 January 1997.

9. After an international protest against the new Days Inn at 'Gush Katif, Israel', the company's president in Israel, Raphael Farber, declared that 'as far as I know, Gush Katif is in the State of Israel', and warned that anyone who disagreed was 'anti-Semitic'. 'Palestinians say hotel conceals its Gaza location', *Reuters*, 4 June 1997.

10. Martin Peretz's article of 7 July 1997 praised Netanyahu's 'Allon Plus' scheme, which would annex around 60% of the West Bank to Israel, as 'a Labor plan', pointing out that the difference between a proposal of Ehud Barak, the new Labour leader, and Netanyahu would be 'a matter more of style than of substance'. For a general account of recent Israeli proposals for annexation of parts of the West Bank, see David Newman, 'Boundaries in flux: the "green line" boundary between Israel and the West Bank – past, present and future', in *Boundary and Territory Briefing*, Vol. 1, No. 7 (1995).

11. See Chapter 3, note 10 and accompanying text.

12. See the press releases of the Israeli public security ministry: 'Closure warning to be issued to Palestinian institutions in eastern Jerusalem' (27 August 1995); 'Chairman of Palestinian Broadcasting and Television Authority signs declaration ceasing activities in Jerusalem' (1 September 1995); and 'Ministry hears arguments against closing Palestinian institutions in eastern Jerusalem' (10 March 1997).

13. 'Bingo tycoon threatens Jerusalem's future', *The Guardian*, 26 July 1997.

14. Netanyahu's 'compromise' plan to site a Palestinian capital in Abu Dis emerged in July 1997 ('Israel plans compromise over Palestinian state', Agence France Presse, 24 July 1997), although the idea is an old one. Yossi Beilin, who supposedly stands at the other end of the mainstream political spectrum, proposed exactly the same plan as part of his joint initiative with Likud

politicians after the Hebron redeployment. See his article 'Consensus, not compromise', in *Jerusalem Post*, 31 January 1997.

15. For a general account of the Palestinian refugee crisis, see Michael Palumbo, *The Palestinian Catastrophe*. Rosemary Sayigh's records of Palestinian refugee life in Lebanon are also invaluable to an understanding of the experience of exiled Palestinians: *Palestinians: From Peasants to Revolutionaries* (London: Zed Books, 1979); and *Too Many Enemies: The Palestinian Experience in Lebanon* (London: Zed Books, 1994).

16. See Elia Zureik's *Palestinian Refugees and the Peace Process* (Washington: Institute for Palestine Studies, 1996), pp. 119–20.

17. In 1995, UNRWA had registered 3.1 million Palestinian refugees, around 2 million of these residing outside the West Bank and Gaza Strip. In the same year, Israeli newspaper *Ha'aretz* estimated the Palestinian population of Jordan, Lebanon and Syria to be around 2.8 million, the vast majority of whom were refugees (Zureik, pp. 14, 18). Zureik's own estimate is of 4 million refugees in total, two-thirds living outside Israel and the occupied territories; p. 116.

18. Paul Findley refers to Israel's 'relentless propaganda campaign to shift the blame onto the Arab states'; *Deliberate Deceptions*, p. 29. Yitzhak Shamir was still engaged in this campaign at the Madrid peace conference; see his speech of 31 October 1991, reprinted in Laqueur and Rubin (eds), pp. 577–82.

19. The initial complaint by Israel was reported in *Ma'ariv*, 15 July 1996. For the IOC's response, decrying Israel's 'last minute political moves', see 'IOC scolds Israel for 11th-hour "Palestine" flap', in *The Atlanta Journal*, 16 July 1996.

20. A Palestinian state was explicitly rejected by the published 'Guidelines' for the new Netanyahu government, 17 June 1996.

21. Netanyahu floated the idea of a Palestinian 'state without powers' in the West Bank and Gaza during an address to various foreign ambassadors to Israel: 'Israeli prime minister wants Palestinian "state without powers"', *Ha'aretz*, 8 November 1996. The Andorran ambassador to Paris, Meritxell Mateu, voiced an official Andorran complaint two weeks later, stressing that the Andorran people did not take kindly to their sovereignty being equated with that of the Palestinians in an Israel-managed state: 'It is important that people should understand that Andorra is not some sort of territory. It is a country.' ('Vexed Andorra ticks off Israel', *The Guardian*, 22 November 1996.)

22. Yitzhak Rabin, for example, was careful to stress throughout his 'peace' overtures that the 'security settlements' of the Jordan Valley would remain in Israel's hands in any permanent settlement. See 'The myth of Rabin's 'security' settlements', *Middle East International*, 21 August 1992.

23. See the *Middle East Economic Digest*'s special report on Palestine, 22 August 1997. The Middle East Economic Strategy Group, a project of the US foreign policy think-tank, the Council on Foreign Relations, counselled investment in Palestinian infrastructure and an untangling of Palestinian/Israeli land and water claims in its 'Recommendations on the Palestinian economy' (New York,

November 1996). The strategy group is chaired by Paul Volcker, former chairman of the US Federal Reserve.

24. See the Palestine National Council resolution of 15 November 1988, reprinted in Laqueur and Rubin (eds), pp. 537–42.

25. The fact that Palestinians have already compromised enormously, in their loss of more than 75% of mandate Palestine to 1949-Israel, will fall from the equation, to be replaced by suggestions that now they should willingly cede around half of the 1967-occupied territories (around 23% of that original Palestine) in the interests of fairness. This will ensure that roughly equal Israeli and Palestinian populations will be given around 90% and 10% of the original pre-1949 Palestinian territory respectively. For a good example of how this highly dubious 'compromise' can be presented as equitable, see Martin Peretz's advocacy of the Allon Plus plan in his 'Off the map', *The New Republic*, 7 July 1997. In Peretz's imagination, the plan to give 50% of the final 23% of Palestine to Israel represents a 'realistic compromise' and is 'responsive to Palestinian political aspirations'.

26. Since the foundation of the Palestinian Authority, Israel has successfully managed to maintain a stranglehold over its actions through such means as closure but also through more subtle restrictions. For example, the Israeli government brought the Palestinian public sector to a standstill in August and September 1997 by refusing to pay the revenues accruing to the PA from Palestinian tax payments. See 'No funds for PA until terror prevented', *Jerusalem Post*, 7 August 1997.

27. See the report of Human Rights Watch/Middle East, 'Israel's closure of the West Bank and Gaza Strip' (New York, July 1996), pp. 44–5; and the report of the UN Special Coordinator in the Occupied Territories (UNSCO) and the World Bank, 'Closure on the West Bank and Gaza, August–September 1997' (Gaza City, October 1997).

28. The report of the Middle East Economic Strategy Group, 'Recommendations on the Palestinian economy', notes that 'the border restrictions ... imposed by the Israeli authorities' have led to 'the near-absence of private investment' in Palestine. Considering the new, draconian closure measures of Shimon Peres in the first months of 1996, the report declares that 'the uncertainties associated with the border closures ... have virtually dried up direct foreign private investment.' The UNSCO/World Bank report, 'Closure', concludes that 'the Palestinian economy's longer term growth potential is likely to be hampered by the disincentive to private investors as a result of the uncertain business environment.' Evidence of the limited ability of the Palestinians to affect Israel through a consumer boycott came in August 1997, when the PA attempted to persuade Palestinians not to buy Israeli goods to punish Israel for its many (and more powerful) punishments of Palestinians. ('Palestinians launch boycott', *Jerusalem Post*, 18 August 1997.) The *Post* wryly noted the potential of this measure: 'Palestinian economists consider their boycott more of a statement than an actual threat, since Israel can prevent the PA from importing goods from other countries.'

29. The World Bank's efforts to try to establish a new Palestinian industrial estate just inside Gaza, for example, have been confounded by Israel's reluctance to offer guarantees of free movement to such an estate, and to exempt it from any future security closures. The World Bank's Ad-Hoc Liaison Committee (AHLC) Secretariat wrote in June 1997 that 'numerous meetings [with Israel] on security arrangements have been held, but no written proposals have yet been forthcoming ... especially on the central issue of a commercially-viable security arrangement for any major issues pertaining to the establishment of industrial zones.' 'Quarterly monitoring report on the tripartite action plan on revenues, expenditures and donor funding for the Palestinian Authority', AHLC Secretariat, 3 June 1997, pp. 9–10.

30. A glimpse into the future was offered by Israeli newspaper *Ma'ariv*, 'Revolutionary plan to hire Palestinians', 15 September 1997. According to the report, the Israeli Construction and Housing Ministry is planning to establish 'large, sophisticated plants' in the occupied territories to allow Palestinian labourers to produce parts for the Israeli construction industry. Railway lines would take the finished parts into 1949-Israel, leaving the workers outside, and ensuring a steady labour supply even if the borders have been closed. 'The aim of the plan is to reduce the number of foreign workers in Israel without lifting the closure.'

31. The Tel Aviv bombing of March 1997 was carried out by a Palestinian who had been working in Israeli restaurants for several years before the attack. ('Suicide bomber: the wrong profile?', *New York Times*, 26 March 1997.)

32. Yossi Beilin, Remarks to the Jerusalem Economic Forum, 31 January 1995.

33. On Israel's shift towards non-Palestinian foreign labourers, see 'Israel holds upper hand in a battle of boycotts', *Christian Science Monitor*, 3 September 1997. Moshe Arens, in an article ominously entitled 'A call for permanent closure', *Jerusalem Post*, 28 March 1997, argued that 'recent years' had 'convincingly demonstrated that Palestinian workers can be replaced by other foreign workers'; and so there is no need ever to recruit a Palestinian again, or to open the occupied territories to Israel. Even Arens notes, in passing, the 'negative effect' this catastrophic measure would have on Palestinians; but 'the welfare of the Palestinian people ... cannot justify allowing people intent on murder to walk the streets of our cities.'

34. This was exactly the conclusion of Yitzhak Rabin's own security and economic experts, who predicted in 1995 that his plan for separation and a fragmented Palestine 'would actually fuel terrorism by denying Palestinian wage-earners access to jobs in Israel.' ('Separation set to fail', *Middle East International*, 31 March 1995.)

35. The comparison between the treatment of native populations in 19th century America and 20th century Palestine is made in Norman G. Finkelstein, *The Rise and Fall of Palestine* (Minneapolis: University of Minnesota Press, 1996), pp. 104–21.

36. Israeli scholar Nur Masalha has chronicled transfer as a Zionist political imperative in his two books on the subject: *Expulsion of the Palestinians* and *A Land without a People*. The first volume covers Zionism up to 1948, the second to the present day.

37. In an interview before an American television audience in November 1997, Netanyahu inadvertently drew the parallel between Israel and the United States by hypothesising the relationship between white settlers in Washington and (non-white) 'terrorists' in neighbouring Bethesda, Maryland. 'Suppose you had terrorists basing themselves in Bethesda, under the authorities in Bethesda, ... organising killer gangs to leave from Bethesda to Washington, to bomb your neighbourhood, to blow up buses, to kill people in markets. I think the first thing you'd say – if you wanted peace with Bethesda – is stop these terrorists and stop these killings. That's exactly what we are saying.' (The News-Hour with Jim Lehrer, 3 November 1997.) Of course, if Netanyahu drew the parallel with historical exactitude, the next stage would be to transfer the 'terrorists', and the civilian population around them, to a place far from Bethesda or Washington, and ultimately to contain them in reservations.

38. Masalah discusses the possibility of Israel implementing transfer during or after a war in *A Land without a People*, pp. 221 ff.

39. Israel's military commanders are adept at presenting threats to Israel's existence from its neighbours, in spite of its overwhelming technical superiority. Army Chief of Staff Amnon Shahak 'set alarm bells ringing' in June 1997 by suggesting, with virtually no evidence to support his conjecture, that Syria was preparing an attack. 'Israeli army chief worries aloud about Syrian intentions', *Agence France Presse*, 10 June 1997.

40. Israeli newspaper *Ma'ariv*, 12 November 1996, reported that the Israeli government was considering ceding the 'little triangle' area of 1949-Israel to the Palestinian Authority, along with its substantial Palestinian population, in return for the PA's agreement to an Israeli annexation of a large part of the West Bank and Gaza (including the settlements and settlers).

41. Thomas Friedman, *From Beirut to Jerusalem* (London: HarperCollins, 1990, 2nd edition), p. 518. Friedman's particular vision of ethnic cleansing was rewarded in the United States with the National Book Award.

42. Fortunately, Friedman's old friend Martin Peretz has given us a more up-to-date formulation of this threat to the Palestinians. In his article on the just 'compromise' of the Allon Plus plan, Peretz stated that '[i]f the Palestinians fail to seize this opportunity for statehood, this chance for a country of their own, it will be a tragedy for them. But it will not be a surprise. ... Will the Palestinians now reject all that is left of the idea of separation? Who will wager not?' ('Off the map', *The New Republic*, 7 July 1997.) For an account of the macabre extent of Peretz's Zionism, see Richard Marius, 'Al Gore and me, or how Marty Peretz saved me from packing my bags for Washington', *Journal of Palestine Studies*, Vol. XXV, No. 2 (Winter 1996), pp. 54–9. Peretz had Marius fired as Al Gore's speechwriter in July 1995 after Marius had attacked the brutality of Israel's secret police in a review article three years earlier.

7 *Alternatives to Oslo*

In its present form, the Oslo process does not provide a stable, let alone a just solution to the Israeli–Palestinian conflict. Even if negotiations continue, and the sides sign further agreements, the consequences will almost certainly be the perpetuation and formalisation of the system of Grand Apartheid which has been Oslo's principal achievement so far. In the longer term, three scenarios present themselves. (1) Transfer of the Palestinian population out of the occupied territories would stabilise the situation, and complete the Zionist project to substitute an entirely Jewish population for the native one. (2) Oslo might be replaced by a genuine two-state solution, based on a sufficient territorial concession by Israel to support an economically viable, sovereign Palestine. (3) The entire territory west of the Jordan river (i.e., Israel and the occupied West Bank and Gaza) might become the basis for a single state, in which the Israelis and Palestinians lived equally in a unitary, non-discriminatory system.

Although any effort to predict the future would be futile, in the remainder of this book we will consider alternatives to Oslo. The prevailing assumption that the current peace process offers the only hope of reconciliation is patently false, and a better understanding of the options will help us to avoid another doomed peace process in the future. However, the idea of wholesale transfer will not here be presented as an alternative to Oslo, even though it remains a possibility and does offer a clear resolution of sorts to the Palestinian 'problem'. As many Israelis would agree, the practical possibility of transfer does not make it a morally viable option.[1] It may be practically possible for Israel to kill every Palestinian, since the Israeli army is militarily unchallenged in the occupied territories; but this theoretical potential does not make genocide a legitimate strategy. Similarly, the transfer of the Palestinians, which would constitute one of the largest acts of ethnic cleansing in this century, should not merit serious discussion as a practical 'alternative' without the reminder that its implementation would be a crime against humanity. In addition to the Palestinian bantustans and ongoing instability, then, we must consider the chances of a political solution based on either two sovereign states or a single, unitary one.

The two-state solution

Since at least the UN partition plan of 1947, it has been argued by many observers that two states, Israel and Palestine, should exist on the territory formerly occupied by Palestine alone. Palestinians found this 'compromise' very difficult to accept, since their land had, through no fault of their own, been taken by foreign settlers and would now be lost forever, were they to sign an agreement recognising 'Israel'. Over time, however, Palestinians have accepted in the main that their moral claims to all of the land west of the Jordan (i.e., what today is Israel) have not empowered them in practice to regain what has been lost. The apparent reluctance of the international community to uphold Palestinian rights, even where it has recognised their validity, forced successive Palestinian leaderships to compromise their calls to justice with pragmatic concessions to Israel's military force. Consequently, the Palestinians set aside their claim for a single Palestinian state and agreed to share the land with Israel. Although both the Israelis and United States have regularly denied this transition, a Palestinian willingness to accept Israel as a neighbour has been a constant factor in the peace initiatives of the past 25 years, and remains a foundational Palestinian assumption today.[2]

Oslo has cynically exploited a Palestinian willingness to compromise by reducing the concept of a Palestinian state to an absurdity. If we retreat from what has happened to what may happen in the future, we have first to imagine a very different concept of Palestinian statehood. Palestine would have to be sufficiently large to ensure genuine independence from Israel, and would need genuine sovereignty over its territory if it were to direct its own destiny. The settlers would therefore have either to return to 1949 Israel or to accept complete immersion in the new Palestinian state, dependent on Palestinian infrastructure and resources and living under Palestinian law. The Israeli army, meanwhile, could exercise no power over the new Palestine, and would be allowed to occupy none of its territory. Although Israel's various strategic specialists frequently refer to Israeli retention of the Jordan Valley as an early warning against a putative Arab invasion, they conveniently disregard the fact that such an arrangement perpetuates an unjust *Israeli* invasion of Palestinian land. Once again, the relationship between Israeli aggression and Arab response is reversed: as in 1967, Israel attacks its foes as a 'defensive' measure. This logic is inimical to a stable resolution of the conflict, and cannot be used to justify further erosion of the territory of a new Palestine.[3]

If Palestine encompassed all the occupied territories, including East

Jerusalem, it would stand a good chance of succeeding as an independent state. Were it able to control its borders with neighbouring Arab countries, it might develop economic partnerships and encourage external investment without the burden of insecurity imposed by Israel's frequent closures. Although they would have to concede their practical claims to all of what had been Palestine before 1948 and recognise Israel formally, Palestinians could look forward to genuine self-determination in at least a part of what had formerly been their land. They would not be forced to rely on Israeli goodwill for their continued survival, or to plead vainly to the international community to uphold their claims. Given the pattern of Israeli domination and discrimination which has marked the occupied territories since 1967, this partial 'liberation' of pre-1948 Palestine represents an attractive alternative to continuing subservience to Israel. In context, at least, a two-state solution seems like the best option remaining.

The principal problem with a two-state solution, then, refers not to the make-up of an independent Palestine but to its likelihood given current reality. Just as most Palestinians have abandoned a solution to the conflict which envisages the transfer of Israeli Jews back to Europe or the US, so we may concede that the material conditions of the occupied territories shape a possible solution to the problem. There is a surrender here to the brilliant and terrible logic of 'fact creation' which, as Moshe Dayan predicted, would not only shape political debate but would 'bind the hands of reality'. A two-state solution which was not able to challenge and overturn the current reality in the occupied territories would not truly produce two states, but rather a situation where Israel was considerably more than one state and 'Palestine' less than half of one.[4]

Even in the best scenario, a withdrawal of Israeli soldiers and settlers from the occupied territories might still offer too limited an area to support a fully sovereign state. Since the new Palestine would comprise less than a quarter of British Mandate Palestine, the Palestinian population would inevitably find itself living in a densely packed area, the more so if any effort were made to repatriate the millions of refugees living outside the occupied territories altogether. The original population would seek to return to a new Palestine occupying a fraction of the former territory, with negative implications for social conditions and an independent Palestinian economy.[5] It is vital that a new Palestine is at least sovereign in the economic sphere, to prevent the development of a cheap labour pool for Israel and, consequently, ongoing dependence.

If Palestinians agree to a separate Palestinian state, they will essentially resign their claims over most of their homeland, and legitimise

Israel's territorial gain and national future. Since no other nation is strong enough or motivated to defend the Palestinians' concept of justice, this concession to Israel is probably unavoidable. But unless the model of Palestinian statehood offered by Israel is functional and viable, the Palestinians have little to gain, and a great deal to lose, by recognising it. Haidar Abdul-Shafi, leader of the Palestinian delegation at the Madrid talks, and subsequently sidelined by the Oslo 'secret channel', spoke strongly for rejecting Oslo, seeing this not as an idealistic aloofness but as a sensible alternative to the agreements signed in 1993:

> The alternative was not to sign. The alternative was not to concede Israel's claim to the occupied territories. And if Israel had remained adamant, so be it, then things would stand there. Things are bad, but at least we wouldn't have conceded our rights.[6]

Israel has, through Oslo, attempted to exploit its 'generosity' towards the Palestinians and its 'desire for peace' to effect its international rehabilitation. Those nations which had previously backed Palestinian claims, in name at least, have rushed to congratulate Israel on its vision and to withdraw their rhetorical or economic reproaches to its actions. The Palestinians have at least some agency over this process, since their leadership's acquiescence in Oslo has been read as a Palestinian endorsement of this model of peace, and of Israel. Advocacy of a two-state solution which did not truly create a second state is therefore dangerous and destructive, and removes from the Palestinian cause the dignity of opposition which it has enjoyed, at least in some circles, for half a century.[7]

In sum, objections to a two-state solution focus more on its feasibility than its prospects once established. If the reality of Israeli settlement truly could be reversed, an independent Palestine would offer an attractive alternative to ongoing economic and political vassalage to Israel. Although the establishment of this state would represent a major compromise of Palestinian claims to the whole of what was once Palestine, it might offer the best pragmatic solution in a political situation where Israel's force of arms and American advocacy crowd out international law and abstract justice. In this sense, it represents a genuine alternative to Oslo; but it would be absolutely necessary to ensure no further territorial compromises or cessions to Israel, lest this solution came to seem more like a continuation of the current Oslo process than a constructive response to it. If Israel is not prepared to reverse its gains of the last 30 years, there is no two-state solution, and talk of one indulges a fantasy which can only help Israel to consolidate its gains.

The one-state solution

Perhaps Oslo's greatest irony has been that, for all Israel's efforts to effect a strict separation between the peoples, its ongoing settlement of the occupied territories has made such a separation more problematic. Although successive Israeli governments have sought to dispossess the Palestinians and to preserve a distinction between Palestinians and Israelis, the success of the first objective has seriously threatened the second. Meron Benvenisti, former deputy mayor of Jerusalem, conceded in his 1995 book *Intimate Enemies* that the model of Palestinian independence envisaged by Oslo was hardly akin to statehood:

> It goes without saying that 'cooperation' based on the current power relationship is no more than permanent Israeli domination in disguise, and that Palestinian self-rule is merely a euphemism for bantustanisation.[8]

From this shrewd assessment of Oslo, Benvenisti rejects a two-state solution as unworkable, and envisages 'a confederated Israel/Palestine' instead:

> But there are both Israeli Jews and Palestinians who dream of Israel/Palestine, undivided in its physical and human landscapes, pluralistic and open; a country in which cultural relations, human interaction, intimate coexistence, and attachment to a common homeland will be stronger than militant tribalism and segregation in national ghettos.[9]

Oslo offers no stable solution; and yet a simple separation of the peoples is incompatible with the extent of coexistence imposed circumstantially by the settlements. For Benvenisti, if Israelis are not prepared to deport the Palestinians en masse, Israel's own actions have created a reality which can be addressed only by a single state. An article by Edward Witten in the *New Republic* in September 1997 put it more urgently: if Israel continues to colonise the land which might become Palestine, then the 'the window of opportunity for a two-state solution will close'.[10]

The chief advantage of a one-state solution is that it recognises a reality which already exists, rather than calling for the invention of a new reality, as a two-state solution would.[11] If Palestinians were able to win equal rights in a single state of Israel-Palestine, they might be better able to undermine Israel's discriminatory and exclusivist policies than if they remain its passive victims in a neighbouring state. Jewish exclusivism is the root cause of the Palestinian problem: the notion that the land and water of the region belongs exclusively to Jews, and should be maintained solely for their use, is a direct challenge to the existence of non-Jews in the same land. If this exclusivism could be abandoned, as a genuinely democratic, single state would demand, a more meaningful and lasting coexistence might be attained than if Palestinians remained under a heavy Israeli influence in an 'independent' state close by.

Under Oslo, Palestinians have seemed to demand national rights even as their civil liberties are taken from them. With the system of bantustans in particular, the Palestinian leadership has accepted an Israeli solution which makes movement around the West Bank and Gaza even more difficult than before the peace process began. If a two-state solution cannot effectively emerge from the current situation, it is vital that Palestinians look beyond the chimeras of autonomy and self-rule, and that they seek an index for their well-being, not in the trappings of sovereignty, but in their economic and social health compared with Israelis. Effectively, a single state already exists, but Palestinians have been discouraged from seeing it as such, and thus from recognising themselves as second-class citizens.

If Palestinians were to demand equality in a single state, the repercussions for Israel would be grave. Zionism, the founding ideology of the state, would have to be abandoned. Land could no longer be held in perpetuity for the exclusive use of Jews, as is now the case. The right of 'return', which has ensured a steady flow of Jews to Israel throughout its history, would be nullified. The fear of these developments can already be detected in some circles; Edward Witten fretted that 'the Israelis are now perilously close to the point of no return':

> How much lasting damage will be done? Concerned parties, including the Israeli public, the American government, the business community, and the Jewish diaspora, should bring pressures aimed at damage control. The real question is whether Netanyahu (or another leader with his outlook) will prevail in Israel's next election. The window of opportunity for a two-state solution is not likely to survive a second term of such leadership.

The 'real question', of course, has little to do with Netanyahu, who is merely following in the footsteps of preceding Labour leaders in his promotion of settlements. Yitzhak Rabin specifically boasted that Oslo allowed for further expansion, and his successor, Ehud Barak, has done nothing to threaten his plan. Witten's fear, however, is instructive. Israel may finally have to come to terms with its own, inadvertent creation: the two populations juxtaposed, intertwined and impossible to disentangle.

A one-state solution might attract Palestinians, therefore, precisely because it is something that Israel and its supporters most fear. If Zionism could be destroyed, and true equality forged for Palestinians in a new Israel-Palestine, Israel's own 'fact creation' would finally be turned on its inventor. The Palestinians of the occupied territories would represent a substantial minority in a new, single state; but with their votes added to those of the existing one million Palestinian citizens of Israel, the Jewish and Arab ratio would be close to fifty-fifty. This could offer Palestinians a real opportunity to ensure that Israel's various discriminatory systems were dismantled, a task which the present Palestinian Israelis have lacked the numbers to carry out. A single state would therefore combine all of the Palestinians currently living to the west of the Jordan in a single struggle to attain freedom and equality. An Israeli nervousness about this prospect is understandable, and itself evidence of the powerful challenge which such a reorientation of the Palestinian struggle could lay down.[12]

Although a one-state solution appears more radical than the creation of a separate Israel and Palestine, and perhaps has more potential to ensure equality between those Israelis and Palestinians who would live in such close proximity, it is also a very dangerous route which should be traversed with great care. Just as we have viewed critically the model of statehood envisaged for a Palestine by the Oslo process, so we should consider the prospects for a single state with the utmost caution. It is by no means true that ethnic populations within a single state always enjoy equality, or that enormous disparities between them cannot be safely masked or happily admitted in practice. If Israelis and Palestinians are to live together as equal members of a unitary state, Palestinians should expect guarantees and evidence from Israel that this equality is more than simply a paper one. An emancipation proclamation for Palestinians will achieve little if the new state's policies are directed towards preserving inequality by other means.

As we have observed, a single state does effectively exist in the occupied territories, with Israeli infrastructure, institutions and settlements penetrating deep into the West Bank and Gaza. However, those who suggest uncritically that this network might form the basis of a single democratic state must confront the fact that the single entity that currently exists was set up to perpetuate Jewish exclusivity: discrimination was its raison d'être. Although one could imagine a situation in which both Israelis and Palestinians enjoyed equal access to resources and infrastructure, one might just as easily, if not more easily, imagine a single state perpetuating the same inequality which now exists. An economic and political disparity between the populations will certainly be the starting point for any planned union; why should Palestinians believe that the existing discriminatory structures will challenge this disparity rather than continue to serve it?

A closer examination of Meron Benvenisti's proposed binational state confirms this suspicion. Although Benvenisti has accepted that Israel's actions have made a measure of coexistence and confederation inevitable, his model for the new state seeks to preserve separation as an organising principle:

> The need to combine political separation with physical unity, separate national self-identity with strong affinity to the shared homeland, points to the need for a confederated Israel/Palestine, which would entail combining a vertical geopolitical partition with a horizontal power-sharing partition. The entire country would have to be cantonized on the basis of ethnic homogeneity, with broad powers granted to each ethnic canton.[13]

Thus Benvenisti's Israel/Palestine looks very much like Oslo revisited, right down to the plan for cantonisation and 'separate national self-identity'. In fact, Benvenisti's vision is probably an even worse fate for Palestinians, since under this new bantustanisation plan, not even a single inch of Palestinian territory would actually be considered Palestine. Benvenisti, who undoubtedly deserves credit for bringing the plight of the occupied territories to the attention of the Israeli public, gives us an idea of just how far Israelis would have to travel to forge an effective, non-discriminatory state. Benvenisti tried for many years to create 'ethnic cantons' in East Jerusalem, hoping to satisfy the Palestinians with local powers and inure them to overall Israeli rule (or a 'vertical geopolitical partition', to put it more opaquely). Now, he would like to succeed on the national level where he failed locally. Located on the fringes of acceptable opinion in Israel, he calls himself a 'dreamer' as he floats his idea of a single, but ethnically segregated state. Since even his vision of fraternity and coexistence is so far from a genuine commitment to equality, we might question seriously whether the will could ever be found in Israeli society to effect a single state, let alone a functional, non-discriminatory one.[14]

As for the existing Israeli Palestinians, their enfranchisement alongside the Palestinians of the occupied territories in a new state could advance the cause of Palestinian rights, and close the gap between Arab and Jewish privileges. However, we might just as easily infer from the failure of this community to end discrimination in Israel that the majority Jewish population will be able to consolidate its privileges even with a much larger Palestinian population. As Uri Davis pointed out in *Israel: An Apartheid State*, Palestinian Israelis have not been assimilated within Israeli society as equals, nor have they been able to transcend their ethnic origin and act effectively as citizens of what remains the Jewish state. Binyamin Netanyahu's 1996 election victory, following his advocacy of what was 'good for the Jews', reminded us again that Israel's ongoing Jewishness, not as an ethnic or religious component but as the political essence of the state, will only marginalise those non-Jews who are unfortunate enough to have been born there. The Palestinian Israelis have made little impact on Israel's conception of itself as a Jewish state, and silently testify to the emptiness of Israel's boast that it is a true 'democracy'.[15] An addition to their ranks will achieve little unless it forces Jewish Israelis to set aside the fiction that they live in an exclusively Jewish state, a psychological and philosophical leap which even liberal Israelis like Benvenisti are still unable to make.

In material terms, a newly cantonised single state would offer the Palestinians exactly what they have received under Oslo: an economic relationship which veers between vassalage and impoverishment, and no means to advance themselves or escape from dependence on Jewish masters. Even in South Africa, where the non-white population is overwhelmingly in the majority, black aspirations have struggled since 1994 against the historical legacy of white supremacy and exclusivism, particularly in the economic sphere.[16] In an Israel-Palestine, where a Jewish majority might still exist after 'unification', it would be even more difficult to overcome the pre-existing hierarchies and inequities. Although Palestinians might have the vote, they would find it almost impossible to level these historical disparities or to challenge the material distribution which has grown up on dispossession and expropriation in the occupied territories. The possibility of Palestinians enjoying formal equality, but living and working in the shadows of the Jewish population, is a real one.

In many respects, the one-state solution would represent the death of one state and the emergence of another. In the most optimistic scenario, Zionism and a Jewish exclusivist state would give way to a genuinely multi-ethnic, secular, democratic successor. This state lays a strong claim to being the best option of all, since it would be constituted on the principle that any form of separation or discrimination is anathema to peace. However, given the fact that Israel and Israelis would be instrumental in effecting the transition to Israel-Palestine, and that even liberal Israelis cling to separation in their definition of a future for Israel's Jews, we must balance our enthusiasm for a single state with the fear that it too will backfire for Palestinians. Instead of the end of Zionism, a single state could easily mark the death of Palestinian aspirations towards a democratic and secular state in which they possessed genuine equality.[17] This outcome would lead not to the creation of a new state but to the expansion of Israel and the permanent confounding of 'Palestine'. Immediately, the Palestinians' claims of land or sovereignty would be silenced; in time, perhaps, the memory of Palestine would fade, and the 'unitary' state would come to resemble many others in which inequality has been institutionalised along ethnic lines. The Palestinians, having already lost three-quarters of their land, would now lose the rest, and a Jewish state would survive, its dimensions expanded and its conscience assuaged.

Prospects

One of the themes of this book has been Israel's absolute agency in any peace process, and the extent to which all negotiations or proposals are dependent upon the prevailing mentality amongst Israelis for their continuation and success. For this reason, the alternatives to Oslo which we have discussed offer as many possibilities for Palestinian disaster as for a redress of Palestinian grievances. It is easy to see that both a two-state arrangement and a unitary state could work in practice, and offer security and prosperity to both Israeli Jews and Palestinians; but we must also concede that Israel retains the power to prejudice both solutions against Palestinian development and in favour of continuing Jewish domination. Given the prevailing political climate in Israel, and the overwhelming consensus on the merits of Zionism and Jewish exclusivism, it is hard to see how either solution could be imposed without concessions to discrimination which would undermine Palestinian citizens in either 'Palestine' or 'Israel-Palestine'. Regardless of the justice or promise of these solutions, a continuing Israeli emphasis on Jewish territorial claims and the necessity of ethnic separation makes it hard to view the future with optimism.

Although some Israelis on the left claim publicly to have made peace with the idea of a Palestinian state, they refuse to make the territorial concessions in the occupied territories which are essential to its existence. Conversely, Israel has made the territorial changes which could lead to a single state of Israel-Palestine, but cannot make the ideological concession that Palestinians should be treated equally alongside Jews within it. As a result, Oslo has revived talk of transfer inside Israel, an option which demands a temporary suspension of morality, but which would at least solve the paradox of Israel's own making. Other Israelis, with Oslo as their guide, will try to present an attenuated version of a genuine one- or two-state solution, hoping to win international approval, tempt Palestinians into a renunciation of their historical rights, and to prop up the exclusivist foundation on which Israel's many mistakes and misdemeanours rest. If a transfer plan is not implemented, Israel will seek a gap in the Palestinians' moral defences and, as with Arafat, attempt to find a Palestinian representative who is prepared to sign up to Israel's vision of peace. That such an agreement will produce no real peace should not surprise us.

From the vantage point of the present, it is hard to see a successful two-state solution emerging from any peace process, and still harder to envisage a functional and stable, single state of Israel-Palestine. However, the strongest argument for the eventual implementation of one of these scenarios is that the existing framework for negotiations cannot secure a lasting peace. As in South Africa, where the white minority and the international community had eventually to conclude that the condition of the black majority was unacceptable, so the destitution and discontent of the Palestinian population will testify in the years ahead to the insufficiency of Oslo and like-minded solutions. An Israeli government with enormous resolve might be able to avoid this reckoning through a massive transfer of the Palestinians from their land to Jordan or Egypt, but any less extreme tactic will not prevent the economic and social collapse which must inevitably follow the division and concentration of the Palestinian population on the West Bank and Gaza. Faced with ongoing protests and violence in the Palestinian bantustans, even Israelis may come to understand the need for a more radical approach to the question of coexistence, and the chances of a more equitable solution may increase. It is only in this context of further bloodshed and despair that we can see beyond the current pessimism, and hope that, as in South Africa, prejudice and reluctance are eventually overcome by reality and experience.

As the Jewish state celebrates its 50th birthday, it can view with pride its record of turning Palestine to Israel. Although the Palestinian population in the occupied territories has remained largely, and stubbornly, in place, the Oslo process has done an excellent job of enlarging Israel and concentrating the Palestinians into areas where they can be more easily contained and controlled. Israel cannot, however, look back so fondly at its record of peacemaking, or its successful integration in the Middle East. Its achievements in one field are the cause of its failure in the other. We should accept Shimon Peres's honest assessment that, for Israelis, Oslo is 'a negotiation with ourselves', and then direct to Israel the question of what kind of region it would like to see in the future. The expansion of the settlements and the Israeli army into the occupied territories, and beyond to the Sinai desert, Golan Heights and south Lebanon, has proved that Israel has the military capacity to reach beyond its 1949 borders. The bombs inside Israel's cities, however, suggest that such a greater Israel will not be a peaceful one.

As it has always been, the choice remains with Israel. The international community has a vital role to play, however, in persuading Israel that its actions are unacceptable and deserving of a collective response. The United States, the banker of Israel's settlement efforts since 1967, continues to channel billions of dollars of direct aid each year, and American taxpayers might justly ask why they should continue to fund an ongoing injustice on the other side of the world. Finally, the Jewish diaspora could use its own experience of integration and success in non-Jewish states to urge the end of Jewish exclusivism in Israel, and to uphold the rights of all human beings, including Jews and Palestinians, against the discriminatory privileging of any one group. Without this effort to engage with and to put pressure on Israel, it is highly unlikely that either Israelis or Palestinians will soon enjoy the peace which, under Oslo, has been conspicuous only in its absence.

Notes

1. Nur Masalha, in *A Land Without A People*, notes the 'large number' of Jewish Israelis – 'journalists, academics, writers and politicians' – who would oppose transfer, for moral and pragmatic reasons; p. 223.

2. The Israeli government, not to mention various Zionist lobbies inside and outside Israel, has claimed repeatedly over the past five years that the Palestinians refuse to recognise it, and continue to call for its destruction. In fact, Arafat made a formal recognition of Israel as a precondition to the signing of the first Oslo Accords in 1993, and declared that those sections of the Palestine National Charter (or the PLO Covenant) relating to the destruction of Israel were now revoked. See Graham Usher, *Palestine in Crisis* (London: Pluto Press, 1995), p. 11. Dilip Hiro has written of Arafat's reluctance to amend the various Palestinian charters individually, since such a move would offer a concession to Israel which many Palestinians (upon whose support Arafat depends) would consider unrequited. *Sharing the Promised Land*, p. 530, points out that Israel's severe closure of February and March 1996 prevented Arafat from convincing the Palestine National Council to modify the Charter. At no stage has Israel recognised 'Palestine', as a national entity or as a sovereign territory.

3. The West Bank and Gaza Strip, and the perceived threat to Israel from Arab armies sweeping across them, have given Israeli strategy wonks many happy field-days. For a sense of their one-track approach to the occupation, see the rugged prose of *Can Israel Survive a Palestinian State* pp. 10ff. ('The geostrategic significance of the West Bank and Gaza'); and *No Trumpets, No Drums: A Two-State Settlement of the Israeli–Palestinian Conflict* (New York: Hill and Wang, 1991), which speaks of the need 'to prevent crippling first strikes by Arab air forces or vertical envelopment by air- or heli-bourne Arab ground forces, for which anti-air defenses situated on the eastern side [of the Jordan Valley] are

necessary'; p. 69. Although this book was co-authored by Palestinian philosophy professor Sari Nusseibeh and Israeli strategic expert Mark Heller, we can safely assume that the threat of 'vertical heli-bourne envelopment' is more the creation of the latter than the former.

4. The bare minimum for a viable two-state solution would be the near-complete withdrawal envisaged in *No Trumpets, No Drums*; in some respects, such as the ongoing Israeli military presence in the Jordan Valley and proposals for a form of local autonomy for those settlers who decided to remain in the occupied territories, even this model is insufficient.

5. For an analysis of the circumstances surrounding the possible return of refugees to a Palestine in the West Bank and Gaza, see Rex Brynen, 'Imagining a solution: final status arrangements and Palestinian refugees in Lebanon', *Journal of Palestine Studies*, Vol. XXVI, No. 2 (Winter 1997), pp. 42–58.

6. 'Interview with Haidar Abdul-Shafi', *Journal of Palestine Studies*, Vol. XXIII, No. 1 (Autumn 1993), pp. 14–19.

7. See Edward Said's quietly damning comparison between Nelson Mandela, who refused to compromise with the white South African government, even on the subject of his own release, and Yasser Arafat, who made his first series of compromises to Israel to win his own return to Gaza and Jericho; *Peace and its Discontents* (New York: Vintage, 1996), p. 63.

8. *Intimate Enemies*, p. 232.

9. Ibid., p. 234.

10. 'Zionism at 100: a symposium', *New Republic*, 8 and 15 September 1997.

11. Edward Witten speaks of the 'de facto binational state that currently exists in Israel and the territories it controls'.

12. Aside from Benvenisti, the one-state solution has also been mooted by Ghada Karmi, 'Is Palestinian autonomy the only alternative?', *Middle East International*, 23 October 1992; Burhan Dajani, 'An alternative to Oslo', *Journal of Palestine Studies*, Vol. XXV, No. 4 (Summer 1996), pp. 5–19; and Marc H. Ellis, 'The future of Israel/Palestine: embracing the broken middle', *Journal of Palestine Studies*, Vol. XXVI, No. 3 (Spring 1997), pp. 56–66, amongst others.

13. *Intimate Enemies*, p. 233.

14. We should not perhaps be surprised that Thomas Friedman penned the Foreword to Benvenisti's book, celebrating the author's advocacy of 'separation based on equality' rather than 'separation based on inequality'. Ibid., p. xii.

15. For confirmation that Israeli Palestinians have seen little improvement in their lives since the publication of Uri Davis's book in 1987, see 'Israel's forgotten Palestinians', *Middle East International*, 8 October 1993; and 'Israeli Arabs and the Netanyahu government', ibid., 10 January 1997. The second article recounts the visit to a conference organised in 1996 by Israeli Palestinians by Dullah Omar, minister of justice in the new South Africa. Omar 'drew parallels between the situation of Palestinians in Israel and the apartheid era in South

Africa and stressed the importance of equality for a society to be truly democratic'.

16. See, for example, the Barclays Bank 'Country report' (London, October 1997), which notes that South Africa still suffers from serious inequalities, mostly drawn along racial lines, with an average national rate of unemployment of 30% rising to 50% or more in the black townships. See also 'Bridging past and future', *Boston Globe*, 31 August 1997, in which South African newspaper editor Aggrey Klaaste puts the problem simply: 'The struggle doesn't end with having the keys to the political kingdom when the economic power is still in the hands of white businessmen.'

17. The Palestinian leadership's espousal of a democratic and secular state is a fact of historical record, but not a consistently or unambiguously asserted position. Yasser Arafat's speech to the UN General Assembly on 13 November 1974 speaks of 'one democaratic state where Christians, Jews and Muslims live in justice, equality, fraternity and progress'. (Laqueur and Rubin (eds), p. 339.) However, the PLO has spoken of an 'independent national state', not necessarily secular or democratic, in other communications; see Noam Chomsky, *Towards a New Cold War* (New York: Pantheon, 1982), pp. 240, 268. This disparity may be partly explained by the perennial vacillation of the PLO; partly by different conceptions of 'Palestine', dependent on whether the new state was created alongside or in place of Israel.

Index

Printed in the United States
87023LV00002B/154-177/A

9 781856 495806